CREATION IN CHRIST

UNSPOKEN SERMONS

GEORGE MACDONALD

EDITED AND ABRIDGED BY
ROLLAND HEIN

REGENT COLLEGE PUBLISHING
Vancouver, British Columbia

Creation in Christ: Unspoken Sermons
Copyright © 1976 by Rolland Hein
All rights reserved.

George MacDonald's *Unspoken Sermons* were first published in three
volumes, 1870, 1885 & 1891

First published in condensed form by Harold Shaw Publishers, 1976

This edition published 2004 by Regent College Publishing
5800 University Boulevard, Vancouver, BC V6T 2E4 Canada
www.regentpublishing.com

Views expressed in works published by Regent College Publishing are
those of the author and do not necessarily represent the official position
of Regent College <www.regent-college.edu>.

National Library of Canada Cataloguing in Publication

Macdonald, George, 1824-1905
    Creation in Christ : unspoken sermons / George MacDonald ;
Rolland Hein, editor.

ISBN 1-57383-299-5 (pbk.)

    1. Sermons, English. I. Hein, Rolland II. Title.

BV4253.M33 2004   252.'058   C2004-900294-5

These Ears of Corn,
gathered and rubbed in my hands
upon broken Sabbaths,
I offer first to my Wife,
and then to my other Friends.

EPIGRAPH FOR FIRST SERIES

CONTENTS

INTRODUCTION

"Why reprint today these writings of over a hundred years ago?" This question must be uppermost in the mind of anyone who picks up this volume with no prior acquaintance with George MacDonald's works, and who is wondering how he may spend most profitably the precious little time he snatches from his busy life for reading. To such a person, I offer the following answers.

"Of all things, turn from a mean, poverty-stricken faith," MacDonald pleads. This material will help the reader so to turn. The publication of this volume is, in a sense, a protest. It is a protest against all unworthy and inadequate thinking concerning the character and working of God. But the intention is positive, not negative. MacDonald's vision of the gracious character of God, and of His creative presence within His children for righteousness' sake, is perhaps unsurpassed in Christian writings. I have not found any material on these subjects that seems more true, or gives greater rejoicing in heart, than does the material here reprinted.

MacDonald was a gadfly in his own day, as he continues to be in ours. In his stern Scottish manner he vehemently criticized certain attitudes and tenets of nineteenth century Evangelicalism. "Theologians," he writes, "have done more to hide the gospel of Christ than any of its adversaries." But his criticisms were motivated by nothing other than a consuming love for Christ and a magnificently stirring concept of the nature of God the Father. The strength and captivating moral beauty of his convictions led him to exercise a righteous scorn of all anemic thinking concerning holy things. In his day, as in ours, not a few self-styled thinkers would attribute to God, under the guise of impressive theological jargon, actions and attitudes which any good man would justly condemn, were he to find them in his fellow man. Such depictions of God create within the devout a secret, mostly subconscious, aversion and fear that stifles what would otherwise be a glad, creative relationship with the Father of the Universe. MacDonald helps us to know God so as to thirst for Him—to use the Psalmist's figure—as a hart longs for flowing streams.

George MacDonald was born on December 10, 1824, the second son of a strong-willed but gentle Scottish tenant farmer, at Huntly, in the Scottish Highlands. His rural upbringing, amid the measureless blessings of a lovingly disciplined and joyous home, instilled within him a fervent love of nature, of the Christian virtues, and of the God who is over all. He was educated in King's College, Aberdeen, and Highbury Theological College, London. In 1851 he married Louisa Powell, daughter of a prosperous London merchant, and he began his career as a minister at Trinity Congregational Church, Arundel. There he worked with conviction and compassion until 1853, when he was forced to resign. A group within the church objected to his hope that the "time of trial" for the heathen did not cease at their death, and to his interest in certain German men of letters, such as Novalis and Hoffmann.

Leaving the pastorate in poverty, he took his growing family—when completed it numbered eleven children—to Manchester and there preached and lectured from rented quarters to all who would listen. Soon he started publishing. His early poetry and fantasies, however, which gave provocative and at times enigmatic expression to his growing perceptions of the grace and purposes of God, met with only a modest reception.

Convinced that he could convey his convictions to a larger popular audience by writing novels, he began in the early 1860's his prolific career in this literary genre. Each novel embodies in the narrative a vision of the loving Father God manifesting Himself in the lives of men and women through nature and circumstance. MacDonald's running commentary of poignant spiritual observations upon the characters and action—although it may be artistically questionable in terms of formalist literary standards—

remains a rich source of Christian insight into why people think and behave the way they do.

Thus George MacDonald applied his remarkable gift for telling stories to the service of Truth. Once, when asked by his son Ronald why he did not write a story simply of human passion and artistic plot, MacDonald replied he would like to, but his conviction of the need of men for his message forbade him. In his sermon "Kingship" he expresses the attitude that characterized all his activities: ". . . I fear only lest, able to see and write these things, I should fail of witnessing, and myself be, after all, a castaway—no king, but a talker; no disciple of Jesus, ready to go with Him to the death, but an arguer about the truth; a hater of the lies men speak for God, and myself a truth-speaking liar, not a doer of the word."

He fulfilled his ministry prodigiously throughout the remainder of the century, publishing some fifty-two volumes. He also lectured widely, touring the United States in 1873. Sickly during much of his long life, first with tuberculosis, then asthma and eczema—and almost constantly poor—he always faced adversity with courage and faith. His anagram, based on the letters of his name, was "Corage, God mend al." He spent many of his later years in Italy, and died in 1905.

Although MacDonald left the formal pulpit early in his life and found in his imaginative writings an effective way of giving concrete expression to his convictions, he remained a preacher at heart. He published three volumes of sermons under the title Unspoken Sermons, Series I *in 1867, II in 1886, and III in 1889. A number of anthologies have been compiled from these, C. S. Lewis's* George MacDonald: An Anthology *being the latest. Written in the more leisurely and repetitious style of the Victorian era, these sermons need a certain compression and distillation for today's reader, which I have tried to effect in this edition. It is hoped that MacDonald's compelling commitment to holiness of life and to glad discipleship are better served thereby.*

The unfailing energies that characterized MacDonald's career were fed by his Scottish indignation against much of the religious climate of his own times. The Church of Scotland, in which MacDonald was raised, had been founded in the sixteenth century by John Knox upon the teachings of John Calvin. In dogma it held by letter to the iron-clad doctrines of the strongly worded Westminster Confession. Through the years to MacDonald's time this church changed not a jot nor tittle, except for a steady narrowing and hardening of attitudes. It was generally separatist, exclusive, and intolerant.

With what dexterity MacDonald confronts and exposes the spiritual paucity of this general mentality I will not attempt to summarize here, anxious that the reader leave this preface and experience the adroitness of MacDonald's thinking for himself. His thinking has sweeping implications, as germane to us as to readers a century ago. Present spiritual poverty may not spring so directly from a popular distortion of Calvinist doctrines, but contemporary tendencies to explain Christianity in terms of a list of simple formulas are as spiritually disastrous to true Christian experience as anything MacDonald opposed. One set of rules is to be applied for instant salvation and another set for sanctification without pain. No one can read long in these pages and remain convinced that holiness is to be pursued and attained in six easy steps. It is, rather, as simple to achieve–and as difficult–as to choose continually the will of God with the whole heart.

The purpose of these sermons is to arouse the reader's will so to choose, by imparting a clearer understanding of what His will is. It is not to argue doctrines intellectually. It is not to formulate a systematic theology. MacDonald's insights are not for the mind alone, but for the heart. They afford the reader glimpses of truths which to the child-heart of the true Christian are undeniable. MacDonald avows: "I believe that no teacher should strive to make men think as he thinks, but to lead them to the living Truth, to the Master Himself, of whom alone they can learn anything, who will make them in themselves know what is true by the very seeing of it." The careful reader (and this material may not be read otherwise) will certainly have such a confrontation with Truth in the pages ahead. More than once reading here has brought sudden tears to my eyes and an involuntary thrill to my breast, and I have seldom had a stronger feeling of certainty that I was standing in the presence of valid insights into the Eternal Mystery than during the reading of these Unspoken Sermons.

In his opposition to certain misconceptions of Christian truth, Mac-Donald insists that he is not interested simply in pitting his opinions against those of other good men. Correct opinions are no substitute for obedience. But it is of grave importance to the spiritual health and growth of the earnest child of God that he not harbor opinions about God which, however inadvertently, attribute evil to Him. Such conceptions result only in grudging service prompted by fear–a fear which renders glad obedience and worship impossible. To know God rightly, MacDonald insists, is to love Him wholly. "The hardest, gladdest thing in the world is, to cry Father! from a full heart. I would help whom I may to call thus upon the Father." He does so by exploring the love and mercies of God as our Heav-

enly Father, whose deepest longings are, and have always been, to forgive and perfect erring man.

There are some who are immediately cautious in the presence of such a vision, fearing that it presents God as one who overlooks sin. The sinner must, they hold, suffer the penalty for his wrongdoing. Such readers will find in these chapters a concept of salvation that is probably far more rigorous than they have yet encountered. MacDonald dares to hope that all men will become God's sons—in another life if not in this—not because God takes a light view of their sin, but because they may eventually come to see themselves and the true nature of their sin as God sees them. Because God is both love and justice together, He will have nothing less than final purity in the lives of all with whom He will fellowship. He is a consuming fire. Some Christians take this fire to mean, for the unsaved, a fire of punishment after condemnation, and, with Dante, hold that they who enter into it abandon all hope. MacDonald sees this fire as he sees adverse events in this life—an expression of God's holy love, which, with infinite patience, will never cease to work for a reorientation of the rebellious wills of men to Himself. The narrow way that leads to life will never be less rugged than it presently is, but the gate at its foot will never be closed. Eternal love will continually work through the coming eons to overcome all resistance, and will not be defeated in the end.

The holiness without which no man shall see God is neither imputed nor self-generated. It is the presence of the living Christ within us, MacDonald points out, that enables us to please God by creating a vital righteousness within our lives. "Christ is our righteousness, not that we should escape punishment, still less escape being righteous, but as the live potent creator of righteousness in us, so that we, with our wills receiving His spirit, shall . . . know in ourselves, as He knows, what a lovely thing is righteousness, what a mean, ugly, unnatural thing is unrighteousness. He is our righteousness, and that righteousness is no fiction, no pretence, no imputation." This love of God is answered by nothing less than our best.

MacDonald, then, differs from most devotional writers who urge us on to perfection in this—that he finds motivation in a most grand and appealing vision of the nature and purposes of God, our Heavenly Father. While in no wise minimizing God's judgment upon sin and human shortcomings, he at the same time motivates us to renewed dedication and effort by removing from our thinking every vestige of the image of God as a tyrant who is pleased with nothing less than the humanly impossible, and who then condemns man for not achieving it. God in truth yearns over the beings He is *presently creating with an infinite mercy, surrounding them with influences that nurture their growth, and gently but strongly urging them to new heights of spiritual experience.*

My work with these sermons has been to condense them by removing repetitious arguments, belabored passages, and elaborate literary figures that have little contemporary appeal. Individual sermons are thereby reduced from perhaps twenty to sixty percent. From the original thirty-six I have omitted two, the essence of their thought already being present in others. Twice I have combined two sermons into one, as the content seemed conducive to such union. And I have capitalized, for clarity's sake, the masculine singular pronouns referring to deity. Scripture quotations have been changed from the King James Version to the Revised Standard Version. The order in which the sermons appear is my own.

It is my prayer that the Spirit of God, whose influences for good are myriad around us all, will cause this volume to be found by sincere people who are seeking—but who have not yet fully discovered—the complete joy that a true apprehension of the God of Truth can bring.

Rolland Hein
April, 1976

I

THE
CHARACTER
OF THE
CREATOR

". . . it cannot be that any creature should know Him as He is and not desire Him."

ONE

THE CREATION IN CHRIST

*A*ll things were made through Him, and without Him was not anything made that was made. In Him was life, and the life was the light of men. (John 1:3, 4. The R.S.V. gives as an alternate reading: ... was not anything made. That which has been made was life in Him.)

Let us look at the passage as I think it ought to be translated, and after that, seek the meaning for the sake of which it was written. "All things were made through Him, and without Him was made not one thing. That which was made in Him was life, and the life was the light of men."

Note the antithesis of the *through* and the *in*.

In this grand assertion seems to me to lie, more than shadowed, the germ of creation and redemption—of all the divine in its relation to all the human.

I believe that Jesus Christ is the eternal Son of the eternal Father; that from the first of firstness Jesus is the Son, because God is the Father. I believe therefore that the Father is the greater, that if the Father had not been, the Son could not have been.

I will not apply logic to the thesis, nor would I state it now but for the sake of what is to follow. The true heart will remember the inadequacy of our speech, and our thought also, to the things that lie near the unknown roots of our existence. In saying what I do, I only say what Paul implies when he speaks of the Lord giving up the kingdom to His Father, that God may be all in all.

I worship the Son as the human God, the divine, the only Man, deriving His being and power from the Father, equal with Him as a son is the equal at once and the subject of his father—but *making Himself the equal of His Father in what is most precious in Godhead, namely, Love.*

The Father, in bringing out of the unseen the things that are seen, made essential use of the Son, so that all that exists was created *through* Him. What the difference between the part in creation of the Father and the part of the Son may be, who can understand? Perhaps we may one day come to see into it a little; for I dare hope that, through our willed sonship, we shall come far nearer ourselves to creating. The word *creation* applied to the loftiest success of human genius, seems to me a mockery of humanity, itself in process of creation.

Let us read the text again: "All things were made *through* Him, and without Him was made not one thing. That which was made *in* Him was life." You begin to see it? The power by which He created the worlds was given Him by His Father; He had in Himself a greater power than that by which He made the worlds. There was something made, not *through* but *in* Him; something brought into being by Himself. Here He creates in His grand way, in Himself, as did the Father. "That which was made *in* Him was *life.*"

What Is This Life?
What was that life, the thing made *in* the Son—made by

Him inside Himself, not outside Him—made not *through*
but *in* Him—the life that was His own, as God's is His own?
It was, I answer, that act in Him that corresponded in
Him, as the Son, to the self-existence of His Father. Now
what is the deepest in God? His power? No, for power could
not make Him what we mean when we say *God*. Evil could,
of course, never create one atom; but let us understand very
plainly, that a being whose essence was only power would be
such a negation of the divine that no righteous worship
could be offered Him: His service must be fear, and fear
only. Such a being, even were He righteous in judgment,
yet could not be God.

The God Himself whom we love could not be righteous
were He not something deeper and better still than we generally mean by the word—but, alas, how little can language
say without seeming to say something wrong! In one word,
God is Love. Love is the deepest depth, the essence of His
nature, at the root of all His being. It is not merely that He
could not be God, if He had made no creatures to whom to
be God; but love is the heart and hand of His creation; it is
His right to create, and His power to create as well. The love
that foresees creation is itself the power to create.

Neither could He be righteous—that is, fair to His creatures—but that His love created them. His perfection is His
love. All His divine rights rest upon His love. Ah, He is not
the great monarch! The simplest peasant loving his cow, is
more divine than any monarch whose monarchy is his
glory. If God would not punish sin, or if He did it for anything but love, He would not be the Father of Jesus Christ,
the God who works as Jesus wrought.

What then, I say once more, is in Christ correspondent
to the creative power of God? It must be something that
comes also of love; and in the Son the love must be to the
already existent. Because of that eternal love which has no
beginning, the Father must have the Son. God could not
love, could not be love, without making things to love. Jesus

has God to love, the love of the Son is responsive to the love of the Father.

The response to self-existent love is self-abnegating love. The refusal of Himself is that in Jesus which corresponds to the creation of God. His love takes action, creates, in self-abjuration, in the death of self as motive; in the drowning of self in the life of God, where it lives only as love.

The life of Christ is this—negatively, that He does nothing, cares for nothing for His own sake; positively, that He cares with His whole soul for the will, the pleasure of His Father. Because His Father is His father, therefore He will be His child. The truth in Jesus is His relation to His Father; the righteousness of Jesus is His fulfilment of that relation.

Meeting this relation, loving His Father with His whole being, He is not merely alive as born of God. Giving Himself with perfect will to God, choosing to die to Himself and live to God, He therein creates in Himself a new and higher life. Standing upon Himself, He has gained the power to awake life, the divine shadow of His own, in the hearts of us His brothers and sisters, who have come from the same birth-home as Himself, namely, the heart of His God and our God, His Father and our Father, but who, without our Elder Brother to do it first, would never have chosen that self-abjuration which is life, never have become alive like Him. To will not from self, but with the Eternal, is to live.

There is no life for any man, other than the same kind that Jesus has; His disciple must live by the same absolute devotion of his will to the Father's; then is his life one with the life of the Father.

We Must Choose
Because we are come out of the divine nature, which chooses to be divine, we must *choose* to be divine, to be of God, to be one with God, loving and living as He loves and lives, and so be partakers of the divine nature, or we perish. Man cannot originate this life; it must be shown him, and he

must choose it. God is the father of Jesus and of us—of every possibility of our being; but while God is the father of His children, Jesus is the father of their sonship. For in Him is made the life which is sonship to the Father—the recognition, namely, in fact and life, that the Father has His claim upon His sons and daughters.

We are not and cannot become true sons without our will willing His will, our doing following His making. It was the will of Jesus to be the thing God willed and meant Him, that made Him the true son of God. He was not the son of God because He could not help it, but because He willed to be in Himself the son that He was in the divine idea.

So with us: we must *be* the sons we are. We are not made to be what we cannot help being; sons and daughters are not after such fashion! We are sons and daughters in God's claim; we must be sons and daughters in our will. And we can be sons and daughters, saved into the original necessity and bliss of our being, only by choosing God for the father He is, and doing His will—yielding ourselves true sons to the absolute Father. Therein lies human bliss—only and essential. The working out of this our salvation must be pain, and the handing of it down to them that are below must ever be in pain; but the eternal form of the will of God in and for us, is intensity of bliss.

The Life Became Light
"And the life was the light of men."

The life of which I have now spoken became light to men in the appearing of Him in whom it came into being. The life became light that men might see it, and themselves live by choosing that life also, by choosing so to live, such to be.

There is always something deeper than anything said—a something of which all human, all divine words, figures, pictures, motion-forms, are but the outer laminar spheres through which the central reality shines more or less plainly. Light itself is but the poor outside form of a deeper, bet-

ter thing, namely, life. The life is Christ. The light too is
Christ, but only the body of Christ. The life is Christ Himself. The light is what we *see* and shall see in Him; the life is
what we may *be* in Him.

Therefore the obedient human God appeared as the
obedient divine man, doing the works of His Father—the
things, that is, which His Father did—doing them humbly
before unfriendly brethren. The Son of the Father must
take His own form in the substance of flesh, that He may be
seen of men, and so become the light of men—not that men
may have light, but that men may have life. Seeing what
they could not originate, they may, through the life that is
in them, begin to hunger after the life of which they are
capable, and which is essential to their being.

Let us not forget that the devotion of the Son could never
have been but for the devotion of the Father, who never
seeks His own glory one atom more than does the Son; who
is devoted to the Son, and to all His sons and daughters,
with a devotion perfect and eternal, with fathomless unselfishness. The bond of the universe, the fact at the root of
every vision, revealing that "love is the only good in the
world," and selfishness the one thing hateful, in the city of
the living God unutterable, is the devotion of the Son to the
Father. It is the life of the universe.

It is not the fact that God created all things, that makes
the universe a whole; but that He through whom He
created them loves Him perfectly, is eternally content in His
Father, is satisfied to be because His Father is with Him. It is
not the fact that God is all in all, that unites the universe; it is
the love of the Son to the Father. For of no onehood comes
unity; there can be no oneness where there is only one. For
the very beginnings of unity there must be two.

Without Christ, therefore, there could be no universe.
The reconciliation wrought by Jesus is not the primary
source of unity, of safety to the world; that reconciliation
was the necessary working out of the eternal antecedent

fact, the fact making itself potent upon the rest of the family
—that God and Christ are one, are father and son, the
Father loving the Son as only the Father can love, the Son
loving the Father as only the Son can love. The prayer of the
Lord for unity between men and the Father and Himself,
springs from the eternal need of love. The more I regard it,
the more I am lost in the wonder and glory of the thing.

Life In Us
But light is not enough; light is for the sake of life. We too
must have life in ourselves. We too must, like the Life Himself, live. We can live in no way but that in which Jesus lived,
in which life was made in Him. That way is, to give up our
life. This is the one supreme action of life possible to us for
the making of life in ourselves. Christ did it of Himself, and
so became light to us, that we might be able to do it in ourselves, after Him, and through His originating act.

We must do it ourselves, I say. The help that He has given
and gives, the light and the spirit-working of the Lord, the
Spirit, in our hearts, is all in order that we may, as we must,
do it ourselves. Till then we are not alive; life is not made in
us. The whole strife and labour and agony of the Son with
every man, is to get him to die as He died. All preaching
that aims not at this, is a building with wood and hay and
stubble. If I say not with whole heart, "My Father, do with
me as you will, only help me against myself and for you,"
then I have not yet laid hold upon that for which Christ has
laid hold upon me.

The faith that a man must put in God reaches above
earth and sky, stretches beyond the farthest outlying star of
the creatable universe. The question is not at present, however, of removing mountains, a thing that will one day be
simple to us, but of waking and rising from the dead *now*.

When a man truly and perfectly says with Jesus, and as
Jesus said it, "Thy will be done," he closes the everlasting
life-circle. The life of the Father and the Son flows through

him. He is a part of the divine organism. Then is the prayer of the Lord in him fulfilled: "I in them and thou in me, that they may be made perfect in one."

Friends, those of you who know, or suspect, that these things are true, let us arise and live—arise even in the darkest moments of spiritual stupidity, when hope itself sees nothing to hope for. Let us not trouble ourselves about the cause of our earthliness, except we know it to be some unrighteousness in us, but go at once to the Life.

Let us comfort ourselves in the thought of the Father and the Son. So long as there dwells harmony, so long as the Son loves the Father with all the love the Father can welcome, all is well with the little ones. God is all right—why should we mind standing in the dark for a minute outside His window? Of course we miss the *inness*, but there is a bliss of its own in waiting.

What if the rain be falling, and the wind blowing? What if we stand alone, or, more painful still, have some dear one beside us, sharing our *outness*? What even if the window be not shining, because of the curtains of good inscrutable drawn across it? Let us think to ourselves, or say to our friend, "God is; Jesus is not dead. Nothing can be going wrong, however it may look so to hearts unfinished in childness."

Your will, O God, be done! Nought else is other than loss, than decay, than corruption. There is no life but that born of the life that the Word made in Himself by doing your will, which life is the light of men. Through that light is born the life of men—the same life in them that came first into being in Jesus. As He laid down His life, so must men lay down their lives, that as He lives they may live also. That which was made in Him was life, and the life is the light of men; and yet His own, to whom He was sent, did not believe Him.

TWO

THE KNOWING OF THE SON

*H*is voice you have never heard, His form you have never seen; and you do not have His word abiding in you, for you do not believe Him whom He has sent (John 5:37b, 38).

If Jesus said these words, He meant more, not less, than lies on their surface. They cannot be mere assertion of what everybody knew; neither can their repetition of similar negations be tautological. They were not intended to inform the Jews of a fact they would not have dreamed of denying. Who among them would say he had ever heard God's voice, or seen His shape? John himself says "No man has ever seen God." What is the tone of the passage? It is reproach. Then He reproaches them that they had not seen God, when no man hath seen God at any time, and Paul says no man can see Him! Is there here any paradox?

The word *see* is used in one sense in the one statement, and in another sense in the other. In the one it means *see with the eyes*; in the other, *with the soul*. The one statement is made of all men; the other is made to certain of the Jews of Jerusalem concerning themselves. It is true that no man has seen God, and true that some men ought to have seen Him. No man has seen Him with his bodily eyes; these Jews ought to have seen Him with their spiritual eyes.

The argument of the Lord was indeed of small weight with, and of little use to, those to whom it most applied, for the more it applied, the more incapable were they of seeing that it did apply; but it would be of great force upon some that stood listening, their minds more or less open to the truth, and their hearts drawn to the Man before them.

His argument was this: "If you had ever heard the Father's voice; if you had ever known His call; if you had ever imagined Him, or a God anything like Him; if you had cared for His will so that His word was at home in your hearts, you would have known me when you saw me— known that I must come from Him, that I must be His messenger, and would have listened to me. The least acquaintance with God, such as any true heart must have, would have made you recognize that I came from the God of whom you knew that something. You would have been capable of knowing me by the light of His word abiding in you; by the shape you had beheld however vaguely; by the likeness of my face and my voice to those of my Father. You would have seen my Father in me; you would have known me by the little you knew of Him. That you do not know me now, as I stand here speaking to you, is that you do not know your own Father, even my Father; that throughout your lives you have refused to do His will, and so have not heard His voice; that you have shut your eyes from seeing Him, and have thought of Him only as a partisan of your ambitions. If you had loved my Father, you would have known His Son."

The Same Is True Today

If the Lord were to appear this day as once in Palestine, He would not come in the halo of the painters. Neither would He probably come as carpenter, or mason, or gardener. He would come in such form and condition as might bear to the present [culture] a relation like that which the form and condition He then came in bore to the motley Judea, Samaria, and Galilee. If He came thus, in form altogether unlooked for, who would they be that recognized and received Him?

The idea involves no absurdity. He is not far from us at any moment—if the old story be indeed more than the best and strongest of the fables that possess the world. He might at any moment appear. Who, I ask, would be the first to receive him? Now, as then, it would of course be the child-like in heart, the truest, the least selfish. They would not be the highest in the estimation of any church, for the child-like are not yet the many. It might not even be those that knew most about the former visit of the Master, that had pondered every word of the Greek Testament.

It would certainly, if any, be those who were likest the Master—those, namely, that did the will of their Father and His Father, that built their house on the rock by hearing and doing His sayings. But are there any enough like Him to know Him at once by the sound of His voice, by the look of His face? There are multitudes who would at once be taken by a false Christ fashioned after their fancy, and would at once reject the Lord as a poor impostor. One thing is certain: they who first recognized Him would be those that most loved righteousness and hated iniquity.

To Receive Him Is To Become Like Him

"And we all, with unveiled face, beholding the glory of the Lord, are being changed into His likeness, from one degree of glory to another; for this comes from the Lord who is the Spirit" (II Cor. 3:18).

Let us see then what Paul teaches us in this passage about the life which is the light of men. It is his form of bringing to bear upon men the truth announced by John.

When Moses came out from speaking with God, his face was radiant; its shining was a wonder to the people, and a power upon them. But the radiance began at once to diminish and die away, as was natural, for it was not indigenous in Moses. Therefore Moses put a veil upon his face that they might not see it fade. As to whether this was right or wise, opinion may differ: it is not my business to discuss the question. When he went again into the tabernacle, he took off his veil, talked with God with open face, and again put on the veil when he came out.

Paul says that the veil which obscured the face of Moses lies now upon the hearts of the Jews, so that they cannot understand him, but that when they turn to the Lord (go into the tabernacle with Moses) the veil shall be taken away, and they shall see God. Then will they understand that the glory is indeed faded upon the face of Moses, but by reason of the glory of Jesus that overshines it.

Paul says that the sight of the Lord will take that veil from their hearts. His light will burn it away. His presence gives liberty. Where He is, there is no more heaviness, no more bondage, no more wilderness or Mount Sinai. The Son makes free with sonship.

Paul's idea is, that when we take into our understanding, our heart, our conscience, our being, the glory of God—namely Jesus Christ as He shows himself to our eyes, our hearts, our consciences—He works upon us, and will keep working, till we are changed to the very likeness we have thus mirrored in us; for with His likeness He comes Himself, and dwells in us. He will work until the same likeness is wrought out and perfected in us, the image, namely, of the humanity of God, in which image we were made at first, but which could never be developed in us except by the indwelling of the perfect likeness. By the power of Christ thus received and at home in us, we are changed—the glory in Him becoming glory in us, His glory changing us to glory.

One With God

But let us note this, that the dwelling of Jesus in us is the power of the Spirit of God upon us; for "the Lord is the Spirit," and "this comes from the Lord who is the Spirit." When we think Christ, Christ comes; when we receive His image into our spiritual mirror, He enters with it.

When our hearts turn to Him, that is opening the door to Him, that is holding up our mirror to Him; then He comes in, not by our thought only, not in our idea only, but He comes Himself, and of His own will. Thus the Lord, the Spirit, becomes the soul of our souls, becomes spiritually what He always was creatively; and as our spirit informs, gives shape to our bodies, in like manner His soul informs, gives shape to our souls.

In this there is nothing unnatural, nothing at conflict with our being. It is but that the deeper soul that willed and wills our souls, rises up, the infinite Life, into the Self we call *I* and *me*, makes the *I* and *me* more and more His, and Himself more and more ours; until at length the glory of our existence flashes upon us, we face full to the sun that enlightens what it sent forth, and know ourselves alive with an infinite life, even the life of the Father. Then indeed we *are*; then indeed we have life; the life of Jesus has, through light, become life in us; the glory of God in the face of Jesus, mirrored in our hearts, has made us alive; we are one with God for ever and ever.

What less than such a splendor of hope would be worthy the revelation of Jesus? Filled with the soul of their Father, men shall inherit the glory of their Father; filled with themselves, they cast Him out, and rot. No other saving can save them. They must receive the Son, and through the Son the Father.

What it cost the Son to get so near to us that we could say

Come in, is the story of His life. He stands at the door and knocks, and when we open to Him He comes in, and dwells with us, and we are transformed to the same image of truth and purity and heavenly childhood. Where power dwells, there is no force; where the spirit-Lord is, there is liberty.

The Lord Jesus, by free, potent communion with their inmost being, will change His obedient brethren till in every thought and impulse they are good like Him, unselfish, neighborly, brotherly like Him, loving the Father perfectly like Him, ready to die for the truth like Him, caring like Him for nothing in the universe but the will of God, which is love, harmony, liberty, beauty, and joy.

I do not know if we may call this having life in ourselves; but it is the waking up, the perfecting in us of the divine life inherited from our Father in heaven, who made us in His own image, whose nature remains in us, and makes it the deepest reproach to a man that he has neither heard His voice at any time, nor seen His shape. He who would thus live must, as a mirror draws into its bosom an outward glory, receive into his "heart of hearts" the inward glory of Jesus Christ, the Truth.

THREE

THE
CHILD
IN THE
MIDST

*M*ark 9:33-37; cf Matt. 18:1-5.

These passages record a lesson our Lord gave His disciples against ambition, against emulation. It is not for the sake of setting forth this lesson that I write about these words of our Lord, but for the sake of a truth, a revelation about God, in which His great argument reaches its height.

He took a little child—possibly a child of Peter; for St. Mark says that the incident fell at Capernaum, and "in the house"—a child therefore with some of the characteristics of Peter, whose very faults were those of a childish nature. We might expect the child of such a father to possess the childlike countenance and bearing essential to the conveyance of the lesson which I now desire to set forth as contained in the passage.

For it must be confessed that there are children who are not childlike. One of the saddest and not least common sights in the world is the face of a child whose mind is so brimful of worldly wisdom that the human childishness has vanished from it, as well as the divine childlikeness. For the *childlike* is the divine.

If the disciples could have seen that the essential childhood was meant, and not a blurred and half-obliterated childhood, the most selfish child might have done as well, but could have done no better than the one we have supposed in whom the true childhood is more evident. But when the child was employed as a manifestation, utterance, and sign of the truth that lay in his childhood, in order that the eyes as well as the ears should be channels to the heart, it was essential—not that the child should be beautiful but— that the child should be childlike.

What Childlikeness Reveals
That this lesson did lie, not in the humanity, but in the childhood of the child, let me now show more fully. The disciples had been disputing who should be the greatest, and the Lord wanted to show them that such a dispute had nothing whatever to do with the way things went in His kingdom. Therefore, as a specimen of His subjects, He took a child and set him before them. It was not to show the scope but the nature of the kingdom.

He told them they could not enter into the kingdom save by becoming little children—by humbling themselves. For the idea of ruling was excluded where childlikeness was the one essential quality. It was to be no more who should rule, but who should serve; no more who should look down upon his fellows from the conquered heights of authority—even of sacred authority, but who should look up honoring humanity, and ministering to it, so that humanity itself might at length be persuaded of its own honor as a temple of the living God. It was to impress this lesson upon them that He showed them the child; therefore, I repeat, the lesson lay in the childhood of the child.

But I now approach my especial object; for this lesson led to the enunciation of a yet higher truth, upon which it was

founded, and from which indeed it sprung. Nothing is required of man that is not first in God. It is because God is
perfect that we are required to be perfect. And it is for the
revelation of God to all the human souls, that they may be
saved by knowing Him, and so becoming like Him, that this
child is thus chosen and set before them in the gospel. He
who, in giving the cup of water or the embrace, comes into
contact with the essential childhood of the child—that is,
embraces the *childish* humanity of it, (not he who embraces
it out of love to humanity, or even love to God as the Father
of it)—is partaker of the meaning, that is, the blessing, of
this passage. It is the recognition of the childhood as divine
that will show the disciple how vain the strife after relative
place of honor in the great kingdom.

For it is *in my name*. This means *as representing me*; and,
therefore, *as being like me*. Our Lord could not commission
any one to be received in His name who could not more or
less represent Him. But a special sense, a lofty knowledge of
blessedness, belongs to the act of embracing a child as the
visible likeness of the Lord Himself. For the blessedness is
the perceiving of the truth—the blessing is the truth itself—
the God-known truth, that the Lord has the heart of a child.
The man who perceives this knows in himself that he is
blessed—blessed because that is true.

But the argument as to the meaning of our Lord's words,
in my name, is incomplete, until we follow our Lord's enunciation to its second and higher stage: "Whoever receives
me, receives not me but Him who sent me." It will be allowed that the connection between the first and second link
of the chain will probably be the same as the connection between the second and third. How is it that he who receives
the Son receives the Father? Because the Son is as the Father; and he whose heart can perceive the essential in
Christ, has the essence of the Father—that is, sees and holds
to it by that recognition, and is one therewith by recognition
and worship.

What, then, next, is the connection between the first and second? I think the same. "He that sees the essential in this child, the pure childhood, sees that which is the essence of me," grace and truth—in a word, childlikeness. It follows not that the former is perfect as the latter, but it is the same in kind, and therefore manifest in the child; it reveals that which is in Jesus.

Then to receive a child in the name of Jesus is to receive Jesus; to receive Jesus is to receive God; therefore to receive the child is to receive God Himself.

To receive the child because God receives it, or for its humanity, is one thing; to receive it because it is like God, or for its childhood, is another. The former will do little to destroy ambition. Alone it might argue only a wider scope to it, because it admits all men to the arena of the strife. But the latter strikes at the very root of emulation. As soon as even service is done for the honor and not for the service sake, the doer is that moment outside the kingdom. But when we receive the child in the name of Christ, the very childhood that we receive to our arms is humanity. We love its humanity in its childhood, for childhood is the deepest heart of humanity—its divine heart; and so in the name of the child we receive all humanity.

The Childlikeness of God ·

But to advance now to the highest point of this teaching of our Lord: "Whoever receives me, receives not me but Him who sent me." To receive a child in the name of God is to receive God Himself. How to receive Him? As alone He can be received—by knowing Him as He is. To know Him is to have Him in us. And that we may know Him, let us now receive this revelation of Him, in the words of our Lord Himself. Here is the argument of highest import founded upon the teaching of our Master in the utterance before us.

God is represented in Jesus, for that God is like Jesus: Jesus is represented in the child, for that Jesus is like the

child. Therefore God is represented in the child, for that
He is like the child. God is child-like. In the true vision of
this fact lies the receiving of God in the child.

Let me ask, do you believe in the Incarnation? And if you
do, let me ask further, was Jesus ever less divine than God?
I answer for you, Never. God is man, and infinitely more.
Our Lord became flesh, but did not *become* man. He took on
Him the form of man: He was man already. And He was,
is, and ever shall be divinely childlike. He could never have
been a child if He would ever have ceased to be a child, for
in Him the transient found nothing. Childhood belongs to
the divine nature. Obedience, then, is as divine as Will, Service as divine as Rule. How? Because they are one in their
nature; they are both a doing of the truth. The love in them
is the same. The Fatherhood and the Sonship are one, save
that the Fatherhood looks down lovingly, and the Sonship
looks up lovingly. Love is all. And God is all in all. He is ever
seeking to get down to us—to be the divine man to us. And
we are ever saying, "That be far from you, Lord!" We are
careful, in our unbelief, over the divine dignity, of which
He is too grand to think.

Let us dare, then, to climb the height of divine truth to
which this utterance of our Lord would lead us. Does it not
lead us up higher: that the devotion of God to His creatures
is perfect? that He does not think about Himself but about
them? that He wants nothing for Himself, but finds His
blessedness in the outgoing of blessedness?

In this, then, is God like the child: that He is simply and
altogether our friend, our father—our more than friend,
father, and mother—our infinite love-perfect God. Grand
and strong beyond all that human imagination can conceive
of poet-thinking and kingly action, He is delicate beyond all
that human tenderness can conceive of husband or wife,
homely beyond all that human heart can conceive of father
or mother.

He has not two thoughts about us. With Him all is simplicity of purpose and meaning and effort and end—namely, that we should be as He is, think the same thoughts, mean the same things, possess the same blessedness. It is so plain that any one may see it, every one ought to see it, every one shall see it. It must be so. He is utterly true and good to us, nor shall anything withstand His will.

How terribly, then, have the theologians misrepresented God! Nearly all of them represent Him as a great King on a grand throne, thinking how grand He is, and making it the business of His being and the end of His universe to keep up His glory, wielding the bolts of a Jupiter against them' that take His name in vain. They would not allow this, but follow out what they say, and it comes much to this.

Brothers, have you found our king? There He is, kissing little children and saying they are like God. There He is at table with the head of a fisherman lying on His bosom, and somewhat heavy at heart that even he, the beloved disciple, cannot yet understand Him well. The simplest peasant who loves his children and his sheep were—no, not a truer, for the other is false, but —a true type of our God beside that monstrosity of a monarch.

The God who is ever uttering Himself in the changeful profusions of nature; who takes millions of years to form a soul that shall understand Him and be blessed; who never needs to be, and never is, in haste; who welcomes the simplest thought of truth or beauty as the return for seed He has sown upon the old fallows of eternity; who rejoices in the response of a faltering moment to the age-long cry of His wisdom in the streets; the God of music, of painting, of building, the Lord of Hosts, the God of mountains and oceans; whose laws go forth from one unseen point of wisdom, and thither return without an atom of loss; the God of history working in time unto Christianity; this God is the God of little children, and He alone can be perfectly abandonedly simple and devoted. The deepest, purest love of a woman has its well-spring in Him. Our longing desires can

no more exhaust the fulness of the treasures of the Godhead, than our imagination can touch their measure. Of
Him not a thought, not a joy, not a hope of one of His creatures can pass unseen; and while one of them remains unsatisfied, He is not Lord over all.

Therefore, with angels and with archangels, with the
spirits of the just made perfect, with the little children of the
kingdom, yea, with the Lord Himself, and for all them that
know Him not, we praise and magnify and laud His name
in itself, saying *Our Father.* We do not draw back for that we
are unworthy, nor even for that we are hard-hearted and
care not for the good. For it is His childlikeness that makes
Him our God and Father. The perfection of His relation to
us swallows up all our imperfections, all our defects, all our
evils; for our childhood is born of His fatherhood. That
man is perfect in faith who can come to God in the utter
dearth of his feelings and his desires, without a glow or an
aspiration, with the weight of low thoughts, failures, neglects, and wandering forgetfulness, and say to Him, "You
are my refuge, because you are my home."

Such a faith will not lead to presumption. The man who
can pray such a prayer will know better than another, that
God is not mocked; that He is not a man that He should repent; that tears and entreaties will not work on Him to the
breach of one of His laws; that for God to give a man because he asked for it that which was not in harmony with
His laws of truth and right, would be to damn him—to cast
him into the outer darkness. And He knows that out of that
prison the childlike, imperturbable God will let no man
come till he has "paid the last penny."

And if he should forget this, the God to whom he belongs
does not forget it, does not forget him. Life is no series of
chances with a few providences sprinkled between to keep
up a justly failing belief, but one providence of God; and
the man shall not live long before life itself shall remind
him, it may be in agony of soul, of that which he has forgot-

ten. When he prays for comfort, the answer may come in dismay and terror and the turning aside of the Father's countenance; for love itself will, for love's sake, turn the countenance away from that which is not lovely; and he will have to read, written upon the dark wall of his imprisoned conscience, the words, awful and glorious, *Our God is a consuming fire.*

FOUR

LIGHT

❦

This is the message we have heard from Him and proclaim to you, that God is light and in Him is no darkness at all (I John 1:5).

And this is the judgment, that the light has come into the world, and men loved darkness rather than light, because their deeds were evil (John 3:19).

We call the story of Jesus, told so differently, yet to my mind so consistently, by four narrators, *the gospel*. What makes this tale *the good news*? Is everything in the story of Christ's life on earth good news? Is it good news that the one only good man was served by his fellow-men as Jesus was served—cast out of the world in torture and shame? Is it good news that He came to His own, and His own received Him not? What makes it fit, I repeat, to call the tale *good news*?

If we asked this or that theologian, we should, in so far as he was a true man, and answered from his own heart and not from the tradition of the elders, understand what he saw in it that made it good news to him, though it might involve what would be anything but good news to some of us. The deliverance it might seem to this or that man to bring, might be founded on such notions of God as to not a few of us contain as little of good as of news.

To share in the deliverance which some men find in what they call the gospel—for all do not apply the word to the tale itself, but to certain deductions made from the epistles and their own consciousness of evil—we should have to believe such things of God as would be the opposite of an evangel to us—yea, a message from hell itself. We must first believe in an unjust God, from whom we have to seek refuge. True, they call Him just, but say He does that which seems to the best in me the essence of injustice. They will tell me I judge after the flesh: I answer, Is it then to the flesh the Lord appeals when He says, "Why do you not judge for yourselves what is right?" Is He not the light that lights every man that comes into the world?

They tell me I was born in sin, and I know it to be true; they tell me also that I am judged with the same severity as if I had been born in righteousness, and that I know to be false. They make it a consequence of the purity and justice of God that He will judge us, born in evil, for which birth we were not accountable, by our sinfulness, instead of by our guilt. They tell me, or at least give me to understand, that every wrong thing I have done makes me subject to be treated as if I had done that thing with the free will of one who had in him no taint of evil—when, perhaps, I did not at the time recognize the thing as evil, or recognized it only in the vaguest fashion.

Is there any gospel in telling me that God is unjust, but that there is a way of deliverance from Him? Show me my God unjust, and you wake in me a damnation from which no power can deliver me—least of all God Himself. It may be good news to such as are content to have a God capable of unrighteousness, if only He be on their side!

Who would not rejoice to hear from Matthew, or Mark, or Luke, what, in a few words, he meant by the word *gospel* —or rather, what in the story of Jesus made him call it *good news*! Each would probably give a different answer to the question, all the answers consistent, and each a germ from which the others might be reasoned; but in the case of John, we have his answer to the question: he gives us in one sentence of two members, not indeed the gospel according to John, but the gospel according to Jesus Christ Himself.

"This is the message," he says, "we have heard from Him, and proclaim to you, that God is light, and in Him is no darkness at all." Ah, my heart, this is indeed the good news for you! This *is* gospel! If God be light, what more, what else can I seek than God, than God Himself! Away with your doctrines! Away with your salvation from the "justice" of a God whom it is a horror to imagine! Away with your iron cages of false metaphysics! I am saved—for God is light!

My God, I come to you. That you should be yourself is enough for time and eternity, for my soul and all its endless need. Whatever seems to me darkness, that I will not believe of my God. If I should mistake, and call that darkness which is light, will He not reveal the matter to me, setting it in the light that lights every man, showing me that I saw but the husk of the thing, not the kernel? Will He not break open the shell for me, and let the truth of it, His thought, stream out upon me?

Where would the good news be if John said, "God is light, but you cannot see His light; you cannot tell, you have no notion, what light is; what God means by light, is not what you mean by light; what God calls light may be horrible darkness to you, for you are of another nature from Him!" Where, I say, would be the good news of that?

It is true, the light of God may be so bright that we see nothing; but that is not darkness, it is infinite hope of light. It is true also that to the wicked "the day of the Lord is darkness, and not light;" but is that because the conscience of the wicked man judges of good and evil oppositely to the conscience of the good man? When he says "Evil, be my good," he means by *evil* what God means by evil, and by *good* he means *pleasure*. He cannot make the meanings change places. To say that what our deepest conscience calls darkness may be light to God, is blasphemy; to say light in God and light in man are of differing kinds, is to speak against the spirit of light.

God is light far beyond what we can see, but what we mean by light, God means by light; and what is light to God is light to us, or would be light to us if we saw it, and will be light to us when we do see it. God means us to be jubilant in the fact that He is light—that He is what His children, made in His image, mean when they say *light*; that what in Him is dark to them, is dark by excellent glory, by too much cause of jubilation; that, however dark it may be to their eyes, it is light even as they mean it, light for their eyes and souls and hearts to take in the moment they are enough of eyes, enough of souls, enough of hearts, to receive it in its very being.

The Beauty of God's Light
To fear the light is to be untrue, or at least it comes of untruth. No being, for himself or for another, needs fear the light of God. Nothing can be in light inimical to our nature, which is of God, or to anything in us that is worthy. All fear of the light, all dread lest there should be something dangerous in it, comes of the darkness still in those of us who do not love the truth with all our hearts; it will vanish as we are more and more interpenetrated with the light.

In a word, there is no way of thought or action which we count admirable in man, in which God is not altogether adorable. There is no loveliness, nothing that makes man dear to his brother man, that is not in God, only it is infinitely better in God. He is God our savior. Jesus is our savior because God is our savior. He is the God of comfort and consolation. He will soothe and satisfy His children better than any mother her infant.

The only thing He will not give them is—leave to stay in the dark. If a child cry, "I want the darkness," and complain that He will not give it, yet He will not give it. He gives what His child needs—often by refusing what he asks. If His child say, "I will not be good; I prefer to die; let me die!" His dealing with that child will be as if He said—"No; I have the right to content you, not giving you your own will but mine, which is your one good. You shall not die; you shall live to thank me that I would not hear your prayer. You know what you ask, but not what you refuse."

There are good things God must delay giving until His child has a pocket to hold them—till he gets His child to make that pocket. He must first make him fit to receive and to have. There is no part of our nature that shall not be satisfied—and that not by lessening it, but by enlarging it to embrace an ever-enlarging enough.

Come to God, then, my brother, my sister, with all your desires and instincts, all your lofty ideals, all your longing for purity and unselfishness, all your yearning to love and be true, all your aspirations after self-forgetfulness and child-life in the breath of the Father; come to Him with all your weaknesses, all your shames, all your futilities; with all your helplessness over your own thoughts; with all your failure, yes, with the sick sense of having missed the tide of true affairs; come to Him with all your doubts, fears, dishonesties, meannesses, paltrinesses, misjudgments, wearinesses, disappointments, and stalenesses: be sure He will take you and all your miserable brood, whether of dragglewinged angels, or covert-seeking snakes, into His care, the angels for life, the snakes for death, and you for liberty in His limitless heart! For He is light, and in Him is no darkness at all.

If He were a king, a governor; if the name that described

Him were *The Almighty*, you might well doubt whether there could be light enough in Him for you and your darkness; but He is your father, and more your father than the word can mean in any lips but His who said, "my father and your father, my God and your God;" and such a father *is* light, an infinite, perfect light. If He were any less or any other than He is, and you could yet go on growing, you must at length come to the point where you would be dissatisfied with Him; but He is light, and in Him is no darkness at all.

If anything seem to be in Him that you cannot be content with, be sure that the ripening of your love to your fellows and to Him, the source of your being, will make you at length know that anything else than just what He is would have been to you an endless loss. Be not afraid to build upon the rock Christ, as if your holy imagination might build too high and heavy for that rock, and it must give way and crumble beneath the weight of your divine idea.

Let no one persuade you that there is in Him a little darkness, because of something He has said which His creature interprets into darkness. The interpretation is the work of the enemy—a handful of tares of darkness sown in the light. Neither let your cowardly conscience receive any word as light because another calls it light, while it looks to you dark. Say either the thing is not what it seems, or God never said or did it. But, of all evils, to misinterpret what God does, and then say the thing as interpreted must be right because God does it, is of the devil.

Do not try to believe anything that affects you as darkness. Even if you mistake and refuse something true thereby, you will do less wrong to Christ by such a refusal than you would by accepting as His what you can see only as darkness. It is impossible you are seeing a true, a real thing —seeing it as it is, I mean—if it looks to you darkness. But let your words be few, lest you say with your tongue what you will afterward repent with your heart. Above all things believe in the light, that it is what you call light, though the darkness in you may give you cause at a time to doubt whether you are verily seeing the light.

John 3:19

"But there is another side to the matter: God is light indeed, but there *is* darkness; darkness is death, and men are in it."

Yes; darkness is death, but not death to him that comes out of it.

It may sound paradoxical, but no man is condemned for anything he has done; he is condemned for continuing to do wrong. He is condemned for not coming out of the darkness, for not coming to the light, the living God, who sent the light, His Son, into the world to guide him home. Let us hear what John says about the darkness.

For here also we have, I think the word of the apostle himself: at the 13th verse he begins, I think, to speak in his own person. In the 19th verse he says, "And this is the judgment"—not that men are sinners—not that they have done that which, even at the moment, they were ashamed of— not that they have committed murder, not that they have betrayed man or woman, not that they have ground the faces of the poor, making money by the groans of their fellows—not for any hideous thing are they condemned, but that they will not leave such doings behind, and do them no more: "This is the judgment, that light has come into the world, and men"would not come out of the darkness to the light, but "loved darkness rather than light, because their deeds were evil."

Choosing evil, clinging to evil, loving the darkness because it suits with their deeds, therefore turning their backs on the inbreaking light, how can they but be condemned— if God be true, if He be light, and darkness be alien to Him! Whatever of honesty is in man, whatever of judgment is left in the world, must allow that their condemnation is in the very nature of things, that it must rest on them and abide.

But it does not follow, because light has come into the world, that it has fallen upon this or that man. He has his portion of the light that lights every man, but the revelation of God in Christ may not yet have reached him. A man might see and pass the Lord in a crowd, nor be to blame like the Jews of Jerusalem for not knowing Him. A man like Nathanael might have started and stopped at the merest glimpse of Him, but all growing men are not yet like him without guile.

Everyone who has not yet come to the light is not necessarily keeping his face turned away from it. We dare not say that this or that man would not have come to the light had he seen it; we do not know that he will not come to the light the moment he does see it. God gives every man time. There is a light that lightens sage and savage, but the glory of God in the face of Jesus may not have shined on this sage or that savage.

The condemnation is of those who, having seen Jesus, refuse to come to Him, or pretend to come to Him but do not the things He says. They have all sorts of excuses at hand; but as soon as a man begins to make excuse, the time has come when he might be doing that from which he excuses himself. How many are there not who, believing there is something somewhere with the claim of light upon them, go on and on to get more out of the darkness! This consciousness, all neglected by them, gives broad ground for the expostulation of the Lord—"Yet you refuse to come to me that you may have life!"

The Unforgivable Sin

"Every sin and blasphemy," the Lord said, "will be forgiven unto men; but the blasphemy against the Spirit will not be forgiven." God speaks, as it were, in this manner: "I forgive you everything. Not a word more shall be said about your sins—only come out of them; come out of the darkness of your exile; come into the light of your home, of your birthright, and do evil no more. Lie no more; cheat no more; oppress no more; slander no more; envy no more; be neither greedy nor vain; love your neighbor as I love you; be my good child; trust in your Father. I am light; come to me, and you shall see things as I see them, and hate the evil thing. I will make you love the thing which now you call good and love not. I forgive all the past."

"I thank you, Lord, for forgiving me, but I prefer staying in the darkness: forgive me that too."

"No; that cannot be. The one thing that cannot be forgiven is the sin of choosing to be evil, of refusing deliverance. It is impossible to forgive that sin. It would be to take part in it. To side with wrong against right, with murder against life, cannot be forgiven. The thing that is past I pass, but he who goes on doing the same, annihilates this my forgiveness, makes it of no effect."

"Let a man have committed any sin whatever, I forgive him; but to choose to go on sinning—how can I forgive that? It would be to nourish and cherish evil! It would be to let my creation go to ruin. Shall I keep you alive to do things hateful in the sight of all true men? If a man refuse to come out of his sin, he must suffer the vengeance of a love that would be no love if it left him there. Shall I allow my creature to be the thing my soul hates?"

There is no excuse for this refusal. If we were punished for every fault, there would be no end, no respite; we should have no quiet wherein to repent; but God passes by all He can. He passes by and forgets a thousand sins, yea, tens of thousands, forgiving them all—only we must begin to be good, begin to do evil no more.

He who refuses must be punished and punished—punished through all the ages—punished until he give way, yields, and comes to the light, that his deeds may be seen by himself to be what they are, and be by himself reproved, and the Father at last have His child again. For the man who in this world resists to the full, there may be, perhaps, a whole age or era in the history of the universe during which his sin shall not be forgiven; but *never* can it be forgiven until he repents. How can they who will not repent be forgiven, save in the sense that God does and will do all He can to make them repent? Who knows but such sin may need for its cure the continuous punishment of an aeon?

FIVE

IT
SHALL
NOT BE
FORGIVEN

And everyone who speaks a word against the Son of man will be forgiven; but he who blasphemes against the Holy Spirit will not be forgiven (Luke 12:10).

Our Lord had no design of constructing a system of truth in intellectual forms. The truth of the moment in its relation to Him, The Truth, was what He spoke. He spoke out of a region of realities which He knew could only be suggested—not represented—in the forms of intellect and speech. With vivid flashes of life and truth His words invade our darkness, rousing us with sharp stings of light to will our awaking, to arise from the dead and cry for the light which He can give, not in the lightning of words only, but in indwelling presence and power.

How, then, must the truth fare with those who, having neither glow nor insight, will build intellectual systems upon the words of our Lord, or of His disciples? A little child would better understand Plato than they St. Paul. The meaning in those great hearts who knew our Lord is too great to enter theirs. The sense they find in the words must be a sense small enough to pass through their narrow doors.

And if mere words, without the interpreting sympathy, may mean, as they may, almost anything the receiver will or can attribute to them, how shall the man, bent at best on the salvation of his own soul, understand, for instance, the meaning of that apostle who was ready to encounter banishment itself from the presence of Christ, that the beloved brethren of his nation might enter in? To men who are not simple, simple words are the most inexplicable of riddles.

If we are bound to search after what our Lord means— and He speaks that we may understand—we are at least equally bound to refuse any interpretation which seems to us unlike Him, unworthy of Him. He Himself says, "Why do you not judge for yourselves what is right?" To accept that as the will of our Lord which to us is inconsistent with what we have learned to worship in Him already, is to introduce discord into that harmony whose end is to unite our hearts, and make them whole.

That part of us which loves Him let us follow, and in its judgments let us trust; hoping, beyond all things else, for its growth and enlightenment by the Lord, who is the Spirit.

Better I say again, to refuse the right *form*, than, by accepting it in misapprehension of what it really is, to refuse the spirit, the truth that dwells therein. Which of these, I pray, is more like to the sin against the Holy Spirit? To mistake the meaning of the Son of man may well fill a man with sadness. But to care so little for Him as to receive as His what the noblest part of our nature rejects as low and poor, or selfish and wrong, that surely is more like the sin against the Holy Spirit that can never be forgiven; for it is a sin against the truth itself, not the embodiment of it in Him.

Words for their full meaning depend upon their source, the person who speaks them. An utterance may even seem commonplace, till you are told that thus spoke one whom you know to be always thinking, always feeling, always acting. Recognizing the mind whence the words proceed, you know the scale by which they are to be understood. So the words of God cannot mean just the same as the words of man. Whatever a good word means, as used by a good man, it means just infinitely more as used by God. And the feeling or thought expressed by that word takes higher and higher forms in us as we become capable of understanding Him—that is, as we become like Him.

I am far less anxious to show what the sin against the Holy Spirit means, than to show what the non-forgiveness means; though I think we may arrive at some understanding of both. I cannot admit for a moment that there is anything in the Bible too mysterious to be looked into; for the Bible is a *revelation*, an unveiling. True, into many things uttered there I can see only a little way. But that little way is the way of life; for the depth of their mystery is God.

The Meaning of Forgiveness

To reach the first position necessary for the final attainment of our end, I will inquire what the divine forgiveness means. And in order to arrive at this naturally, I will begin by asking what the human forgiveness means; for, if there be any meaning in the Incarnation, it is through the human that we must climb up to the Divine.

I do not know that it is of much use to go back to the Greek or the English word for any primary idea of the act—the one meaning *a sending away*, the other *a giving away*. It will be enough if we look at the feelings associated with the exercise of what is called *forgiveness*.

A man will say: "I forgive, but I cannot forget. Let the fellow never come in my sight again." To what does such a forgiveness reach? To the remission or sending away of the penalties which the wronged believes he can claim from the wrong-doer.

But there is no sending away of the wrong itself from between them.

Again, a man will say: "He has done a very mean action, but he has the worst of it himself in that he is capable of doing so. I despise him too much to desire revenge. I will take no notice of it. I forgive him. I don't care."

Here, again, there is no sending away of the wrong from between them—no *remission* of the sin.

A third will say: "I suppose I must forgive him; for if I do not forgive him, God will not forgive me."

This man is a *little* nearer the truth, inasmuch as a ground of sympathy, though only that of common sin, is recognized as between the offender and himself.

One more will say: "He has wronged me grievously. It is a dreadful thing to me, and more dreadful still to him, that he should have done it. He has hurt me, but he has nearly killed himself. He shall have no more injury from it that I can save him. I cannot feel the same towards him yet; but I will try to make him acknowledge the wrong he has done me, and so put it away from him. Then, perhaps, I shall be able to feel towards him as I used to feel. For this end I will show him all the kindness I can, not forcing it upon him, but seizing every fit opportunity; not, I hope, from a wish to make myself great through bounty to him, but because I love him so much that I want to love him more in reconciling him to his true self. I would destroy this evil deed that has come between us. I send it away. And I would have him destroy it from between us too, by abjuring it utterly."

Which comes nearest to the divine idea of forgiveness? nearest, though with the gulf between, wherewith the heavens are higher than the earth?

For the Divine creates the human, has the creative power in excess of the human. It is the Divine forgiveness that, originating itself, creates our forgiveness, and therefore can do so much more. It can take up all our wrongs, small and great, with their righteous attendance of griefs and sorrows, and carry them away from between our God and us.

Christ is God's Forgiveness.

Before we approach a little nearer to this great sight, let us consider the human forgiveness in a more definite embodiment—as between a father and a son. For although God is so much more to us, and comes so much nearer to us than a father can be or come, yet the fatherhood is the last height of the human stair whence our understandings can see Him afar off, and where our hearts can first know that He is nigh, even in them.

There are various kinds and degrees of wrong-doing, which need varying kinds and degrees of forgiveness. An outburst of anger in a child, for instance, scarcely wants forgiveness. The wrong in it may be so small, that the parent has only to influence the child for self-restraint, and the rousing of the will against the wrong. The father will not feel that such a fault has built up any wall between him and his child.

But suppose that he discovered in him a habit of sly cruelty towards his younger brothers, or the animals of the house, how differently would he feel! Could his forgiveness be the same as in the former case? Would not the different evil require a different *form* of forgiveness? I mean, would not the forgiveness have to take the form of that kind of punishment fittest for restraining, in the hope of finally rooting out, the wickedness? Could there be true love in any other kind of forgiveness than this? A passing-by of the offence might spring from a poor human kindness, but never from divine love. It would not be *remission*. Forgiveness can never be indifference. Forgiveness is love towards the unlovely.

Let us look a little closer at the way a father might feel, and express his feelings. One child, the moment the fault was committed, the father would clasp to his bosom, knowing that very love in its own natural manifestation would destroy the fault in him, and that, the next moment, he would be weeping. The father's hatred of the sin would burst forth

in his pitiful tenderness towards the child who was so
wretched as to have done the sin, and so destroy it. The fault
of such a child would then cause no interruption of the
interchange of sweet affections. The child is forgiven at
once.

But the treatment of another upon the same principle
would be altogether different. If he had been guilty of base-
ness, meanness, selfishness, deceit, self-gratulation in the
evil brought upon others, the father might *say* to himself:
"I cannot forgive him. This is beyond forgiveness." He
might *say* so, and keep saying so, while all the time he was
striving to let forgiveness find its way that it might lift him
from the gulf into which he had fallen.

His love might grow yet greater because of the wandering and loss of his son. For love is divine, and then most
divine when it loves according to *needs* and not according to
merits. But the forgiveness would be but in the process of
making, as it were, or of drawing nigh to the sinner. Not till
his opening heart received the divine flood of destroying
affection, and his own affection burst forth to meet it and
sweep the evil away, could it be said to be finished, to have
arrived, could the son be said to *be* forgiven.

God is forgiving us every day—sending from between
Him and us our sins and their fogs and darkness. Witness
the shining of His sun and the falling of His rain, the filling
of their hearts with food and gladness, that He loves them
that love Him not. When some sin that we have committed
has clouded all our horizon, and hidden Him from our
eyes, He, forgiving us, ere we are, and that we may be, forgiven, sweeps away a path for this His forgiveness to reach
our hearts, that it may by causing our repentance destroy
the wrong, and make us able even to forgive ourselves. For
some are too proud to forgive themselves, till the forgiveness of God has had its way with them.

But, looking upon forgiveness, then, as the perfecting of
a work ever going on, as the contact of God's heart and ours,

in spite and in destruction of the intervening wrong, we may say that God's love is ever in front of His forgiveness. God's love is the prime mover, ever seeking to perfect His forgiveness, which latter needs the human condition for its consummation. The love is perfect, working out the forgiveness. God loves where He cannot yet forgive—where forgiveness in the full sense is as yet simply impossible, because no contact of hearts is possible, because that which lies between has not yet begun to yield to His holy destruction.

Some things, then, between the Father and His children, as between a father and his child, may comparatively, and in a sense, be made light of—I do not mean made light of in themselves: away they must go—inasmuch as, evils or sins though they be, they yet leave room for the dwelling of God's Spirit in the heart, forgiving and cleansing away the evil. When a man's evil is thus fading out of him, and he is growing better and better, that is the forgiveness coming into him more and more. Perfect in God's will, it is having its perfect work in the mind of the man.

When the man has, with his whole nature, cast away his sin, there is no room for forgiveness any more, for God dwells in him, and he in God. With the voice of Nathan, "You are the man," the forgiveness of God laid hold of David, the heart of the king was humbled to the dust; and when he thus awoke from the moral lethargy that had fallen upon him, he found that he was still with God. "When I awake," he said, "I am still with thee."

Our Unforgiveness toward Others
But there are two sins, not of individual deed, but of spiritual condition, which *cannot be forgiven*; that is, as it seems to me, which cannot be excused, passed by, made little of by the tenderness even of God, inasmuch as they will allow no forgiveness to come into the soul, they will permit no good influence to go on working alongside of them; they shut God out altogether. Therefore the man guilty of these can

never receive into himself the holy renewing saving influences of God's forgiveness. God is outside of him in every sense, save that which springs from His creating relation to him, by which, thanks be to God, He yet keeps a hold of him, although against the will of the man who will not be forgiven. The one of these sins is against man; the other against God.

The former is unforgivingness to our neighbor; the shutting of him out from our mercies, from our love—so from the universe, as far as we are a portion of it—the murdering therefore of our neighbor. It may be an infinitely less evil to murder a man than to refuse to forgive him. The former may be the act of a moment of passion: the latter is the heart's choice. It is *spiritual* murder, the worst, to hate, to brood over the feeling that excludes, that kills the image, the idea of the hated.

We listen to the voice of our own hurt pride or hurt affection to the injury of the evil-doer. In as far as we can, we quench the relations of life between us; we close up the passages of possible return. This is to shut out God, the Life, the One. For how are we to receive the forgiving presence while we shut out our brother from our portion of the universal forgiveness, the final restoration, thus refusing to let God be All in all? If God appeared to us, how could He say, "I forgive you," while we remained unforgiving to our neighbor? Suppose it possible that He should say so, His forgiveness would be no good to us while we were uncured of our unforgivingness. It would not touch us.

Nay, it would hurt us, for we should think ourselves safe and well, while the horror of disease was eating the heart out of us. Tenfold the forgiveness lies in the words, "If you do not forgive men their trespasses, neither will your Father forgive your trespasses." Those words are kindness indeed. God holds the unforgiving man with His hand, but turns His face away from him. If, in his desire to see the face of his Father, he turns his own towards his brother, then the face of God turns round and seeks his, for then the man may look upon God and not die. With our forgiveness to our neighbor, in flows the consciousness of God's forgiveness to us; or even with the effort, we become capable of believing that God can forgive us.

If God said, "I forgive you," to a man who hated his brother, and if (as is impossible) that voice of forgiveness should reach the man, what would it mean to him? How would the man interpret it? Would it not mean to him, "You may go on hating. I do not mind it. You have had great provocation, and are justified in your hate"? No doubt God takes what wrong there is, and what provocation there is, into the account; but the more provocation, the more excuse that can be urged for the hate, the more reason, if possible, that the hater should be delivered from the hell of his hate, that God's child should be made the loving child that He meant him to be.

The man would think, not that God loved the sinner, but that He forgave the sin, which God never does. *Every* sin meets with its due fate—inexorable expulsion from the paradise of God's Humanity. He loves the sinner so much that He cannot forgive him in any other way than by banishing from his bosom the demon that possesses him, by lifting him out of that mire of his iniquity.

No one, however, supposes for a moment that a man who has once refused to forgive his brother, shall therefore be condemned to endless unforgiveness and unforgivingness. What is meant is, that while a man continues in such a mood, God cannot be with him as his friend; not that He will not be his friend, but the friendship being all on one side—that of God—must take forms such as the man will not be able to recognize as friendship. Forgiveness, as I have said, is not love merely, but love *conveyed as love* to the erring, so establishing peace towards God, and forgiveness towards our neighbor.

God's Unforgiveness

To return then to our immediate text: Is the refusal of forgiveness contained in it a condemnation to irrecoverable impenitence? Strange righteousness would be the decree, that because a man has done wrong—let us say has done wrong so often and so much that he *is* wrong—he shall forever remain wrong! Do not tell me the condemnation is only negative—a leaving of the man to the consequences of his own will, or at most a withdrawing from him of the Spirit which he has despised. God will not take shelter behind such a jugglery of logic or metaphysics. He is neither schoolman nor theologian, but our Father in heaven. He knows that that in Him would be the same unforgivingness for which He refuses to forgive man.

The only tenable ground for supporting such a doctrine is, that God *cannot* do more; that Satan has overcome; and that Jesus, amongst His own brothers and sisters in the image of God, has been less strong than the adversary, the destroyer. What then shall I say of such a doctrine of devils as that, even if a man did repent, God would not or could not forgive him?

Let us look at "*the* unpardonable sin," as this mystery is commonly called, and see what we can find to understand about it.

All sin is unpardonable. There is no compromise to be made with it. We shall not come out except clean, except having paid the "last penny." But the special unpardonableness of those sins, the one of which I have spoken and that which we are now considering, lies in their shutting out God from His *genial*, His especially spiritual, influences upon the man. Possibly in the case of the former sin, I may have said this too strongly; possibly the love of God may have some part even in the man who will not forgive his brother, although, if he continues unforgiving, that part must decrease and die away; possibly resentment against our brother, might yet for a time leave room for some divine influences by its side, although either the one or the other must speedily yield; but the man who denies truth, who consciously resists duty, who says there is no truth, or that the truth he sees is not true, who says that which is good is of Satan, or that which is bad is of God, supposing him to know that it is good or is bad, denies the Spirit, shuts out the Spirit, and therefore cannot be forgiven.

For without the Spirit no forgiveness can enter the man to cast out the Satan. Without the Spirit to witness with his spirit, no man could know himself forgiven, even if God appeared to him and said so. The full forgiveness is, as I have said, when a man feels that God is forgiving him; and this cannot be while he opposes himself to the very essence of God's will.

As far as we can see, the men of whom this was spoken were men who resisted the truth with some amount of perception that it was the truth. They were men so set, from selfishness and love of influence, against one whom they saw to be a good man, that they denied the goodness of what they knew to be good, in order to put down the man whom they knew to be good, because He had spoken against them, and was ruining their influence and authority with the people by declaring them to be no better than they knew themselves to be. Is not this to be Satan? Was not this their *condition* unpardonable? How, through all this mass of falsehood, could the pardon of God reach the essential humanity within it?

Crying as it was for God's forgiveness, these men had almost separated their humanity from themselves, had taken their part with the powers of darkness. Forgiveness while they were such was an impossibility. No. Out of that they must come, else there was no word of God for them. But the very word that told them of the unpardonable state in which they were, was just the one form the voice of mercy could take in calling on them to repent. They must hear and be afraid. I dare not, cannot think that they refused the truth, knowing *all* that it was; but I think they refused the truth, knowing that it was true. They were not carried away, as I have said, by wild passion, but by cold self-love, and envy, and avarice, and ambition; they were not merely doing wrong knowingly, but setting their whole natures knowingly against the light.

Of this nature must the sin against the Holy Spirit surely be. "This is the judgment," (not the sins that men have committed, but the condition of mind in which they choose to remain,) "that the light has come into the world, and men loved darkness rather than light because their deeds were evil." In this sin against the Holy Spirit, I see no single act alone, although it must find expression in many acts, but a wilful condition of mind,

> *As far removed from God and light of heaven,*
> *As from the centre thrice to the utmost pole.*

But can a man really fall into such a condition of spiritual depravity?

That is my chief difficulty. But I think it may be. And wiser people than I have thought so. I have difficulty in believing it, I say; yet I think it must be so. But I do not believe that it is a fixed, a final condition. I do not see why it should be such any more than that of the man who does not forgive his neighbor. If you say it is a worse offence, I say, Is it too bad for the forgiveness of God?

But is God able to do anything more with the man? Or how is the man ever to get out of this condition? If the Spirit of God is shut out from his heart, how is he to become better?

The Rebel In Extremity

The Spirit of God is the Spirit whose influence is known by its witnessing with our spirit. But may there not be other powers and means of the Spirit preparatory to this its highest office with man? God who has made us can never be far from any man who draws the breath of life—nay, must be in him: not necessarily in his heart, as we say, but still in him. May not then one day some terrible convulsion from the centre of his being, some fearful earthquake from the hidden gulfs of his nature, shake such a man so that through all the deafness of his death, the voice of the Spirit may be faintly heard, the still small voice that comes after the tempest and the earthquake? May there not be a fire that even such can feel? Who shall set bounds to the consuming of the fire of our God, and the purifying that dwells therein?

The only argument that I can think of, which would with me have weight against this conclusion, is, that the revulsion of feeling in any one who had thus sinned against the truth, when once brought to acknowledge his sin, would be so terrible that life would never more be endurable, and the kindest thing God could do would be to put such a man out of being, because it had been a better thing for him never to have been born. But He who could make such a man repent, could make him so sorrowful and lowly, and so glad that he had repented, that he would wish to live ever that he might ever repent and ever worship the glory he now beheld. When a man gives up self, his past sins will no longer oppress him. It is enough for the good of life that God lives, that the All-perfect exists, and that we can behold Him.

"Father, forgive them, for they know not what they do," said the Divine, making excuse for His murderers, not after it was all over, but at the very moment when He was dying by their hands. Then Jesus had forgiven them already. His prayer the Father must have heard, for He and the Son are one. When the Father succeeded in answering His prayer, then His forgiveness in the hearts of the murderers broke out in sorrow, repentance, and faith. Here was a sin dreadful enough surely—but easy for our Lord to forgive. All that excuse for the misled populace! Lord Christ be thanked for that! That was like thee!

But must we believe that Judas, who repented even to agony, who repented so that his high-prized life, self, soul, became worthless in his eyes and met with no mercy at his own hand—must we believe that he could find no mercy in such a God? I think, when Judas fled from his hanged and fallen body, he fled to the tender help of Jesus, and found it —I say not how. He was in a more hopeful condition now than during any moment of his past life, for he had never repented before. But I believe that Jesus loved Judas even when he was kissing Him with the traitor's kiss; and I believe that He was his Savior still.

If any man remind me of His words, "It had been good for that man if he had not been born," I had not forgotten them, though I know that I now offer nothing beyond a conjectural explanation of them when I say: Judas had got none of the good of the world into which he had been born. He had not inherited the earth. He had lived an evil life, out of harmony with the world and its God. Its love had been lost upon him. He had been brought to the very Son of God, and had lived with Him as his own familiar friend; and he had not loved Him more, but less than himself. Therefore it had been all useless. "It had been good for that man if he had not been born"; for it was all to try over again, in some other way—inferior perhaps, in some other world, in a lower school.

He had to be sent down the scale of creation which is ever ascending towards its Maker. But I will not, cannot believe, O my Lord, that you would not forgive your enemy, even when he repented, and did you right. Nor will I believe that your holy death was powerless to save your foe—that it could not reach to Judas. Have we not heard of those, your own, taught of you, who could easily forgive their betrayers in your name? And if you forgive, will not your forgiveness find its way at last in redemption and purification?

Look for a moment at the clause preceding my text: "He who denies me before men will be denied before the angels of God." What does it mean? Does it mean—"Ah! you are mine, but not of my sort. You denied me. Away to the outer darkness"? Not so. "Everyone who speaks a word against the Son of man will be forgiven"; for He may be but the truth revealed *without* him. Only he must have shame before the universe of the loving God, and may need the fire that burns and consumes not.

But for him that speaks against the Spirit of Truth, against the Son of God revealed *within* him, he is beyond the teaching of that Spirit now. For how shall he be forgiven? The forgiveness would touch him no more than a wall of stone. Let him know what it is to be without the God he has denied. Away with him to the Outer Darkness! Perhaps *that* will make him repent.

My friends, I offer this as only a contribution towards the understanding of our Lord's words. But if we ask Him, He will lead us into all truth. And let us not be afraid to think, for He will not take it ill.

But what I have said must be at least a part of the truth.

No amount of discovery in His words can tell us more than *we* have discovered, more than we have seen and known to be true. For all the help the best of His disciples can give us is only to discover, to see for ourselves.

And beyond all our discoveries in His words and being, there lie depths within depths of truth that we cannot understand, and yet shall be ever going on to understand. Yea, even now sometimes we seem to have dim glimpses into regions from which we receive no word to bring away.

The fact that some things have become to us so much more simple than they were, and that great truths have come out of what once looked common, is ground enough for hope that such will go on to be our experience through the ages to come. Our advance from our former ignorance can measure but a small portion of the distance that lies, and must ever lie, between our childishness and His manhood, between our love and His love, between our dimness and His mighty vision.

SIX

JUSTICE

❦

...*A*nd that to thee, O Lord, be-
longs steadfast love. For thou dost require a man according to his
work (Psalm 62:12).

Some of the translators make it *kindness* and *goodness;* but
I presume there is no real difference among them as to the
character of the word which here, in the English Bible, is
translated *mercy* [RSV: steadfast love].

The religious mind, however, educated upon the
theories yet prevailing in the so-called religious world, must
here recognize a departure from the presentation to which
they have been accustomed. To make the psalm speak
according to prevalent theoretic modes, the verse would
have to be changed thus: "To thee, O Lord, belongs *justice*,
for thou dost require a man according to his work."

Let us endeavour to see plainly what we mean when we
use the word *justice*, and whether we mean what we ought to
mean when we use it—especially with reference to God. Let

us come nearer to knowing what we ought to understand by justice, that is, the justice of God. For His justice is the live, active justice, giving existence to the idea of justice in our minds and hearts. Because He is just, we are capable of knowing justice; it is because He is just, that we have the idea of justice so deeply imbedded in us.

What do we most often mean by *justice*? Is it not the carrying out of the law, the infliction of penalty assigned to offense? By a just judge we mean a man who administers the law without prejudice, without favor or dislike; and where guilt is manifest, punishes as much as, and no more than, the law has in the case laid down. It may not be that justice has therefore been done. The law itself may be unjust, and the judge may mistake; or, which is more likely, the working of the law may be foiled by the parasites of law for their own gain. But even if the law be good, and thoroughly administered, it does not necessarily follow that justice is done.

Illustration
Suppose my watch has been taken from my pocket. I lay hold of the thief. He is dragged before the magistrate, proved guilty, and sentenced to a just imprisonment. Must I walk home satisfied with the result? Have I had justice done me? The thief may have had justice done him—but where is my watch? That is gone, and I remain a man wronged. Who has done me the wrong? The thief. Who can set right the wrong? The thief, and only the thief; nobody but the man that did the wrong. God may be able to move the man to right the wrong, but God Himself cannot right it without the man.

Suppose my watch found and restored, is the account settled between me and the thief? I may forgive him, but is the wrong removed? By no means. But suppose the thief repents. He has, we shall say, put it out of his power to return the watch, but he comes to me and says he is sorry he stole it, and begs me to accept for the present what little he is able to bring, as a beginning of atonement. How should I then regard the matter?

Should I not feel that he had gone far to make atonement —done more to make up for the injury he had inflicted upon me, than the mere restoration of the watch, even by himself, could reach to? Would there not lie, in the thief's confession and submission and initial restoration, an appeal to the divinest in me—to the eternal brotherhood? Would it not indeed amount to a sufficing atonement as between man and man? If he offered to bear what I chose to lay upon him, should I feel it necessary, for the sake of justice, to inflict some certain suffering as demanded by righteousness? I should still have a claim upon him for my watch, but should I not be apt to forget it? He who commits the offense can make up for it—and he alone.

One thing must surely be plain—that the punishment of the wrong-doer makes no atonement for the wrong done. How could it make up to me for the stealing of my watch that the man was punished? The wrong would be there all the same. Punishment may do good to the man who does the wrong, but that is a thing as different as important.

Another thing plain is, that, even without the material rectification of the wrong where that is impossible, repentance removes the offense which no suffering could. I at least should feel that I had no more quarrel with the man. I should even feel that the gift he had made me, giving into my heart a repentant brother, was infinitely beyond the restitution of what he had taken from me. True, he owed me both himself and the watch, but such a greater does more than include such a less.

It may be objected, "You may forgive, but the man has sinned against God!" Then it is not a part of the divine to be merciful, I return, and a man may be more merciful than his maker! A man may do that which would be too merciful in God! Then mercy is not a divine attribute. It must not be infinite; therefore, it cannot be God's own.

What Is God's Justice?

"Mercy may be against justice." Never—if you mean by justice what I mean by justice. If anything be against justice, it cannot be called mercy, for it is cruelty.... "*to thee, O Lord, belongs steadfast love. For thou dost requite a man according to his work.*" There is *no* opposition, *no* strife whatever, between mercy and justice. Those who say justice means the punishing of sin, and mercy the not punishing of sin, and attribute both to God, would make a schism in the very idea of God. And this brings me to the question, What is meant by divine justice?

Human justice may be a poor distortion of justice, a mere shadow of it; but the justice of God must be perfect. We cannot frustrate it in its working; are we just to it in our idea of it? In God shall we imagine a distinction of office and character? God is one; and the depth of foolishness is reached by that theology which talks of God as if He held different offices, and differed in each. It sets a contradiction in the very nature of God Himself. It represents Him, for instance, as having to do that as a magistrate which as a father He would not do! The love of the father makes Him desire to be unjust as a magistrate!

Oh the folly of any mind that would explain God before obeying Him! that would map out the character of God, instead of crying, Lord, what would you have me to do? God is no magistrate; but, if He were, it would be a position to which His fatherhood alone gave Him the right; His rights as a father cover every right He can be analytically supposed to possess.

The justice of God is this, that—to use a boyish phrase, the best the language will now afford me because of misuse —He gives every man, woman, child, and beast—everything that has being—*fair play*. He renders to every man according to his work. And therein lies His perfect mercy, for nothing else would be merciful to the man, and nothing but mercy could be fair to him. God does nothing of which any just man, the thing set fairly and fully before him so that he understood, would not say, "That is fair."

Who would, I repeat, say a man was a just man because he insisted on prosecuting every offender? A scoundrel might do that. Yet the justice of God, forsooth, is His punishment of sin! A just man is one who cares, and tries, and always tries, to give fair play to everyone in everything. When we speak of the justice of God, let us see that we do mean justice! Punishment of the guilty may be involved in justice, but it does not constitute the justice of God one atom more than it would constitute the justice of a man.

The Lord of Life complains of men for not judging right. To say on the authority of the Bible that God does a thing no honorable man would do, is to lie against God; to say that it is therefore right, is to lie against the very Spirit of God. To uphold a lie for God's sake is to be against God, not for Him. God cannot be lied for. He is the truth. The truth alone is on His side. While His child could not see the rectitude of a thing, He would infinitely rather, even if the thing were right, have him say, "God could not do that thing," than have him believe that He did it.

If it be said by any that God does a thing, and the thing seems to me unjust, then either I do not know what the thing is, or God does not do it. The saying cannot mean what it seems to mean, or the saying is not true. If, for instance, it be said that God visits the sins of the fathers on the children, a man who takes *visits upon* to mean *punishes*, and *the children* to mean *the innocent children*, ought to say, "Either I do not understand the statement, or the thing is not true, whoever says it." God *may* do what seems to a man not right, but it must so seem to him because God works on higher, on divine, on perfect principles, too right for a selfish, unfair, or unloving man to understand. But least of all must we accept some low notion of justice in a man, and argue that God is just in doing after that notion.

Does God Punish Sin?

The common idea, then, is, that the justice of God consists in punishing sin: it is in the hope of giving a larger idea of the justice of God that I ask, "*Why is God bound to punish sin?*"

"How could He be a just God and not punish sin?"

Mercy is a good and right thing, I answer, and but for sin there could be no mercy. We are enjoined to forgive, to be merciful, to be as our Father in heaven. Two rights cannot possibly be opposed to each other. If God punish sin, it must be merciful to punish sin; and if God forgive sin, it must be just to forgive sin. We are required to forgive, with the argument that our Father forgives. It must, I say, be right to forgive. Every attribute of God must be infinite as Himself. He cannot be sometimes merciful, and not always merciful. He cannot be just, and not always just. Mercy belongs to Him, and needs no contrivance of theologic chicanery to justify it.

"Then you mean that it is wrong to punish sin; therefore, God does not punish sin?"

By no means; God does punish sin, but there is no opposition between punishment and forgiveness. The one may be essential to the possibility of the other. *Why*, I repeat, does God punish sin? That is my point.

"Because in itself sin deserves punishment."

Then how can He tell us to forgive it?

"He punishes, and having punished He forgives?"

That will hardly do. If sin demands punishment, and the righteous punishment is given, then the man is free. Why should he be forgiven?

"He needs forgiveness because no amount of punishment will meet his deserts."

(I avoid for the present, as anyone may perceive, the probable expansion of this reply.)

Then why not forgive him at once if the punishment is not essential—if part can be pretermitted? And again, can that be required which, according to your showing, is not adequate? You will perhaps answer, "God may please to take what little He can have," and this brings me to the fault in the whole idea.

Punishment is *nowise* an *offset* to sin. Foolish people sometimes, in a tone of self-gratulatory pity, will say, "If I have sinned I have suffered." Yes, verily, but what of that? What merit is there in it? Even had you laid the suffering upon yourself, what did that do to make up for the wrong? That you may have bettered by your suffering is well for you, but what atonement is there in the suffering? The notion is a false one altogether. Punishment, or deserved suffering, is no equipoise to sin.

If it were an offset to wrong, then God would be bound to punish for the sake of the punishment; but He cannot be, for He forgives. Then it is not for the sake of the punishment, as a thing that in itself ought to be done, but for the sake of something else, as a means to an end, that God punishes. It is not directly for justice, else how could He show mercy, for that would involve injustice?

God's Obligation

Primarily, God is not bound to *punish* sin; He is bound to *destroy* sin. If He were not the Maker, He might not be bound to destroy sin—I do not know. But seeing He has created creatures who have sinned, and therefore sin has, by the creating act of God, come into the world, God is, in His own righteousness, bound to destroy sin.

"But that is to have no mercy."

You mistake. God does destroy sin; He is always destroying sin. In Him I trust that He is destroying sin in me. He is always saving the sinner from his sins, and that is destroying sin. But vengeance on the sinner, the law of a tooth for a tooth, is not in the heart of God, neither in His hand. If the sinner and the sin in him, are the concrete object of the divine wrath, then indeed there can be no mercy. Then indeed there will be an end put to sin by the destruction of the sin and the sinner together. But thus would no atonement be wrought—nothing be done to make up for the wrong God has allowed to come into being by creating man. There must be an atonement, a making-up, a bringing together—an atonement which, I say, cannot be made except by the man who has sinned.

Punishment, I repeat, is not the thing required of God, but the absolute destruction of sin. What better is the world, what better is the sinner, what better is God, what better is the truth, that the sinner should suffer—continue suffering to all eternity? Would there be less sin in the universe? Would there be any making up for sin? Would it show God justified in doing what He knew would bring sin into the world, justified in making creatures who He knew would sin? What setting-right would come of the sinner's suffering?

If justice demand it, if suffering be the equivalent for sin, then the sinner must suffer, then God is bound to exact his suffering, and not pardon; and so the making of man was a tyrannical deed, a creative cruelty. But grant that the sinner has deserved to suffer, no amount of suffering is any atonement for his sin. To suffer to all eternity could not make up for one unjust word.

Does that mean, then, that for an unjust word I deserve to suffer to all eternity? The unjust word is an eternally evil thing; nothing but God in my heart can cleanse me from the evil that uttered it; but does it follow that I saw the evil of what I did so perfectly, that eternal punishment for it would be just?

Sorrow and confession and self-abasing love will make up for the evil word; suffering will not. For evil in the abstract, nothing can be done. It is eternally evil. But I may be saved from it by learning to loathe it, to hate it, to shrink from it with an eternal avoidance. The only vengeance worth having on sin is to make the sinner himself its executioner.

Sin and punishment are in no antagonism to each other
in man, any more than pardon and punishment are in God;
they can perfectly co-exist. The one naturally follows the
other, punishment being born of sin, because evil exists
only by the life of good, and has no life of its own, being in
itself death. Sin and suffering are not natural opposites; the
opposite of evil is good, not suffering; the opposite of sin is
not suffering, but righteousness. The path across the gulf
that divides right from wrong is not the fire, but
repentance.

Take any of those wicked people in Dante's hell, and ask
wherein is justice served by their punishment. Mind, I am
not saying it is not right to punish them; I am saying that
justice is not, never can be, satisfied by suffering—nay,
cannot have any satisfaction in or from suffering. Human
resentment, human revenge, human hate may.

Such justice as Dante's keeps wickedness alive in its most
terrible forms. The life of God goes forth to inform, or at
least give a home to victorious evil. Is He not defeated every
time that one of those lost souls defies Him? God is
triumphantly defeated, I say, throughout the hell of His
vengeance. Although against evil, it is but the vain and
wasted cruelty of a tyrant. There is no destruction of evil
thereby, but an enhancing of its horrible power in the midst
of the most agonizing and disgusting tortures a *divine*
imagination can invent.

If sin must be kept alive, then hell must be kept alive; but
while I regard the smallest sin as infinitely loathsome, I do
not believe that any being, never good enough to see the
essential ugliness of sin, could sin so as to *deserve* such punishment. I am not now, however, dealing with the question
of the duration of punishment, but with the idea of punishment itself; and would only say in passing, that the notion
that a creature born imperfect, nay, born with impulses to
evil not of his own generating, and which he could not help
having, a creature to whom the true face of God was never

presented, and by whom it never could have been seen, should be thus condemned, is as loathsome a lie against God as could find place in heart too undeveloped to understand what justice is, and too low to look up into the face of Jesus. It never in truth found place in any heart, though in many a pettifogging brain. There is but one thing lower than deliberately to believe such a lie, and that is to worship the God of whom it is believed.

The Purpose of Punishment

The one deepest, highest, truest, fittest, most wholesome suffering must be generated in the wicked by a vision, a true sight, more or less adequate, of the hideousness of their lives, of the horror of the wrongs they have done. Physical suffering may be a factor in rousing this mental pain; but "I would I had never been born!" must be the cry of Judas, not because of the hell-fire around him, but because he loathes the man that betrayed his Friend, the world's Friend.

When a man loathes himself, he has begun to be saved. Punishment tends to this result. Not for its own sake, not as a make-up for sin, not for divine revenge—horrible words —not for any satisfaction to justice, can punishment exist. Punishment is for the sake of amendment and atonement. God is bound by His love to punish sin in order to deliver His creature: He is bound by His justice to destroy sin in His creation.

Love is justice—is the fulfilling of the law, for God as well as for His children. This is the reason of punishment; this is why justice requires that the wicked shall not go unpunished—that they, through the eye-opening power of pain, may come to see and do justice, may be brought to desire and make all possible amends, and so become just. Such punishment concerns justice in the deepest degree. For Justice, that is God, is bound in Himself to see justice done by His children—not in the mere outward act, but in their very being. He is bound in Himself to make up for wrong done by His children, and He can do nothing to make up for wrong done but by bringing about the repentance of the wrong-doer.

When the man says, "I did wrong; I hate myself and my deed; I cannot endure to think that I did it!" then, I say, is atonement begun. Without that, all that the Lord did would be lost. He would have made no atonement. Repentance, restitution, confession, prayer for forgiveness, righteous dealing thereafter, is the sole possible, the only true make-up for sin. For nothing less than this did Christ die.

When a man acknowledges the right he denied before; when he says to the wrong, "I abjure, I loathe you; I see now what you are; I could not see it before because I would not; God forgive me; make me clean, or let me die!" then justice, that is God, has conquered—and not till then.

What Atonement Is There?

There is every atonement that God cares for; and the work of Jesus Christ on earth was the creative atonement, because it works atonement in every heart. He brings and is bringing God and man, and man and man, into perfect unity: "I in them and thou in me, that they may be made perfect in one."

"That is a dangerous doctrine!"

More dangerous than you think to many things—to every evil, to every lie, and to every false trust in what Christ did, instead of in Christ Himself. Paul glories in the cross of Christ, but he does not trust in the cross: he trusts in the living Christ and His living Father.

Justice then requires that sin should be put an end to; and not that only, but that it should be atoned for; and where punishment can do anything to this end, where it can help the sinner to know what he has been guilty of, where it can soften his heart to see his pride and wrong and cruelty, justice requires that punishment shall not be spared. And the more we believe in God, the surer we shall be that He will spare nothing that suffering can do to deliver His child from death.

If suffering cannot serve this end, we need look for no more hell, but for the destruction of sin by the destruction of the sinner. That, however, would, it appears to me, be for God to suffer defeat, blameless indeed, but defeat.

If God be defeated, He must destroy, that is, He must withdraw life. How can He go on sending forth His life into irreclaimable souls, to keep sin alive in them throughout the ages of eternity? But then, I say, no atonement would be made for the wrongs they have done. God remains defeated, for He has created that which sinned, and which would not repent and make up for its sin.

But those who believe that God will thus be defeated by many souls, must surely be of those who do not believe He cares enough to do His very best for them. He *is* their Father; He had power to make them out of Himself, separate from Himself, and capable of being one with Him: surely He will somehow save and keep them! Not the power of sin itself can close *all* the channels between creating and created.

The Grip of False Idea

The notion of suffering as an offset for sin, the foolish idea that a man by suffering borne may get out from under the hostile claim to which his wrong-doing has subjected him, comes first of all, I think, from the satisfaction we feel when wrong comes to grief. Why do we feel this satisfaction? Because we hate wrong, but, not being righteous ourselves, more or less hate the wronger as well as his wrong, hence are not only righteously pleased to behold the law's disapproval proclaimed in his punishment, but unrighteously pleased with his suffering, because of the impact upon us of his wrong. In this way the inborn justice of our nature passes over to evil.

It is no pleasure to God, as it so often is to us, to see the wicked suffer. To regard any suffering with satisfaction, save it be sympathetically with its curative quality, comes of evil, is human because undivine, is a thing God is incapable of. His nature is always to forgive, and just because He forgives, He punishes.

Because God is so altogether alien to wrong, because it is to Him a heart-pain and trouble that one of His little ones should do the evil thing, there is, I believe, no extreme of suffering to which, for the sake of destroying the evil thing in them He would not subject them. A man might flatter, or bribe, or coax a tyrant; but there is no refuge from the love of God; that love will, for very love, insist upon the "last penny."

"That is not the sort of love I care about!"

No; how should you? I well believe it! You cannot care for it until you begin to know it. But the eternal love will not be moved to yield you to the selfishness that is killing you. You may sneer at such love, but the Son of God who took the weight of that love, and bore it through the world, is content with it, and so is everyone who knows it. The love of the Father is a radiant perfection. Love and not self-love is lord of the universe.

Justice demands your punishment, because justice demands, and will have, the destruction of sin. Justice demands your punishment because it demands that your Father should do His best for you. God, being the God of justice, that is of fair-play, and having made us what we are, apt to fall and capable of being raised again, is in Himself bound to punish in order to deliver us—else is His relation to us poor beside that of an earthly father. "To thee, O Lord, belongs steadfast love for thou dost requite a man according to his work." A man's work is his character; and God in His mercy is not indifferent, but treats him according to his work.

The notion that the salvation of Jesus is a salvation from

the consequences of our sins, is a false, mean, low notion. The salvation of Christ is salvation from the smallest tendency or leaning to sin. It is a deliverance into the pure air of God's ways of thinking and feeling. It is a salvation that makes the heart pure, with the will and choice of the heart to be pure. To such a heart, sin is disgusting. It sees a thing as it is,—that is, as God sees it, for God sees everything as it is. The souls thus saved would rather sink into the flames of hell than steal into heaven and skulk there under the shadow of an imputed righteousness. No soul is saved that would not prefer hell to sin. Jesus did not die to save us from punishment; He was called Jesus because He should save His people from their sins.

MacDonald's Creed

I believe in Jesus Christ, the eternal Son of God, my elder brother, my lord and master; I believe that He has a right to my absolute obedience whereinsoever I know or shall come to know His will; that to obey Him is to ascend the pinnacle of my being; that not to obey Him would be to deny Him.

I believe that He died that I might die like Him—die to any ruling power in me but the will of God—live ready to be nailed to the cross as He was, if God will it. I believe that He is my Savior from myself, and from all that has come of loving myself, from all that God does not love, and would not have me love—all that is not worth loving; that He died that the justice, the mercy of God, might have its way with me, making me just as God is just, merciful as He is merciful, perfect as my Father in heaven is perfect.

I believe and pray that He will give me what punishment I need to set me right, or keep me from going wrong. I believe that He died to deliver me from all meanness, all pretence, all falseness, all unfairness, all poverty of spirit, all cowardice, all fear, all anxiety, all forms of self-love, all trust or hope in possession; to make me merry as a child, the child of our Father in heaven, loving nothing but what is lovely, desiring nothing I should be ashamed to let the universe of God see me desire.

I believe that God is just like Jesus, only greater yet, for Jesus said so. I believe that God is absolutely, grandly beautiful, even as the highest soul of man counts beauty, but infinitely beyond that soul's highest idea—with the beauty that creates beauty, not merely shows it, or itself exists beautiful. I believe that God has always done, is always doing His best for every man; that no man is miserable because God is forgetting him; that he is not a God to crouch before, but our Father, to whom the child-heart cries exultant, "Do with me as you will."

I believe that there is nothing good for me or for any man but God, and more and more of God, and that alone through knowing Christ can we come nigh to Him.

I believe that no man is ever condemned for any sin except one—that he will not leave his sins and come out of them, and be the child of Him who is his father.

I believe that justice and mercy are simply one and the same thing; without justice to the full there can be no mercy, and without mercy to the full there can be no justice; that such is the mercy of God that He will hold His children in the consuming fire of His distance until they pay the last penny, until they drop the purse of selfishness with all the dross that is in it, and rush home to the Father and the Son, and the many brethren—rush inside the centre of the life-giving fire whose outer circles burn. I believe that no hell will be lacking which would help the just mercy of God to redeem His children.

I believe that to him who obeys, and thus opens the doors of his heart to receive the eternal gift, God gives the Spirit of His Son, the Spirit of Himself, to be in him, and lead him to the understanding of all truth; that the true disciple shall thus always know what he ought to do, though not necessarily what another ought to do; that the Spirit of the Father and the Son enlightens by teaching righteousness.

I believe that no teacher should strive to make men think as he thinks, but to lead them to the living Truth, to the Master Himself, of whom alone they can learn anything, who will make them in themselves know what is true by the very seeing of it. I believe that the inspiration of the Almighty alone gives understanding. I believe that to be the disciple of Christ is the end of being; that to persuade men to be His disciples is the end of teaching.

Atonement

"The sum of all this is that you do not believe in the atonement?"

I believe in Jesus Christ. Nowhere am I requested to believe *in* any thing, or *in* any statement, but everywhere to believe in God and in Jesus Christ. I believe that Jesus Christ *is* our atonement; that through Him we are reconciled to, made one with God. There is not one word in the New Testament about reconciling God to us; it is we that have to be reconciled to God.

I am not writing, neither desire to write, a treatise on the atonement, my business being to persuade men to be atoned to God; but I will go so far to meet my questioner as to say—without the slightest expectation of satisfying him, or the least care whether I do so or not, for his *opinion* is of no value to me, though his truth is of endless value to me and to the universe—that, even in the sense of the atonement being a making-up for the evil done by men toward God, I believe in the atonement.

Did not the Lord cast Himself into the eternal gulf of evil yawning between the children and the Father? Did He not bring the Father to us, let us look on our eternal Sire in the face of His true Son, that we might have that in our hearts which alone could make us love Him—a true sight of Him? Did He not insist on the one truth of the universe, the one saving truth, that God was just what He was? Did He not hold to that assertion to the last, in the face of contradiction and death? Did He not thus lay down His life persuading us to lay down ours at the feet of the Father? Has not His very life by which He died passed into those who have received Him, and re-created theirs, so that now they live with the life which alone is life? Did He not foil and slay evil by letting all the waves and billows of its horrid sea break upon Him, go over Him, and die without rebound—spend their rage, fall defeated, and cease? Verily, He made atonement.

We sacrifice to God!—it is God who has sacrificed His own Son to us; there was no way else of getting the gift of Himself into our hearts. Jesus sacrificed Himself to His Father and the children to bring them together—all the love on the side of the Father and the Son, all the selfishness on the side of the children. If the joy that alone makes life worth living, the joy that God is such as Christ, be a true thing in my heart, how can I but believe in the atonement of Jesus Christ? I believe it heartily, as God means it.

Then again, as the power that brings about a making-up for any wrong done by man to man, I believe in the atonement. Who that believes in Jesus does not long to atone to his brother for the injury he has done him? What repentant child, feeling he has wronged his father, does not desire to make atonement? Who is the mover, the causer, the persuader, the creator of the repentance of the passion that restores fourfold?—Jesus, our propitiation, our atonement. He is the head and leader, the prince of the atonement.

He could not do it without us, but He leads us up to the Father's knee: He makes us make atonement. Learning Christ, we are not only sorry for what we have done wrong, we not only turn from it and hate it, but we become able to serve both God and man with an infinitely high and true service, a soul-service. We are able to offer our whole being to God to whom by deepest right it belongs.

Have I injured anyone? With Him to aid my justice, new risen with Him from the dead, shall I not make good

amends? Have I failed in love to my neighbor? Shall I not
now love him with an infinitely better love than was possible
to me before? That I will and can make atonement, thanks
be to Him who is my atonement, making me at one with
God and my fellows! He is my life, my joy, my lord, my
owner, the perfecter of my being by the perfection of His
own. I dare not say with Paul that I am the slave of Christ;
but my highest aspiration and desire is to be the slave of
Christ.

God's Forgiving Nature

"But you do not believe that the sufferings of Christ, as sufferings, justified the Supreme Ruler in doing anything
which He would not have been at liberty to do but for those
sufferings?"

I do not. I believe the notion is unworthy of man's belief,
as it is dishonoring to God. It has its origin doubtless in a
salutary sense of sin; but sense of sin is not inspiration,
though it may lie not far from the temple-door. It is indeed
an opener of the eyes, but upon home-defilement, not
upon heavenly truth; it is not the revealer of secrets.

Also, there is another factor in the theory, and that is unbelief—incapacity to accept the freedom of God's forgiveness; incapacity to believe that it is God's chosen nature to
forgive, that He is bound in His own divinely willed nature
to forgive. No atonement is necessary to Him but that men
should leave their sins and come back to His heart.

But men cannot believe in the forgiveness of God.
Therefore they need, therefore He has given them a
mediator. And yet they will not know Him. They think of
the Father of Souls as if He had abdicated His fatherhood
for their sins, and assumed the judge. If He put off His
fatherhood, which He cannot do, for it is an eternal fact,
he puts off with it all relation to us. He cannot repudiate the
essential and keep the resultant. Men cannot, or will not, or
dare not see that nothing but His being our Father gives

Him any right over us—that nothing but that could give Him a perfect right.

They regard the Father of their spirits as their governor! They yield the idea of the Ancient of Days, "the glad creator," and put in its stead a miserable, puritanical martinet of a God, caring not for righteousness, but for His rights; not for the eternal purities, but the goody proprieties. The prophets of such a God take all the glow, all the hope, all the color, all the worth, out of life on earth, and offer you instead what they call eternal bliss—a pale, tearless hell. Of all things, turn from a mean, poverty-stricken faith. But, if you are straitened in your own mammon-worshipping soul, how shall you believe in a God any greater than can stand up in that prison-chamber?

I desire to wake no dispute, will myself dispute with no man, but for the sake of those whom certain *believers* trouble, I have spoken my mind. I love the one God seen in the face of Jesus Christ. From all copies of Jonathan Edwards's portrait of God, however faded by time, however softened by the use of less glaring pigments, I turn with loathing. Not such a God is He concerning whom was the message John heard from Jesus, that He is light, and in Him is no darkness at all.

SEVEN

THE
FEAR
OF
GOD

*A*nd when I saw Him, I fell at
*His feet as though dead. And He laid his right hand upon me, say-
ing, 'Fear not; I am the First and the Last and the Living One'
(Rev. 1:17, 18).*

It is not alone the first beginnings of religion that are full
of fear. So long as love is imperfect, there is room for torment. That love only which fills the heart—and nothing but
love can fill any heart—is able to cast out fear, leaving no
room for its presence. What we find in the beginnings of religion, will hold in varying degree, until the religion, that is
the love, be perfected.

Those fear Him most who most imagine Him like their
own evil selves, only beyond them in power, easily able to
work His arbitrary will with them. That they hold Him but a
little higher than themselves, tends nowise to unity with
Him: who so far apart as those on the same level of hate and
distrust? Power without love, dependence where is no

righteousness, wake a worship without devotion, a loathliness of servile flattery.

Neither, where the notion of God is better, but the conscience is troubled, will His goodness do much to exclude apprehension. The same consciousness of evil and of offense which gave rise to the bloody sacrifice is still at work in the minds of most who call themselves Christians. Naturally the first emotion of man towards the being he calls God, but of whom he knows so little, is fear.

The Use of Fear

Where it is possible that fear should exist, it is well it should exist, cause continual uneasiness, and be cast out by nothing less than love. In him who does not know God, and must be anything but satisfied with himself, fear towards God is as reasonable as it is natural, and serves powerfully towards the development of his true humanity. Neither the savage, nor the self-sufficient sage, is rightly human. It matters nothing whether we regard the one or the other as degenerate or as undeveloped—neither I say is human; the humanity is there, but has to be born in each, and for this birth everything natural must do its part.

Fear is natural, and has a part to perform nothing but itself could perform in the birth of the true humanity. Until love, which is the truth towards God, is able to cast out fear, it is well that fear should hold; it is a bond, however poor, between that which is and that which creates—a bond that must be broken, but a bond that can be broken only by the tightening of an infinitely closer bond.

He will not abolish their fear except with the truth of His own being. Till they apprehend that, and in order that they may come to apprehend it, He receives their sacrifices of blood, the invention of their sore need, only influencing for the time the modes of them. He will destroy the lie that is not all a lie only by the truth which is all true. Although He loves them utterly, He does not tell them there is nothing in

Him to make them afraid. That would be to drive them from Him forever. While they are such as they are, there is much in Him that cannot but affright them; they ought, they do well to fear Him. It is, while they remain what they are, the only true relation between them.

To remove that fear from their hearts, save by letting them know His love with its purifying fire, a love which for ages, it may be, they cannot know, would be to give them up utterly to the power of evil. Persuade men that fear is a vile thing, that it is an insult to God, that He will none of it—while yet they are in love with their own will, and slaves to every movement of passionate impulse, and what will the consequence be? That they will insult God as a discarded idol, a superstition, a falsehood, as a thing under whose evil influence they have too long groaned, a thing to be cast out and spit upon. After that how much will they learn of Him?

Nor would it be long ere the old fear would return—with this difference, perhaps, that instead of trembling before a live energy, they would tremble before powers which formerly they regarded as inanimate, and have now endowed with souls after the imagination of their fears. Then would spiritual chaos with all its monsters be come again.

God being what He is, a God who loves righteousness; a God who, rather than do an unfair thing, would lay down His Godhead, and assert Himself in ceasing to be; a God who, that His creature might not die of ignorance, died as much as a God could die (and that is divinely more than man can die) to give him Himself; such a God, I say, may well look fearful from afar to the creature who recognizes in himself no imperative good; who fears only suffering, and has no aspiration—only wretched ambition.

But in proportion as such a creature comes nearer, grows towards Him in and for whose likeness he was begun; in proportion, that is, as the eternal right begins to disclose itself to him; in proportion as he becomes capable of the idea that his kind belongs to Him as he could never belong to himself; approaches the capacity of seeing and understanding that his individuality can be perfected only in the love of his neighbor, and that his being can find its end only in oneness with the source from which it came; in proportion, I do not say as he sees these things, but as he nears the possibility of seeing them, will his terror at the God of his life abate; though far indeed from surmising the bliss that awaits him, he is drawing more nigh to the goal of his nature, the central secret joy of sonship to a God who loves righteousness and hates iniquity, does nothing He would not permit in His creature, demands nothing of His creature He would not do Himself.

Fear of the Fire
The fire of God, which is His essential being, His love, His creative power, is a fire unlike its earthly symbol in this, that it is only at a distance it burns—that the farther from Him, it burns the worse, and that when we turn and begin to approach Him, the burning begins to change to comfort, which comfort will grow to such bliss that the heart at length cries out with a gladness no other gladness can reach, "Whom have I in heaven but thee? and there is nothing upon earth that I desire besides thee!"

The glory of being, the essence of life and its joy, shining upon the corrupt and deathly, must needs, like the sun, consume the dead, and send corruption down to the dust. That which it burns in the soul is not of the soul, yea, is at utter variance with it; yet so close to the soul is the foul fungus growth sprung from and subsisting upon it, that the burning of it is felt through every spiritual nerve. When the evil parasites are consumed away, that is when the man yields his self and all that self's low world, and returns to his lord and God, then that which, before, he was aware of only as burning, he will feel as love, comfort, strength—an eternal, ever-growing life in him. For now he lives, and life cannot hurt life; it can only hurt death, which needs and ought to be destroyed.

God is life essential, eternal, and death cannot live in His sight; for death is corruption, and has no existence in itself, living only in the decay of the things of life. If then any child of the Father finds that he is afraid before Him, that the thought of God is a discomfort to him, or even a terror, let him make haste—let him not linger to put on any garment, but rush at once in his nakedness, a true child, for shelter from his own evil and God's terror, into the salvation of the Father's arms, the home whence he was sent that he might learn that it was home. What father being evil would it not win to see that child with whom he was vexed running to his embrace? How much more will not the Father of our spirits, who seeks nothing but His children themselves, receive him with open arms!

Self, accepted as the law of self, is the one demon-enemy of life; God is the only Savior from it, and from all that is not God; for God is life, and all that is not God is death. Life is the destruction of death, of all that kills, of all that is of death's kind.

John's Fear

When John saw the glory of the Son of Man, he fell at His feet as one dead. In what way John saw Him, whether in what we vaguely call a vision, or in as human a way as when he leaned back on His bosom and looked up in His face, I do not now care to ask. It would take all glorious shapes of humanity to reveal Jesus, and He knew the right way to show Himself to John. It seems to me that such words as were spoken can have come from the mouth of no mere vision, can have been allowed to enter no merely tranced ear, that the mouth of the very Lord Himself spoke them, and that none but the living present Jesus could have spoken or may be supposed to speak them; while plainly John received and felt them as a message he had to give again.

There are also, strangely as the whole may affect us, various points in his description of the Lord's appearance which commend themselves even to our ignorance by their grandeur and fitness. Why then was John overcome with terror? We recall the fact that something akin to terror overwhelmed the minds of the three disciples who saw His glory on the mount; but since then John had leaned on the bosom of his Lord, had followed Him to the judgment seat and had not denied His name, had borne witness to His resurrection and suffered for His sake—and was now "in the island called Patmos on account of the word of God and the testimony of Jesus," why, I say, was he, why *should* he be afraid?

No glory even of God should breed terror; when a child of God is afraid, it is a sign that the word *Father* is not yet freely fashioned by the child's spiritual mouth. The glory can breed terror only in him who is capable of being terrified by it; while he is such it is well the terror should be bred and maintained, until the man seek refuge from it in the only place where it is not—in the bosom of the glory.

There is one point not distinguishable in the Greek: whether is meant, "one like *the* Son of Man," or, "one like *a* son of Man." The Authorized Version has the former, the Revised prefers the latter. I incline to the former, and think that John saw Him like the man he had known so well, and that it was the too much glory, dimming his vision, that made him unsure, not any perceived unlikeness mingling with the likeness. Nothing blinds so much as light, and their very glory might well render him unable to distinguish plainly the familiar features of *The* Son of Man.

But the appearance of The Son of Man was not intended to breed terror in the son of man to whom He came. Why then was John afraid? why did the servant of the Lord fall at His feet as one dead? Joy to us that he did, for the words that follow—surely no phantasmic outcome of uncertain vision or blinding terror! They bear best sign of their source. However given to his ears, they must be from the heart of our great Brother, the one Man, Christ Jesus, divinely human!

It was still and only the imperfection of the disciple, unfinished in faith, so unfinished in everything a man needs, that was the cause of his terror. This is surely implied in the words the Lord said to him when he fell! The thing that made John afraid, He speaks of as the thing that ought to have taken from him all fear.

For the glory that he saw, the head and hair pouring from it such a radiance of light that they were white as white wool—snow-white, as His garments on mount Hermon; in the midst of the radiance His eyes like a flame of fire, and His countenance as the sun shines in his strength; the darker glow of the feet, yet as of fine brass burning in a furnace—as if they, in memory of the twilight of His humiliation, touching the earth took a humbler glory than His head high in the empyrean of undisturbed perfection; the girdle under His breast golden between the snow and the brass—what were they all but the effulgence of His glory who was Himself the effulgence of the Father's, the poor expression of the unutterable verity which was itself the reason why John ought not to be afraid? "He laid His right hand upon me, saying, 'Fear not, I am the First and the Last, and the Living One.' "

Endless must be our terror, until we come heart to heart with the fire-core of the universe, the First and the Last and the Living One!

But oh, the joy to be told, by Power Himself, the First and the Last, the Living One—told what we can indeed then see *must* be true, but which we are so slow to believe—that the cure for trembling is the presence of Power; that fear cannot stand before Strength; that the visible God is the destruction of death; that the one and only safety in the universe, is the perfect nearness of the Living One!

God is being; death is nowhere! What a thing to be taught

by the very mouth of Him who knows! He told His servant
Paul that strength is made perfect in weakness; here He instructs His servant John that the thing to be afraid of is
weakness, not strength. All appearances of strength, such
as might rightly move terror, are but false appearances; the
true Strong is the *One*, even as the true Good is the *One*. The
Living One has the power of life; the Evil One but the
power of death—whose very nature is a self-necessity for
being destroyed.

But the glory of the mildest show of the Living One is
such, that even the dearest of His apostles, the best of the
children of men, is cowed at the sight. He has not yet
learned that glory itself is a part of his inheritance, yea is of
the natural condition of his being; that there is nothing in
the man made in the image of God alien from the most
glorious of heavenly shows. He has not learned this yet, and
falls as dead before it—when lo, the voice of Him that was
and is and is forevermore, telling him not to be afraid—for
the very reason, the one only reason, that He is the First and
the Last, the Living One.

For what shall be the joy, the peace, the completion of
him that lives, but closest contact with his Life?—a contact
close as ere he issued from that Life, only in infinitely higher kind, inasmuch as it is now willed on *both* sides. He who
has had a beginning, needs the indwelling power of that
beginning to make his being complete—not merely complete to his consciousness, but complete in itself—justified,
rounded, ended where it began—with an "endless ending."
Then is it complete even as God's is complete, for it is one
with the self-existent, blossoming in the air of that world
wherein it is rooted, wherein it lives and grows.

Far indeed from trembling because He on whose bosom
he had leaned when the light of His love was all but shut in
now stands with the glory of that love streaming forth, John
Boanerges ought to have felt the more joyful and safe as the
strength of the Living One was more manifested. It was

never because Jesus was clothed in the weakness of the flesh that He was fit to be trusted, but because He was strong with a strength able to take the weakness of the flesh for the garment wherein it could best work its work. That strength was now shining out with its own light, so lately pent within the revealing veil.

Had John been as close in spirit to the Son of Man as he had been in bodily presence, he would have indeed fallen at His feet, but not as one dead—as one too full of joy to stand before the life that was feeding his; he would have fallen, but not to lie there senseless with awe the most holy; he would have fallen to embrace and kiss the feet of Him who had now a second time, as with a resurrection from above, arisen before him, in yet heavenlier plenitude of glory.

In those then who believe that good is the one power, and that evil exists only because for a time it subserves, cannot help subserving the good, what place can there be for fear? The strong and the good are one; and if our hope coincides with that of God, if it is rooted in His will, what should we do but rejoice in the effulgent glory of the First and the Last?

EIGHT

THE
TRUTH
IN
JESUS

But you did not so learn Christ; assuming that you have heard about Him and were taught in Him, as the truth is in Jesus. Put off your old nature which belongs to your former manner of life and is corrupt through deceitful lusts . . . (Eph. 4:2022).

How have we learned Christ? It ought to be a startling thought, that we may have learned Him wrong. That must be far worse than not to have learned Him at all: His place is occupied by a false Christ, hard to exorcize! The point is, whether we have learned Christ as He taught Himself, or as men have taught Him who thought they understood, but did not understand Him. Do we think we know Him—with notions fleshly, after low, mean human fancies and explanations, or do we indeed know Him—after the spirit, in our measure as God knows Him?

The Christian religion, throughout its history, has been open to more corrupt misrepresentation than ever the Jewish could be, for as it is higher and wider, so must it yield larger scope to corruption. Have we learned Christ in false statements and corrupted lessons about Him, or have we learned *Himself?* Nay, true or false, is only our brain full of things concerning Him, or does He dwell Himself in our hearts, a learned, and ever being learned lesson, the power of our life?

I have been led to what I am about to say, by a certain utterance of one in the front rank of those who assert that we can know nothing of the "Infinite and Eternal energy from which all things proceed," and the utterance is this:

> The visiting on Adam's descendants through hundreds of generations dreadful penalties for a small transgression which they did not commit; the damning of all men who do not avail themselves of an alleged mode of obtaining forgiveness, which most men have never heard of; and the effecting a reconciliation by sacrificing a son who was perfectly innocent, to satisfy the assumed necessity for a propitiatory victim; are modes of action which, ascribed to a human ruler, would call for expressions of abhorrence; and the ascription to them to the Ultimate Cause of things even now felt to be full of difficulties, must become impossible.

I do not quote the passage with the design of opposing either clause of its statement, for I entirely agree with it. Almost it feels an absurdity to say so. Neither do I propose addressing a word to the writer of it, or to any who hold with him. The passage bears out what I have often said—that I never yet heard a word from one of that way of thinking, which even touched anything I hold. One of my earliest recollections is of beginning to be at strife with the false system here assailed. Such paganism I scorn as heartily in the name of Christ, as I scorn it in the name of righteousness.

But had I to do with the writer, I should ask how it comes that, refusing these dogmas as abominable, and in themselves plainly false, yet knowing that they are attributed to men whose teaching has done more to civilize the world than that of any men besides—how it comes that, seeing such teaching as this could not have done so, he has not taken such pains of inquiry as must surely have satisfied a man of his faculty that such was not their teaching. It was indeed so different, and so good, that even the forced companionship of such horrible lies as those he has recounted, has been unable to destroy its regenerative power.

I suppose he will allow that there was a man named Jesus, who died for the truth He taught. Can he believe He died for such alleged truth as that? Would it not be well for me to ask him to inquire what He did really teach, according to the primary sources of our knowledge of Him? If he answered that the question was uninteresting to him, I should have no more to say. Nor did I now start to speak of him save with the object of making my position plain to those to whom I would speak—those, namely, who call themselves Christians.

If of them I should ask, "How comes it that such opinions are held concerning the Holy One, whose ways you take upon you to set forth?" I should be met by most with the answer, "Those are the things He tells us Himself in His word; we have learned them from the Scriptures."

Of those whose presentation of Christian doctrine is represented in the quotation above, there are two classes—such as are content it should be so, and such to whom those things are grievous, but who do not see how to get rid of them. To the latter it may be of some little comfort to have one who has studied the New Testament for many years and loves it beyond the power of speech to express, declare to them his conviction that there is not an atom of such teaching in the whole lovely, divine utterance. Such things are all and altogether the invention of men. Honest invention, in part at least, I grant, but yet not true. Thank God, we are nowise bound to accept any man's explanation of

God's ways and God's doings, however good the man may be, if it do not commend itself to our conscience. The man's conscience may be a better conscience than ours, and his judgment clearer; nothing the more can we accept while we cannot see good. To do so would be to sin.

Expostulation

I desire to address those who call themselves Christians, and expostulate with them thus:

Whatever be your *opinions* on the greatest of all subjects, is it well that the impression with regard to Christianity made upon your generation should be that of your opinions, and not of something beyond opinion? Is Christianity capable of being represented by opinion, even the best? If it were, how many of us are such as God would choose to represent His thoughts and intents by our opinions concerning them? Who is there of his friends whom any thoughtful man would depute to represent his thoughts to his fellows? If you answer, "The opinions I hold and by which I represent Christianity, are those of the Bible," I reply, that none can understand, still less represent, the opinions of another, but such as are of the same mind with him—certainly none who mistake his whole scope and intent so far as in supposing *opinion* to be the object of any writer in the Bible. Is Christianity a system of articles of belief, let them be correct as language can give them? Never. So far am I from believing it, that I would rather have a man holding, as numbers of you do, what seem to me the most obnoxious untruths, opinions the most irreverent and gross, if at the same time he *lived* in the faith of the Son of God, that is, trusted in God as the Son of God trusted in Him, than I would have a man with every one of whose formulas of belief I utterly coincided, but who knew nothing of a daily life and walk with God. The one, holding doctrines of devils, is yet a child of God; the other, holding the doctrines of Christ is of the world, yea, of the devil.

"How! a man hold the doctrine of devils, and yet be of God?"

Yes; for to hold a thing with the intellect, is not to believe it. A man's real belief is that which he lives by; and that which the man I mean lives by, is the love of God, and obedience to His law, so far as he has recognized it. What a man believes, is the thing he does. This man would shrink with loathing from actions such as he thinks God justified in doing; like God, he loves and helps and saves. Will the living God let such a man's opinions damn him? No more than He will let the correct opinions of another, who lives for himself, save him. The best salvation even the latter could give would be but damnation.

What I come to and insist upon is, that—supposing your theories right, and containing all that is to be believed—yet those theories are not what makes you Christians, if Christians indeed you are. On the contrary, they are, with not a few of you, just what keeps you from being Christians. For when you say that, to be saved, a man must hold this or that, then you are leaving the living God and His will, and putting trust in some notion about Him or His will.

While the mind is occupied in inquiring, "Do I believe or feel this thing right?" the true question is forgotten: "Have I left all to follow Him?"

To the man who gives himself to the living Lord, every belief will necessarily come right; the Lord Himself will see that His disciple believe aright concerning him. If a man cannot trust Him for this, what claim can he make to faith in Him? It is because he has little or no faith, that he is left clinging to preposterous and dishonoring ideas, the traditions of men concerning His Father, and neither His teaching nor that of His apostles. The living Christ is to them but a shadow; the all but obliterated Christ of their theories no soul can thoroughly believe in. The disciple of such a Christ rests on His work, or His merits, or His atonement!

What I insist upon is, that a man's faith shall be in the living, loving, ruling, helping Christ, devoted to us as much as ever He was, and with all the powers of the Godhead for the salvation of His brethren. It is not faith that He did this, that His work wrought that—it is faith in the Man who did and is doing everything for us that will save him. Without this He cannot work to heal spiritually, any more than He would heal physically, when He was present to the eyes of men.

Do you ask, "What is faith in Him?" I answer, the leaving of your way, your objects, your self, and the taking of His and Him; the leaving of your trust in men, in money, in opinion, in character, in atonement itself, *and doing as He tells you.* I can find no words strong enough to serve the weight of this necessity—this obedience. It is the one terrible heresy of the church, that it has always been presenting something else than obedience as faith in Christ.

The work of Christ is not the Working Christ, any more than the clothing of Christ is the body of Christ. If the woman who touched the hem of His garment had trusted in the garment and not in Him who wore it, would she have been healed? And the reason that so many who believe *about* Christ rather than in Him, get the comfort they do, is that, touching thus the mere hem of His garment, they cannot help believing a little in the live man inside the garment.

Some even ponder the imponderable—whether they are of the elect, whether they have an interest in the blood shed for sin, whether theirs is a saving faith—when all the time the Man who died for them is waiting to begin to save them from every evil, and first from this self which is consuming them with trouble about its salvation. He will set them free, and take them home to the bosom of the Father—if only they will mind what He says to them—which is the beginning, middle, and end of faith. If they would but awake and arise from the dead, and come out into the light which Christ is waiting to give them, He would begin at once to fill them with the fulness of God.

The Primacy of Obedience

"But I do not know how to awake and arise!"

I will tell you. Get up, and do something the Master tells you; so make yourself His disciple at once. Instead of asking yourself whether you believe or not, ask yourself whether you have this day done one thing because He said, Do it, or once abstained because He said, Do not do it. It is simply absurd to say you believe, or even want to believe in Him, if you do not anything He tells you. If you can think of nothing He ever said as having had an atom of influence on your doing or not doing, you have too good ground to consider yourself no disciple of His.

But you can begin at once to *be* a disciple of the Living One—by obeying Him in the first thing you can think of in which you are not obeying Him. We must learn to obey Him in everything, and so must begin somewhere. Let it be at once, and in the very next thing that lies at the door of our conscience! Oh fools and slow of heart, if you think of nothing but Christ, and do not set yourselves to do His words! You but build your houses on the sand.

What have those teachers not to answer for who have turned your regard away from the direct words of the Lord Himself, which are spirit and life, to contemplate plans of salvation tortured out of the words of His apostles, even were those plans as true as they are false! There is but one plan of salvation, and that is to believe in the Lord Jesus Christ; that is, to take Him for what He is—our Master, and His words as if He meant them, which assuredly He did. To do His words is to enter into vital relation with Him, to obey Him is the only way to be one with Him.

The relation between Him and us is an absolute one; it can nohow begin to *live* but in obedience: it *is* obedience. There can be no truth, no reality, in any initiation of at-one-ment with Him, that is not obedience. What! have I the poorest notion of a God, and dare think of entering into relations with Him, the very first of which is not that what

He says, I will do? The thing is eternally absurd, and comes of the father of lies.

I know what Satan whispers to those to whom such teaching as this is distasteful: "It is the doctrine of works!" But one word of the Lord humbly heard and received will suffice to send all the demons of false theology into the abyss. He says the man that does not do the things He tells him, builds his house to fall in utter ruin. He instructs His messengers to go and baptize all nations, "teaching them to observe all that I have commanded you." Tell me it is faith He requires: do I not know it? and is not faith the highest act of which the human mind is capable? But faith in what? Faith in what He is, in what He says—a faith which can have no existence except in obedience—a faith which *is* obedience.

What have you done this day because it was the will of Christ? Have you dismissed, once dismissed, an anxious thought for the morrow? Have you ministered to any needy soul or body, and kept your right hand from knowing what your left hand did? Have you begun to leave all and follow Him? Did you set yourself to judge righteous judgment? Are you being wary of covetousness? Have you forgiven your enemy? Are you hungering and thirsting after righteousness? Have you given to some one that asked of you?

Tell me something that you have done, are doing, or are trying to do because He told you. If you do nothing that He says, it is no wonder that you cannot trust in Him, and are therefore driven to seek refuge in the atonement, as if something He had done, and not He Himself in His doing were the atonement. *That is not as you understand it?* What does it matter how you understand, or what you understand, so long as you are not of one mind with the Truth, so long as you and God are not *at one*, do not atone together? How should you understand?

Knowing that you do not heed His word, why should I heed your explanation of it? You do not His will, and so you cannot understand Him; you do not know Him, that is why

you cannot trust in Him. It is the heart of the child that
alone can understand the Father.

Do you suppose He ever gave a commandment knowing
it was of no use for it could not be done? He tells us a thing
knowing that we must do it, or be lost; that not His Father
Himself could save us but by getting us at length to do
everything He commands, for not otherwise can we know
life, can we learn the holy secret of divine being. He knows
that you can try, and that in your trying and failing He will
be able to help you, until at length you shall do the will of
God even as He does it Himself. He takes the will in the imperfect deed, and makes the deed at last perfect.

We must forsake all our fears and distrusts for Christ. We
must receive His teaching heartily, nor let the interpretation of it attributed to His apostles make us turn aside from
it. I say interpretation attributed to them; for what they
teach is never against what Christ taught, though very often
the exposition of it is—and that from no fault in the apostles; but from the grievous fault of those who would understand, and even explain, rather than obey.

We may be sure of this, that no man will be condemned
for any sin that is past. If he be condemned, it will be because he would not come to the light when the light came to
him; because he would not cease to do evil and learn to do
well; because he hid his unbelief in the garment of a false
faith, and would not obey; because he imputed to himself a
righteousness that was not his; because he preferred
imagining himself a worthy person, to confessing himself
everywhere in the wrong, and repenting. We may be sure
also of this, that if a man becomes the disciple of Christ, He
will not leave him in ignorance as to what he has to believe;
he shall know the truth of everything it is needful for him to
understand. If we do what He tells us, His light will go up in
our hearts. Till then we could not understand even if He ex-
plained to us.

Leaving All

Is there then anything you will not leave for Christ? You cannot know Him—and yet He is the Truth, the one thing alone that can be known! Do you not care to be imperfect? Would you rather keep this or that, with imperfection, than part with it to be perfect? You cannot know Christ, for the very principle of His life was the simple absolute relation of realities; His one idea was to be a perfect child to His Father. He who will not part with all for Christ, is not worthy of Him, and cannot know Him; and the Lord is true, and cannot acknowledge him.

How could He receive to His house, as one of His kind, a man who prefers something to His Father; a man who is not for God; a man who will strike a bargain with God, and say, "I will give up so much, if you will spare me"! To yield all to Him who has only made us and given us everything, yea His very self by life and by death, such a man counts too much. His conduct says, "I never asked you to do so much for me, and I cannot make the return you demand." The man will have to be left to himself. He must find what it is to be without God! Those who know God, or have but begun to catch a far-off glimmer of His gloriousness, of what He is, regard life as insupportable save God be the All in all, the first and the last.

To let their light shine, not to force on them their interpretations of God's designs, is the duty of Christians towards their fellows. If you who set yourselves to explain the theory of Christianity, had set yourselves instead to do the will of the Master, the one object for which the Gospel was preached to you, how different would now be the condition of that portion of the world with which you come into contact! Had you given yourselves to the understanding of His word that you might do it, and not to the quarrying from it of material wherewith to buttress your systems, in many a heart by this time would the name of the Lord be loved where now it remains unknown. The word of life would then by you have been held out indeed.

Men, undeterred by your explanations of Christianity—for you would not be forcing them on their acceptance—and attracted by your behavior, would be saying to each other, as Moses said to himself when he saw the bush that burned with fire and was not consumed, "I will turn aside and see this great sight!" They would be drawing nigh to behold how these Christians loved one another, and how just and fair they were to every one that had to do with them! to note that their goods were the best, their weight surest, their prices most reasonable, their word most certain! that in their families was neither jealousy nor emulation! that their children were as diligently taught to share, as some are to save, or to lay out only upon self—their mothers more anxious lest a child should hoard than lest he should squander; that in no house of theirs was religion one thing, and the daily life another.

Obedience Leads Us to Truth

If any of you tell me my doctrine is presumptuous, that it is contrary to what is taught in the New Testament, and what the best of men have always believed, I will not therefore proceed to defend even my beliefs, the principles on which I try to live—how much less my opinions! I appeal to you instead, whether or not I have spoken the truth concerning our paramount obligation to do the word of Christ. If you answer that I have not, I have nothing more to say; there is no other ground on which we can meet. But if you allow that it is a prime, even if you do not allow it *the* prime duty, then what I insist upon is, that you should do it, so and not otherwise recommending the knowledge of Him.

I do not attempt to change your opinions; if they are wrong, the obedience alone on which I insist can enable you to set them right; I only pray you to obey, and assert that thus only can you fit yourselves for understanding the mind of Christ. I say none but he who does right, can think right;

you cannot *know* Christ to be right until you do as He does, as He tells you to do; neither can you set Him forth, until you know Him as He means Himself to be known, that is, as He is.

The true heart must see at once, that, however wrong I may or may not be in other things, at least I am right in this, that Jesus must be obeyed, and at once obeyed, in the things He did say: it will not long imagine to obey Him in things He did not say. If a man do what is unpleasing to Christ, believing it His will, he shall yet gain thereby, for it gives the Lord a hold of him, which He will use; but before he can reach liberty, he must be delivered from that falsehood. The Lord will leave no man to his own way, however much he may prefer it.

The Lord did not die to provide a man with the wretched heaven he may invent for himself, or accept invented for him by others; He died to give him life, and bring him to the heaven of the Father's peace. The children must share in the essential bliss of the Father and the Son. This is and has been the Father's work from the beginning—to bring us into the home of His heart, where He shares the glories of life with the Living One, in whom was born life to light me back to the original life. This is our destiny; and however a man may refuse, he will find it hard to fight with God—useless to kick against the goads of His love.

For the Father is goading him, or will goad him, if needful, into life by unrest and trouble; hell-fire will have its turn if less will not do. Can any need it more than such as will neither enter the kingdom of heaven themselves, nor suffer them to enter it that would? The old race of the Pharisees is by no means extinct. They were St. Paul's great trouble, and are yet to be found in every religious community under the sun.

The one only thing truly to reconcile all differences is to walk in the light. So St. Paul teaches us in his epistle to the Philippians, the third chapter and sixteenth verse. After setting forth the loftiest idea of human endeavor in declaring the summit of his own aspiration, he says——not, "This must be your endeavor also, or you cannot be saved," but, "If in anything you are otherwise minded, God will reveal that also to you. Only let us hold true to what we have attained." Observe what widest conceivable scope is given by the apostle to honest opinion, even in things of grandest import! The one only essential point with him is that whereto we have attained, what we have seen to be true, *we walk by that.*

In such walking, and in such walking only, love will grow, truth will grow; the soul, then first in its genuine element and true relation towards God, will see into reality that was before but a blank to it; and He who has promised to teach, will teach abundantly. Faster and faster will the glory of the Lord dawn upon the hearts and minds of His people so walking—then His people indeed. Fast and far will the knowledge of Him spread, for truth of action, both preceding and following truth of word, will prepare the way before Him.

The man walking in that whereto he has attained, will be able to think aright. The man who does not think right, is unable because he has not been walking right. Only when he begins to do the thing he knows, does he begin to be able to think aright; then God comes to him in a new and higher way, and works along with the spirit He has created.

II

THE
CREATION
OF
SONS

"We are not and cannot become true sons without our will willing His will, our doing following His making."

NINE

THE
WAY

*I*f you would be perfect . . . (Matt.
19:16-22).

Let us regard the story. As Jesus went out of a house (see
Mark 10:10, 17), the young man came running to Him, and
kneeling down in the way, addressed Him as "Good
Master".

The words with which the Lord interrupts his address reveal the whole attitude of the Lord's being. At that moment,
at every and each moment, just as much as when in the garden of Gethsemane, or encountering any of those hours
which men call crises of life, His whole thought, His whole
delight, was in the thought, in the will, in the being of His
Father.

The Father was all in all to the Son, and the Son no more
thought of His own goodness than an honest man thinks of
his honesty. When the good man sees goodness, he thinks
of his own evil. Jesus had no evil to think of, but neither

does He think of His goodness; He delights in His Father's. "Why do you ask me about what is good? One there is who is good."

Checked thus, the youth turns to the question which, working in his heart, had brought him running, and made him kneel: what good thing shall he do that he may have eternal life? It is unnecessary to inquire precisely what he meant by *eternal life*. Whatever shape the thing took to him, that shape represented a something he needed and had not got—a something which, it was clear to him, could be gained only in some path of good. But he thought to gain a thing by a doing, when the very thing desired was a *being*; he would have that as a possession which must possess him.

The Lord cared neither for isolated truth nor for orphaned deed. It was truth in the inward parts, it was the good heart, the mother of good deeds, He cherished. It was the live, active, knowing, breathing good He came to further. He cared for no speculation in morals or religion. It was good men He cared about, not notions of good things, or even good actions, save as the outcome of life, save as the bodies in which the primary live actions of love and will in the soul took shape and came forth. Could He by one word have set at rest all the questionings of philosophy as to the supreme good and the absolute truth, I venture to say that word He would not have uttered. But He would die to make men good and true. His whole heart would respond to the cry of sad publican or despairing pharisee, "How am I to be good?"

When the Lord says, "Why do you ask me about what is good?" we must not put emphasis on the *me*, as if the Lord refused the question, as He had declined the epithet. He was the proper person to ask, only the question was not the right one. The good thing was a small matter; the good Being was all in all. "Why ask me about the good thing? There is one living good, in whom the good thing, and all good, is alive and ever operant. Ask me not about the good thing, but the good person, the good being—the origin of all good"—who, because He is, can make good. He is the one live good, ready with His life to communicate living good, the power of being, and so doing good, for He makes good itself to exist.

We have to do with Him to whom no one can look without the need of being good waking up in his heart; to think about Him is to begin to be good. To do a good thing is to do a good thing; to know God is to be good. It is not to make us do all things right He cares, but to make us hunger and thirst after a righteousness possessing which we shall never need to think of what is or is not good, but shall refuse the evil and choose the good by a motion of the will which is at once necessity and choice.

Observe, the question in the young man's mind is not about the doing or not doing of something he knows to be right. Had such been the case, the Lord would have permitted no question at all. The one thing He insists upon is the *doing* of the thing we know we ought to do. In the instance present—the youth looking out for some unknown good thing to do—He sends him back to the doing of what he knows, and that in answer to his question concerning the way to eternal life.

A man must have something to do in the matter, and may well ask such a question of any teacher! The Lord does not for a moment turn away from it, and only declines the form of it to help the youth to what he really needs. He has, in truth, already more than hinted where the answer lies, namely, in God Himself, but that the youth is not yet capable of receiving. He must begin with him farther back: "If you would enter life, keep the commandments," for verily, if the commandments have nothing to do with entering into life, why were they ever given to men? This is his task—he must keep the commandments.

Then the road to eternal life is the keeping of the commandments! Had the Lord *not* said so, what man of common moral sense would ever dare say otherwise? What else can be the way into life but the doing of what the Lord of life tells the creatures He has made, and whom He would have live forever, that they must do? It is the beginning of the way.

If a man had kept all those commandments, yet would he not therefore have in him the life eternal; nevertheless, without keeping of the commandments there is no entering into life. The keeping of them is the path to the gate of life. It is not life, but it is the way—so much of the way to it. No, the keeping of the commandments, consciously or unconsciously, has closest and essential relation to eternal life.

Objections
The Lord says nothing about the first table of the law. Why does He not tell this youth as He did the lawyer, that to love God is everything? He had given him a glimpse of the essence of His own life, had pointed the youth to the heart of all—for him to think of afterwards. He was not ready for it yet. He wanted eternal life: to love God with all our heart, and soul, and strength, and mind, is to know God, and to know Him *is* eternal life. That is the end of the whole saving matter; it is no human beginning, it is the grand end and eternal beginning of all things. But the youth was not capable of it. To begin with that would be as sensible as to say to one asking how to reach the top of some mountain, "Just set your foot on that shining snow-clad peak, high there in the blue, and you will at once be where you wish to go."

"Love God with all your heart, and eternal life is yours." That would have been to mock him. Why, he could not yet see or believe that that was eternal life! He was not yet capable of looking upon life even from afar! How many *Christians* are? How many know that they are not? How many care that they are not? The Lord answers his question directly, tells him what to do—a thing he can do—to enter into life: he must keep the commandments! And when he asks

"Which?" the Lord specifies only those that have to do with his neighbor, ending with the highest and most difficult of them.

"But no man can perfectly keep a single commandment of the second table any more than of the first."

Surely not—else why should they have been given? But is there no meaning in the word *keep*, or *observe*, except it be qualified by perfectly? Is there no keeping but a perfect keeping?

"None that God cares for."

There I think you utterly wrong. That no keeping but a perfect one will satisfy God, I hold with all my heart and strength; but that there is none else He cares for, is one of the lies of the enemy. What father is not pleased with the first tottering attempt of his little one to walk? What father would be satisfied with anything but the manly step of the full-grown son?

When the Lord has definitely mentioned the commandments He means, the youth returns at once that he *has* observed those from his youth up. Are we to take his word for it? The Lord at least takes his word for it: He looked on him and loved him. Was the Lord deceived in him? Did he tell an untruth? Or did the Master believe he had kept the commandments perfectly? There must be a keeping of the commandments, which, although anything but perfect, is yet acceptable to the heart of Him from whom nothing is hid. In that way the youth had kept the commandments. He had for years been putting forth something of his life-energy to keep them. Nor, had he missed the end for which they were given to keep.

For the immediate end of the commandments never was that men should succeed in obeying them, but that, finding the more they tried the more was required of them, they should be driven to the source of life and law—to seek from Him such reinforcement of life as should make the fulfillment of the law as possible, yea, as natural, as necessary.

This result had been achieved in the youth. His observance had given him no satisfaction. He was not at rest; but he desired eternal life—of which there was no word in the law. The keeping of the law had served to develop a hunger which no law or its keeping could fill. Must not the imperfection of his keeping of the commandments, even in the lower sense in which he read them, have helped to reveal how far they were beyond any keeping of his, how their implicit demands rose into the infinitude of God's perfection?

Perfection

Having kept the commandments, the youth needed and was ready for a further lesson. The Lord would not leave him where he was; He had come to seek and to save. He saw him in sore need of perfection—the thing the commonplace Christian thinks he can best do without—the thing the elect hungers after with an eternal hunger.

To gain the perfection he desired, the one thing lacking was, that he should sell all that he had, give it to the poor, and follow the Lord! Could this be all that lay between him and entering into life? God only knows what the victory of such an obedience might at once have wrought in him! Much, much more would be necessary before perfection was reached, but certainly the next step, to sell and follow, would have been the step into life. Had he taken it, in the very act would have been born in him that whose essence and vitality is eternal life, needing but process to develop it into the glorious consciousness of oneness with The Life.

I do not suppose that the youth was one whom ordinary people would call a lover of money. I do not believe he was covetous, or desired even the large increase of his possessions. I imagine he was just like most good men of property: he valued his possessions—looked on them as a good. I suspect that in the case of another, he would have regarded such possession almost as a merit, a desert. He would value

a man more who had *means*, value a man less who had none
—like most of my readers. They have not a notion how
entirely they will one day have to alter their judgment, or
have it altered for them, in this respect. Well for them if
they alter it for themselves!

From this false way of thinking, and all the folly and un-
reality that accompany it, the Lord would deliver the young
man. As the thing was, he was a slave; for a man is in bondage to whatever he cannot part with that is less than himself.
He could have taken his possessions from him by an exercise of His own will, but there would have been little good in
that. He wished to do it by the exercise of the young man's
will. That would be a victory indeed for both! So would he
enter into freedom and life, delivered from the bondage of
Mammon by the lovely will of the Lord in him, one with his
own. By the putting forth of the divine energy in him, he
would escape the corruption that is in the world through
lust—that is, the desire or pleasure of *having*.

The young man would not.

His Refusal

Was the Lord then premature in His demand on the youth?
I do not believe it. He gave him the very next lesson in the
divine education for which he was ready. It was possible for
him to respond, to give birth, by obedience, to the redeemed and redeeming will, and so be free. It was time the
demand should be made upon him. Do you say, "But he
would not respond, he would not obey!"? Then it was time,
I answer, that he should refuse—that he should know what
manner of spirit he was of—and meet the confusions of
soul, the sad searchings of heart that must follow. A time
comes to every man when he must obey, or make such refusal—*and know it.*

Shall I then be supposed to mean that the refusal of the
young man was of necessity final? That he was therefore
lost? That because he declined to enter into life the door of

life was closed against him? Verily, I have not so learned Christ. And that the lesson was not lost, I see in this, that he went away sorrowful. Was such sorrow, in the mind of an earnest youth, likely to grow less or to grow more? Was all he had gone through in the way of obedience to be of no good to him? Could the nature of one who had kept the commandments be so slight that, after having sought and talked with Jesus—held communion with Him who is the Life—he would care less about eternal life than before?

And how now would he go on with his keeping of the commandments? Would he not begin to see more plainly his shortcomings, the larger scope of their requirements? Might he not feel the keeping of them more imperative than ever, yet impossible without something he had not? The commandments can never be kept while there is a strife to keep them: the man is overwhelmed in the weight of their broken pieces. It needs a clean heart to have pure hands, all the power of a live soul to keep the law—a power of life, not of struggle; the strength of love, not the effort of duty.

One day the truth of his conduct must dawn upon him with absolute clearness. Bitter must be the discovery. He had refused the life eternal! had turned his back upon The Life! In deepest humility and shame, yet with the profound consolation of repentance, he would return to the Master and lament his unteachableness. There are those who, like St. Paul, can say, "I did wrong, but I did it in ignorance; my heart was not right, and I did not know it." The remorse of such must be very different from that of one who, brought to the point of being capable of embracing the truth, turned from it and refused to be set free. To him the time will come, God only knows its hour, when he will see the nature of his deed, *with the knowledge that he was dimly seeing it so even when he did it.* The alternative had been put before him. And all those months, or days, or hours, or moments, he might have been following the Master, hearing the words He spoke, through the windows of His eyes looking into the very gulfs of Godhead!

TEN

THE HARDNESS OF THE WAY

*C*hildren, how hard it is! (Mark 10:24).

I suspect there is scarcely a young man rich and thoughtful who is not ready to feel our Lord's treatment of this young man is hard. He is apt to ask, "Why should it be difficult for a rich man to enter into the kingdom of heaven?" He is ready to look upon the natural fact as an arbitrary decree, arising, shall I say, from some prejudice in the divine mind, or at least from some objection to the joys of wellbeing, as regarded from the creatures' side. Why should the rich fare differently from other people in respect of the world to come? They do not perceive that the law is they *shall* fare like other people, whereas they want to fare as rich people.

A condition of things in which it would be easy for a rich man to enter into the kingdom of heaven is to me inconceivable. There is no kingdom of this world into which a rich man may not easily enter—in which, if he be but rich enough, he may not be the first. A kingdom into which it would be easy for a rich man to enter could be no kingdom of heaven. The rich man does not by any necessity of things belong to the kingdom of Satan, but into that kingdom he is especially welcome, whereas into the kingdom of heaven he will be just as welcome as another man.

I suspect also that many a rich man turns from the record of this incident with the resentful feeling that there lies in it a claim upon his whole having; while there are many, and those by no means only of the rich, who cannot believe the Lord really meant to take the poor fellow's money from him. To the man born to riches they seem merely a natural, but an essential condition of well-being; and the man who has *made* his money, feels it his by the labor of his soul. Each feels a right to have and to hold the things he possesses.

A Rich Young Man of Today

I can well imagine an honest youth, educated in Christian forms, thus reasoning with himself: "Is this demand made upon me? If I make up my mind to be a Christian, shall I be required to part with all I possess? It must have been comparatively easy in those times to give up the kind of things they had! If I had been he, I am sure I should have done it—at the demand of the Savior in person. Things are very different now! Wealth did not then imply the same social relations as now! I should be giving up so much more! Neither do I love money as he was in danger of doing.

"Besides, am I not a Christian already? Why should the same thing be required of me as of a young Jew? If every one who, like me, has a conscience about money, and cares to use it well, had to give up all, the power would at once be in the hands of the irreligious; they would have no opposition, and the world would go to the devil. We read often in the Bible of rich men, but never of any other who was desired to part with all that he had!

"Besides, the Lord said, 'If you would be perfect, go, sell what you possess.' I cannot be perfect; it is hopeless; and He does not expect it."

It would be more honest if he said, "I do not want to be perfect; I am content to be saved." Such as he do not care for being perfect as their Father in heaven is perfect, but for being what they call *saved*. They little think that without perfection there is no salvation—that perfection *is* salvation. They are one.

I say then to the youth: "Have you kept—have you been keeping the commandments?"

"I will not dare to say that," I suppose him to answer. "I ought to know better than that youth how much is implied in the keeping of the commandments!"

"But," I ask insisting, "does your answer imply that, counting the Lord a hard master, you have taken the less pains to do as He would have you? or that, bending your energies to the absolute perfection He requires, you have the more perceived the impossibility of fulfilling the law? Can you have failed to note that it is the youth who has been for years observing the commandments on whom the further, and to you startling, command is laid, to part with all that he has? Surely not!

"Are you then one on whom, because of correspondent condition, the same command could be laid? Have you, in any sense like that in which the youth answered the question, kept the commandments? Have you, unsatisfied with the result of what keeping you have given them, and filled with desire to be perfect, gone kneeling to the Master to learn more of the way to eternal life? or are you so well satisfied with what you are, that you have never sought eternal life, never hungered and thirsted after the righteousness of God, the perfection of your being?

"If this latter be your condition, then be comforted; the Master does not require of you to sell what you have and give to the poor. *You* follow Him! *You* go with Him to preach good tidings!—you who care not for righteousness! You are not one whose company is desirable to the Master. Be comforted, I say: He does not want you; He will not ask you to open your purse for Him; you may give or withhold; it is nothing to Him. What! is He to be obliged to one outside His kingdom—to the untrue, the ignoble, for money? Bring Him a true heart, an obedient hand: He has given His lifeblood for that; but your money—He neither needs it nor cares for it."

"Pray, do not deal harshly with me. I confess I have not been what I ought, but I want to repent, and would enter into life."

"Once more, then, *go and keep the commandments*. It is not come to your money yet. The commandments are enough for you. You are not yet a child in the kingdom. You do not care for the arms of your Father; you value only the shelter of His roof. As to your money, let the commandments direct you how to use it.

"It is in you but pitiable presumption to wonder whether it is required of you to sell all that you have. When in keeping the commandments you have found the great reward of loving righteousness—the further reward of discovering that, with all the energy you can put forth, you are but an unprofitable servant; when you have come to know that the law can be kept only by such as need no law; when you have come therefore to the Master with the cry, 'What shall I do that I may inherit eternal life?' it may be He will then say to you, 'Sell all that you have and give to the poor, and come follow me.'

"If He do, then will you be of men most honorable if you obey—of men most pitiable if you refuse. Till then you would be no comfort to Him, no pleasure to His friends. For the young man to have sold all and followed Him would have been to accept God's patent of peerage: to you it is not offered."

"But I do not trust in my riches; I trust in the merits of my Lord and Savior. I trust in His finished work. I trust in the sacrifice He has offered."

"Yes; yes! you will trust in anything but the Man Himself who tells you it is hard to be saved! Not all the merits of God and His Christ can give you eternal life; only God and His Christ can; and they cannot, would not if they could, without your keeping the commandments. The knowledge of the living God *is* eternal life. What have you to do with His merits? You have to know His being, Himself.

"And as to trusting in your riches—who ever imagined he could have eternal life by his riches? No man with half a conscience, half a head, and no heart at all, could suppose that any man trusting in his riches to get him in, could enter the kingdom. That would be too absurd."

"You forget yourself; you are criticizing the Lord's own words: He said, 'How hard is it *for them that trust in riches* to enter into the kingdom of heaven!' "

"I do not forget myself; to this I have been leading you: —our Lord, I believe, never said those words. The reading of both the Sinaitic and the Vatican manuscripts, the oldest two we have, is, "Children, how hard is it to enter into the kingdom of God!" These words I take to be those of the Lord.

"Some copyist, with the mind at least of a rich man, dissatisfied with the Lord's way of regarding money, and like yourself anxious to compromise, must affix his marginal gloss—to the effect that it is not the possessing of riches, but the trusting in them, that makes it difficult to enter into the kingdom! *Difficult?* Why, it is eternally impossible for the man who trusts in his riches to enter into the kingdom! it is for the man who *has* riches it is difficult. Is the Lord supposed to teach that for a man who trusts in his riches it is *possible* to enter the kingdom? that, though impossible with men, this is possible with God? God take the Mammon-worshipper into His glory! No! the Lord never said it.

"The annotation of Mr. Facingbothways crept into the text, and stands in the English version. Our Lord was not in the habit of explaining away His hard words. He let them stand in all the glory of the burning fire wherewith they would purge us. Where their simplicity finds corresponding simplicity, they are understood. The twofold heart must mistake. It is hard for a rich man, just because he is a rich man, to enter into the kingdom of heaven."

Take then the Lord's words thus: "Children, how hard is it to enter into the kingdom of God!" It is quite like His way of putting things. Calling them first to reflect on the original difficulty for every man of entering into the kingdom of God, He reasserts in yet stronger phrase the difficulty of the rich man: "It is easier for a camel to go through the eye of a needle than for a rich man to enter the kingdom of God." It always was, always will be, hard to enter into the kingdom of heaven. It is hard even to believe that one must be born from above—must pass into a new and unknown consciousness. The law-faithful Jew, the ceremonial Christian, shrinks from the self-annihilation, the life of grace and truth, the upper air of heavenly delight, the all-embracing love that fills the law full and sets it aside. They cannot accept a condition of being as in itself eternal life.

And hard to believe in, this life, this kingdom of God, this simplicity of absolute existence, is hard to enter. How hard? As hard as the Master of salvation could find words to express the hardness: "If any man comes to me, and does not hate . . . even his own life, he cannot be my disciple." And the rich man must find it harder than another to hate his own life. There is so much associated with it to swell out the self of his consciousness, that the difficulty of casting it from him as the mere ugly shadow of the self God made, is vastly increased.

None can know how difficult it is to enter into the kingdom of heaven, but those who have tried—tried hard, and have not ceased to try. I care not to be told that one may pass at once into all possible sweetness of assurance; it is not assurance I desire, but the thing itself; not the certainty of eternal life, but eternal life. I care not what other preachers may say, while I know that in St. Paul the spirit and the flesh were in frequent strife.

They only, I repeat, know how hard it is to enter into life, who are in conflict every day, are growing to have this conflict every hour—nay, begin to see that no moment is life, without the Presence that makes strong. Let any tell me of peace and content, yea, joy unspeakable, as the instant result of the new birth; I deny no such statement, refuse no such testimony; all I care to say is, that, if by salvation they mean less than absolute oneness with God, I count it no salvation, neither would be content with it if it included every joy in the heaven of their best imagining.

If they are not righteous even as He is righteous, they are not saved, whatever be their gladness or their content; they are but on the way to be saved.

The Tyranny of Things

Possessions are *Things*, and *Things* in general, save as affording matter of conquest and means of spiritual annexation, are very ready to prove inimical to the better life. The man who for consciousness of well-being depends upon anything but life, the life essential, is a slave; he hangs on what is less than himself. He is not perfect who, deprived of every *thing*, would not sit down calmly content, aware of a well-being untouched; for none the less would he be possessor of all things, the child of the Eternal.

Things are given us, this body first of things, that through them we may be trained both to independence and true possession of them. We must possess them; they must not possess us. Their use is to mediate—as shapes and manifestations in lower kind of the things that are unseen, that is, in themselves unseeable, the things that belong, not to the world of speech, but the world of silence, not to the world of showing, but the world of being, the world that cannot be shaken, and must remain.

These things unseen take form in the things of time and space—not that they may exist, for they exist in and from eternal Godhead, but that their being may be known to those in training for the eternal; these things unseen the sons and daughters of God must possess. But instead of reaching out after them, they grasp at their forms, regard the things seen as the things to be possessed, fall in love with the bodies instead of the souls of them.

There are good people who can hardly believe that, if the young man had consented to give up his wealth, the Lord would not then have told him to keep it; they too seem to think the treasure in heaven insufficient as a substitute. They cannot believe he would have been better off without his wealth. "Is not wealth power?" they ask. It is indeed power, and so is a wolf hid in the robe; it is power, but as of a brute machine, of which the owner ill knows the handles and cranks, valves and governor. The multitude of those who read the tale are of the same mind as the youth himself—in his worst moment, as he turned and went—with one vast difference, that they are not sorrowful.

Things can never be really possessed by the man who cannot do without them—who would not be absolutely, divinely content in the consciousness that the cause of his being is within it—and *with him*. I would not be misunderstood: no man can have the consciousness of God with him and not be content; I mean that no man who has not the Father so as to be eternally content in Him alone, can possess a sunset or a field of grass or a mine of gold or the love of a fellow-creature according to its nature—as God would have him possess it—in the eternal way of inheriting, having, and holding.

He who has God, has all things, after the fashion in which He who made them has them. To man, woman, and child, I say—if you are not content, it is because God is not with you as you need Him, not with you as He would be with you, as you *must* have Him; for you need Him as your body never needed food or air, need Him as your soul never hungered after joy, or peace, or pleasure.

The Tyranny of Things in Death

It is imperative on us to get rid of the tyranny of *things*. See how imperative: let the young man cling with every fiber to his wealth, what God can do He will do; His child shall not be left in the hell of possession!

Does Death serve him—ransom him?

Not so!—for then first, I presume, does the man of things become aware of their tyranny. When a man begins to abstain, then first he recognizes the strength of his passion; it may be, when a man has not a thing left, he will begin to know what a necessity he had made of things; and if then he begin to contend with them, to cast out of his soul what Death has torn from his hands, then first will he know the full passion of possession, the slavery of prizing the worthless part of the precious.

Wherein then lies the service of Death?

In this: it is not the fetters that gall, but the fetters that soothe, which eat into the soul. When the fetters of gold are gone, on which the man delighted to gaze, though they held him fast to his dungeon-wall, buried from air and sunshine, then first will he feel them in the soreness of their lack, in the weary indifference with which he looks on earth and sea, on space and stars.

When the truth begins to dawn upon him that those fetters were a horror and a disgrace, then will the good of saving death appear, and the man begin to understand that *having* never was, never could be well-being; that it is not by possessing we live, but by life we possess. In this way is the loss of the things he thought he had, a motioning, hardly *towards*, yet in favor of deliverance. It may seem to the man the first of his slavery when it is in truth the beginning of his freedom. Never soul was set free without being made to feel its slavery; nothing but itself can enslave a soul, nothing without itself free it.

When the drunkard, free of his body, but retaining his desire unable to indulge it, has time at length to think, surely there dawns for him then at last a fearful hope! Not until, by the power of God and his own obedient effort, he is raised into such a condition that, be the temptation what it might, he would not yield for an immortality of unrequited drunkenness—all its delights and not one of its penalties—is he saved.

Thus death may give a new opportunity—with some hope for the multitude counting themselves Christians, who are possessed by *things* as by a legion of devils; who stand well in their church; whose lives are regarded as stainless; who are kind, friendly, give largely, believe in the redemption of Jesus, talk of the world and the church; yet whose care all the time is to heap up, to make much into more, to add house to house and field to field, burying themselves deeper and deeper in the ash-heap of *Things*.

But it is not the rich man only who is under the dominion of things; they too are slaves who, having no money, are unhappy from the lack of it. The man who is ever digging his grave is little better than he who already lies mouldering in it. The money the one has, the money the other would have, is in each the cause of an eternal stupidity. To the one as to the other comes the word, "How is it that you do not understand?"

ELEVEN

ABBA, FATHER

❦❧

...T he spirit of sonship. When we cry, 'Abba, Father' ... (Rom. 8:15).

The hardest, gladdest thing in the world is to cry Father! from a full heart. I would help whom I may to call thus upon the Father.

There are things in all forms of the systematic teaching of Christianity to check this outgoing of the heart—with some to render it simply impossible. Such a cold wind blowing at the very gate of heaven—thank God, *outside* the gate! —is the so-called doctrine of *Adoption*. When a heart hears —and believes, or half believes—that it is not the child of God by origin, from the first of its being, but may possibly be adopted into His family, its love sinks at once in a cold faint: where is its own father, and who is this that would adopt it?

Let us look at the passage where Paul reveals his use of the word. It is in another of his epistles, Galatians 4:1-7.

From the passage it is as plain as St. Paul could make it, that, by the word translated *adoption*, he means the raising of a father's own child from the condition of tutelage and subjection to others—a state which, he says, is no better than that of a slave—to the position and rights of a son. None but a child could become a son; the idea is—a spiritual coming of age; *only when the child is a man is he really and fully a son*.

The thing holds in the earthly relation. How many children of good parents—good children in the main too—never know those parents, never feel towards them as children might, until, grown up, they have left the house—until, perhaps, they are parents themselves, or are parted from them by death! To be a child is not necessarily to be a son or daughter. The childship is the lower condition of the upward process towards the sonship, the soil out of which the true sonship shall grow, the former without which the latter were impossible.

God can no more than an earthly parent be content to have only children: He must have sons and daughters—children of His soul, of His spirit, of His love—not merely in the sense that He loves them, or even that they love Him, but in the sense that they love like Him, love as He loves. For this He does not adopt them. He dies to give them Himself, thereby to raise His own to His heart. He gives them a birth from above; they are born again out of Himself and into Himself—for He is the one and the all.

His children are not His real, true sons and daughters until they think like Him, feel with Him, judge as He judges, are at home with Him, and without fear before Him because He and they mean the same thing, love the same things, seek the same ends. Nothing will satisfy Him, or do for us, but that we be one with our Father! What else could serve! How else should life ever be a good! Because we are the sons of God, we must become the sons of God.

In my own childhood and boyhood my father was the refuge from all the ills of life, even sharp pain itself. Therefore I say to son or daughter who has no pleasure in the name *Father*, "You must interpret the word by all that you have missed in life. All that human tenderness can give or desire in the nearness and readiness of love, all and infinitely more must be true of the perfect Father—of the maker of fatherhood, the Father of all the fathers of the earth, specially the Father of those who have specially shown a father-heart."

He has made us, but we have to be. All things were made *through* the Word, but that which was made *in* the Word was life, and that life is the light of men. They who live by this light, that is, live as Jesus lived—by obedience, namely, to the Father, have a share in their own making. The light becomes life in them; they are, in their lower way, alive with the life that was first born in Jesus, and through Him has been born in them—by obedience they become one with the godhead. He does not *make* them the sons of God, but He gives them power to become the sons of God: in choosing and obeying the truth, man becomes the true son of the Father of lights.

Adoption of the Body

It remains to note yet another passage.

That never in anything he wrote was it St. Paul's intention to contribute towards a system of theology, it were easy to show: one sign of the fact is, that he does not hesitate to use this word he has perhaps himself made, in different, and apparently opposing, though by no means contradictory senses. His meanings always vivify each other. At one time he speaks of the sonship as being the possession of the Israelite, at another as his who has learned to cry *Abba, Father;* and here, in the passage I have now last to consider, that from the 18th to the 25th verse of this same eighth chapter of his epistle to the Romans, he speaks of the "adoption" as yet to come—and as if it had to do, not with our spiritual, but our bodily condition. This use of the

word, however, though not the same use as we find anywhere else, is nevertheless entirely consistent with his other
uses of it.

The 23rd verse says, "And not only the creation, but we
ourselves, who have the first fruits of the Spirit, groan in-
wardly as we wait for adoption as sons, the redemption of
our bodies."

It is nowise difficult to discern that the ideas in this and
the main use are necessarily associated and more than consistent. The putting of a son in his true, his foreordained
place, has outward relations as well as inward reality. The
outward depends on the inward, arises from it, and reveals
it. When the child whose condition under tutors had passed
away took his position as a son, he would naturally change
his dress and modes of life. When God's children cease to be
slaves doing right from law and duty, and become His sons
doing right from the essential love of God and their neighbor, they too must change the garments of their slavery for
the robes of liberty, lay aside the body of this death, and
appear in bodies like that of Christ, with whom they inherit
of the Father.

But many children who have learned to cry *Abba, Father*,
are yet far from the liberty of the sons of God. Sons they are
and no longer children, yet they groan as being still in bondage! Plainly the apostle has no thought of working out an
idea; with burning heart he is writing a letter. He gives,
nevertheless, lines plentifully sufficient for us to work out
his idea, and this is how it takes clear shape:

We are the sons of God the moment we lift up our hearts,
seeking to be sons—the moment we begin to cry *Father*. But
as the world must be redeemed in a few of its thoughts and
wants and ways to begin with: it takes a long time to finish
the new creation of this redemption. Shall it have taken millions of years to bring the world up to the point where a few
of its inhabitants shall desire God, and shall the creature of
this new birth be perfected in a day? The divine process

may indeed now go on with tenfold rapidity, for the new factor of man's fellow-working, for the sake of which the whole previous array of means and forces existed, is now developed; but its end is yet far below the horizon of man's vision.

The apostle speaks at one time of the thing as to come, at another time as done—when it is but commenced. Our ways of thought are such. A man's heart may leap for joy the moment when, amidst the sea-waves, a strong hand has laid hold of the hair of his head. He may cry aloud, "I am saved," and he may be safe, but he is not saved; this is far from a salvation to suffice. So are we sons when we begin to cry Father, but we are far from perfected sons. So long as there is in us the least taint of distrust, the least lingering of hate or fear, we have not received the sonship; we have not such life in us as raised the body of Jesus; we have not attained to the resurrection of the dead—by which word, in his epistle to the Philippians (3:2), St. Paul means, I think, the same thing as here he means by the sonship which he puts in apposition with the redemption of the body.

Until our outward condition is that of sons royal, sons divine; so long as the garments of our souls, these mortal bodies, are mean—torn and dragged and stained; so long as we groan under sickness and weakness and weariness, old age, forgetfulness and all heavy things; so long we have not yet received the sonship in full—we are but getting ready. We groan being burdened; we groan, waiting for the sonship—to wit, the redemption of the body—the uplifting of the body to be a fit house and revelation of the indwelling spirit—nay, like that of Christ, a fit temple and revelation of the deeper indwelling God. For we shall always need bodies to manifest and reveal us to each other—bodies, then, that fit the soul with absolute truth of presentment and revelation. Hence the revealing of the sons of God, spoken of in the 19th verse, is the same thing as the redemption of the body. The body is redeemed when it is made fit for the sons of God; then it is a revelation of them—the thing it was meant for, and always, more or less imperfectly, was. Such it shall be, when truth is strong enough in the sons of God to make it such—for it is the soul that makes the body. When we are the sons of God in heart and soul, then shall we be the sons of God in body too: "we shall be like Him, for we shall see Him as He is."

I care little to speculate on the kind of this body; two things only I will say, as needful to be believed, concerning it: first, that it will be a body to show the same self as before but, second, a body to show the being truly—without the defects, that is, and imperfections of the former bodily revelation. Even through their corporeal presence shall we then know our own infinitely better, and find in them endlessly more delight, than before. These things we must believe, or distrust the Father of our spirits.

To see how the whole utterance hangs together, read from the 18th verse to the 25th, especially noticing the 19th: "For the creation waits with eager longing for the revealing" (*the out-shining*) "of the sons of God." When the sons of God show as they are, taking, with the character, the appearance and the place that belong to their sonship; when the sons of God sit with *the* Son of God on the throne of their Father; then shall they be in potency of fact the lords of the lower creation, the bestowers of liberty and peace upon it. Then shall the creation, subjected to vanity for their sakes, find its freedom in their freedom, its gladness in their sonship. The animals will glory to serve them, will joy to come to them for help.

Let the heartless scoff, the unjust despise! the heart that cries *Abba, Father*, cries to the God of the sparrow and the oxen; nor can hope go too far in hoping what that God will do for the creation that now groans and travails in pain because our higher birth is delayed. Shall not the Judge of all the earth do right? Shall my heart be more compassionate than His?

Thus have both Jesus Christ and His love-slave Paul represented God—as a Father perfect in love, grand in self-forgetfulness, supreme in righteousness, devoted to the lives He has uttered. I will not believe less of the Father than I can conceive of glory after the lines He has given me, after the radiation of His glory in the face of His Son. He is the express image of the Father, by which we, His imperfect images, are to read and understand Him: imperfect, we have yet perfection enough to spell towards the perfect.

Summary

It comes to this then, after the grand theory of the apostle. The world exists for our education. It is the nursery of God's children, served by troubled slaves, troubled because the children are themselves slaves—children, but not good children. Beyond its own will or knowledge, the whole creation works for the development of the children of God into the sons of God. When at last the children have arisen and gone to their Father; when they are clothed in the best robe, with a ring on their hands and shoes on their feet, shining out at length in their natural, their predestined sonship; then shall the mountains and the hills break forth before them into singing, and all the trees of the field shall clap their hands.

Then shall the wolf dwell with the lamb, and the leopard lie down with the kid and the calf, and the young lion and the fatling together, and a little child shall lead them. Then shall the fables of a golden age, which faith invented, and unbelief threw into the past, unfold their essential reality, and the tale of paradise prove itself a truth by becoming a fact. Then shall every ideal show itself a necessity, aspiration although satisfied put forth yet longer wings, and the hunger after righteousness know itself blessed. Then first shall we know what was in the Shepherd's mind when He said, "I came that they may have life, and have it abundantly."

TWELVE

KINGSHIP

*P*ilate said to him, 'So you are a king?' Jesus answered, 'You say that I am a king. For this I was born, and for this I have come into the world, to bear witness to the truth. Every one who is of the truth hears my voice.' (John 18:37).

Pilate asks Jesus if He is a king. The question is called forth by what the Lord had just said concerning His kingdom, closing with the statement that it was not of this world. He now answers Pilate that He is a king indeed, but shows him that His kingdom is of a very different kind from what is called kingdom in this world.

The rank and rule of this world are interesting to Him. He might have had them. Calling His disciples to follow Him, and His twelve legions of angels to help them, He might soon have driven the Romans into the abyss, piling them on the heap of nations they had tumbled there before. What easier for Him than thus to have cleared the way, and

over the tributary world reigned the just monarch that was
the dream of the Jews, never seen in Israel or elsewhere,
but haunting the hopes and longings of the poor and their
helpers! He might from Jerusalem have ruled the world,
not merely dispensing what men call justice, but compelling
atonement.

He did not care for government. No such kingdom
would serve the ends of His Father in heaven, or comfort
His own soul. What was perfect empire to the Son of God,
while He might teach one human being to love his neighbor, and be good like his Father! To be love-helper to one
heart, for its joy, and the glory of His Father, was the beginning of true kingship! The Lord would rather wash the
feet of His weary brothers, than be the one only perfect
monarch that ever ruled in the world. It was empire He rejected when He ordered Satan behind Him like a dog to His
heel. Government, I repeat, was to Him flat, stale, unprofitable.

What then is the kingdom over which the Lord cares to
reign, for He says He came into the world to be a king? I
answer, A kingdom of kings, and no other. Where every
man is a king, there and there only does the Lord care to
reign, in the name of His father. As no king in Europe
would care to reign over a cannibal, a savage, or an animal
race, so the Lord cares for no kingdom over anything this
world calls a nation. A king must rule over his own kind.

Jesus is a king in virtue of no conquest, inheritance, or
election, but in right of essential being; and He cares for no
subjects but such as are His subjects in the same right. His
subjects must be of His own kind, in their very nature and
essence kings. To understand His answer to Pilate, see
wherein consists His kingship; what it is that makes Him a
king; what manifestation of His essential being gives Him a
claim to be king.

The Lord's is a kingdom in which no man seeks to be
above another: ambition is of the dirt of this world's king-

doms. He says, "I am a king, for I was born for the purpose, I came into the world with the object of bearing witness to the truth. Everyone that is of my kind, that is of the truth, hears my voice. He is a king like me, and makes one of my subjects."

Pilate thereupon—as would most Christians nowadays, instead of setting about being true—requests a definition of truth, a presentation to his intellect in set terms of what the word "truth" means. But instantly, whether confident of the uselessness of the inquiry, or intending to resume it when he has set the Lord at liberty, goes out to the people to tell them he finds no fault in Him. Whatever interpretation we put on his action here, he must be far less worthy of blame than those "Christians" who, instead of setting themselves to be pure "even as He is pure," to be their brother and sister's keeper, and to serve God by being honorable in shop and counting-house and labor-market, proceed to "serve" Him, some by going to church or chapel, some by condemning the opinions of their neighbors, some by teaching others what they do not themselves heed.

Neither Pilate nor they ask the one true question, "How am I to be a true man? How am I to become a man worth being a man?" The Lord is a king because His life, the life of His thoughts, of His imagination, of His will, of every smallest action, is true—true first to God in that He is altogether His, true to Himself in that He forgets Himself altogether, and true to His fellows in that He will endure anything they do to Him, nor cease declaring Himself the son and messenger and likeness of God. They will kill Him, but it matters not: the truth is as He says!

Jesus is a king because His business is to bear witness to the truth. What truth? All truth; all verity of relation throughout the universe—first of all, that His Father is good, perfectly good; and that the crown and joy of life is to desire and do the will of the eternal source of will, and of all life.

Principle of Hell Opposed

He deals thus the death-blow to the power of hell. For the one principle of hell is—"I am my own. I am my own king and my own subject. *I* am the center from which go out my thoughts; *I* am the object and end of my thoughts; back upon *me* as the alpha and omega of life, my thoughts return. My own glory is, and ought to be, my chief care; my ambition, to gather the regards of men to the one center, myself. My pleasure is *my* pleasure. My kingdom is—as many as I can bring to acknowledge my greatness over them. My judgment is the faultless rule of things. My right is—what I desire. The more I am all in all to myself, the greater I am. The less I acknowledge debt or obligation to another; the more I close my eyes to the fact that I did not make myself; the more self-sufficing I feel or imagine myself—the greater I am. I will be free with the freedom that consists in doing whatever I am inclined to do, from whatever quarter may come the inclination. To do my own will so long as I feel anything to be my will, is to be free, is to live."

To all these principles of hell, or of this world—they are the same thing, and it matters nothing whether they are asserted or defended so long as they are acted upon—the Lord, the king, gives the direct lie. It is as if He said: "I ought to know what I say, for I have been from all eternity the son of Him from whom you issue, and whom you call your father, but whom you will not have your father: I know all He thinks and is; and I say this, that my perfect freedom, my pure individuality, rests on the fact that I have not another will than His. My will is all for His will, for His will is right. He is righteousness itself.

"His very being is love and equity and self-devotion, and He will have His children such as Himself—creatures of love, of fairness, of self-devotion to Him and their fellows. I was born to bear witness to the truth—in my own person to be the truth visible—the very likeness and manifestation of the God who is true. My very being is His witness. Every fact of me witnesses Him. He is the truth, and I am the truth. Kill me, but while I live I say, Such as I am He is.

"If I said I did not know Him, I should be a liar. I fear nothing you can do to me. Shall the king who comes to say what is true, turn his back for fear of men? My Father is like me; I know it, and I say it. You do not like to hear it because you are not like Him. I am low in your eyes which measure things by their show; therefore you say I blaspheme. I should blaspheme if I said He was such as anything you are capable of imagining Him, for you love show, and power, and the praise of men. I do not, and God is like me.

"I came into the world to show Him. I am a king because He sent me to bear witness to His truth, and I bear it. Kill me, and I will rise again. You can kill me, but you cannot hold me dead. Death is my servant; you are the slaves of Death because you will not be true, and let the truth make you free. Bound, and in your hands, I am free as God, for God is my father. I know I shall suffer, suffer unto death, but if you knew my father, you would not wonder that I am ready; you would be ready too. He is my strength. My father is greater than I."

Remember, friends, I said, "It is as if He said." I am daring to present a shadow of the Lord's witnessing, a shadow surely cast by His deeds and His very words! If I mistake, He will forgive me. I do not fear Him; I fear only lest, able to see and write these things, I should fail of witnessing, and myself be, after all, a castaway—no king, but a talker; no disciple of Jesus, ready to go with Him to the death, but an arguer about the truth; a hater of the lies men speak for God, and myself a truth-speaking liar, not a doer of the word.

The truth is *God*; the witness to the truth is Jesus. The kingdom of the truth is the hearts of men. The bliss of men is the true God. The thought of God is the truth of everything. All well-being lies in true relation to God. The man who knows these things and does not order life and action, judgment and love by them, is of the worst of the lying. With hand, and foot, and face he casts scorn upon that which his tongue confesses.

Is every Christian expected to bear witness? A man content to bear no witness to the truth is not in the kingdom of heaven. One who believes must bear witness. One who sees the truth, must live witnessing to it. Is our life, then, a witnessing to the truth? Do we carry ourselves in bank, on farm, in house or shop, in study or chamber or workshop, as the Lord would, or as the Lord would not?

Are we careful to be true? Or are we mean, self-serving, world-flattering, fawning slaves? When contempt is cast on the truth, do we smile? Wronged in our presence, do we make no sign that we hold by it? I do not say we are called upon to dispute, and defend with logic and argument, but we are called upon to show that we are on the other side.

But when I say *truth*, I do not mean *opinion*: to treat opinion as if that were truth, is grievously to wrong the truth. The soul that loves the truth and tries to be true, will know when to speak and when to be silent; but the true man will never look as if he did not care. We are not bound to say all we think, but we are bound not even to look what we do not think.

THIRTEEN

THE
TRUTH

❦

I am ... the truth (John 14:6).

I desire to help those whom I may to understand more of what is meant by *the truth*, not for the sake of definition, or logical discrimination, but that, when they hear the word from the mouth of the Lord, the right idea may rise in their minds. Let us endeavor to arrive at His meaning by a gently ascending stair.

A thing being so, the word that says it is so, is the truth. But the fact may be of no value in itself, and our knowledge of it of no value either. Of most facts it may be said that the truth concerning them is of no consequence. For instance, it cannot be in itself important whether on a certain morning I took one side of the street or the other. It may be of importance to someone to know which I took, but in itself it is of none. It would therefore be felt unfit if I said, "It is *a truth* that I walked on the sunny side." The correct word would be *a fact*, not *a truth*.

Let us go up now from the region of facts that seem casual, to those facts that are invariable, by us unchangeable, which therefore involve what we call *law*. It will be seen at once that the *fact* here is of more dignity, and the truth or falsehood of a statement in this region of more consequence in itself. It is a small matter whether the water in my jug was frozen on such a morning; but it is a fact of great importance that at thirty-two degrees of Fahrenheit water always freezes. Is it a truth that water freezes at thirty-two degrees? I think not. Call it a law if you will—a law of nature if you choose—that it always is so, but not a truth.

Tell us why it *must* be so, and you state a truth. When we come to see that a law is such, because it is the embodiment of a certain eternal thought, beheld by us in it, a fact of the being of God, the facts of which alone are truths, then indeed it will be to us, not a law merely, but an embodied truth. A law of God's nature is a way He would have us think of Him; it is a necessary truth of all being. When we say, "I understand that law. I see why it ought to be. It is just like God," then it rises [to become] a revelation of character, nature, and will in God. It is a picture of something in God, a word that tells a fact about God, and is therefore far nearer being called a truth than anything below it.

I believe that every fact in nature is a revelation of God, is there such as it is because God is such as He is; and I suspect that all its facts impress us so that we learn God unconsciously. From the moment when first we come into contact with the world, it is to us a revelation of God, His things seen, by which we come to know the things unseen.

How should we imagine what we may of God, without the firmament over our heads, a visible sphere, yet a formless infinitude! What idea could we have of God without the sky? The truth of the sky is what it makes us feel of the God that sent it out to our eyes.

Poet vs. Scientist

We are here in a region far above that commonly claimed for science, open only to the heart of the child and the child-like man and woman—a region in which the poet is among his own things, and to which he has often to go to fetch them. For things as they are, not as science deals with them, are the revelation of God to His children.

I would not be misunderstood: there is no fact of science not yet incorporated in a law, no law of science that has got beyond the hypothetic and tentative, that has not in it the will of God, and therefore may not reveal God; but neither fact nor law is there for the sake of fact or law; each is but a means to an end; in the perfected end we find the intent, and there God—not in the laws themselves, save as His means.

For that same reason, human science cannot discover God; for human science is but the backward undoing of the tapestry-web of God's science, works with its back to Him, and is always leaving Him—His intent, that is, His perfected work—behind it, always going farther and farther away from the point where His work culminates in revelation. Doubtless it thus makes some small intellectual approach to Him, but at best it can come only to His back; science will never find the fact of God.

Analysis is well, as death is well; analysis is death, not life. It discovers a little of the way God walks to His ends, but in so doing it forgets and leaves the end itself behind. I do not say the man of science does so, but the very process of his work is such a leaving of God's ends behind.

Ask a man of mere science, what is the truth of a flower: he will pull it to pieces, show you its parts, explain how they minister each to the life of the flower; he will tell you what changes are wrought in it by scientific cultivation; where it lives originally, where it can live; the effects upon it of another climate; what part the insects bear in its varieties—and doubtless many more facts about it.

Ask the poet what is the truth of the flower, and he will answer: "Why, the flower itself, the perfect flower, and what it cannot help saying to him who has ears to hear it." The truth of the flower is, not the facts about it, be they correct as ideal science itself, but the shining, glowing, gladdening, patient thing throned on its stalk—the compeller of smile and tear from the child and prophet.

The man of science laughs at this, because he is only a man of science, and does not know what it means. The children of God must always be mocked by the children of the world. Those that hold love the only good in the world, understand and smile at the world's children, and can do very well without anything they have got to tell them. In the higher state to which their love is leading them, they will speedily outstrip the men of science, for they have that which is at the root of science, that for the revealing of which God's science exists. What shall it profit a man to know all things, and lose the bliss, the consciousness of well-being, which alone can give value to his knowledge?

The truth *of a thing*, then, is the blossom of it, the thing it is made for. Truth in a man's imagination is the power to recognize this truth of a thing. Wherever, in anything that God has made, in the glory of it, be it sky or flower or human face, we see the glory of God, there a true imagination is beholding a truth of God. And now we must advance to a yet higher plane.

Becoming a True Person

We have seen that the moment whatever goes by the name of truth comes into connection with man, the moment the knowledge of it affects or ought to affect his sense of duty, it becomes a thing of far nobler import. A fact which in itself is of no value, becomes at once a matter of life and death— moral life and death, when a man has the choice, the imperative choice of being true or false concerning it.

When the truth, the heart, the summit, the crown of a

thing, is perceived by a man, he approaches the fountain of truth whence the thing came, and perceiving God by understanding what is, becomes more of a man, more of the being he was meant to be. In virtue of this truth perceived, he has relations with the universe undeveloped in him till then. But far higher will the doing of the least, the most insignificant duty raise him. He begins thereby to be a true man.

A man may delight in the vision and glory of a truth, and not himself be true. The man whose vision is weak, but who, as far as he sees, and desirous to see farther, does the thing he sees, is a true man. If a man knows what is, and says it is not, his knowing does not make him less than a liar. The man who recognizes the truth of any human relation, and neglects the duty involved, is not a true man. The man who knows the laws of nature, and does not heed them, the more he teaches them to others, the less is he a true man. But he may obey them all and be the falsest of men, because of far higher and closer duties which he neglects. The man who takes good care of himself and none of his brother and sister, is false.

Man is man only in the doing of the truth, perfect man only in the doing of the highest truth, which is the fulfilling of his relations to his origin. But he has relations with his fellow man, closer infinitely than with any of the things around him, and to many a man far plainer than his relations with God. The very nature of a man depends upon or is one with these relations. They are *truths*, and the man is a true man as he fulfils them. Fulfilling them perfectly, he is himself a *truth*, a living truth.

The man is a true man who chooses duty; he is a perfect man who at length never thinks of duty, who forgets the name of it. The duty of Jesus was the doing in lower forms than the perfect that which He loved perfectly, and did perfectly in the highest forms also. Thus He fulfilled all righteousness. One who went to the truth by mere impulse, would be a holy animal, not a true man. Relations, truths, duties, are shown to the man away beyond him, that he may choose them, and be a child of God, choosing righteousness like Him. Hence the whole sad victorious human tale, and the glory to be revealed!

The facts of human relation, then, are truths indeed, and of awfullest import. "Anyone who hates his brother is a murderer, and you know that no murderer has eternal life abiding in him!" The man who lives a hunter after pleasure, not a laborer in the fields of duty, who thinks of himself as if he were alone on the earth, is in himself a lie. Instead of being the man he looks, the man he was made to be, he lives as the beasts seem to live—with this difference, I trust, that they are rising, while he, so far as lies in himself, is sinking. But he cannot be allowed to sink beyond God's reach; hence all the holy—that is, healing—miseries that come upon him, of which he complains as so hard and unfair: they are for the compelling of the truth he will not yield—a painful persuasion to be himself, to be a truth.

The highest truth to the intellect, the abstract truth, is the relation in which man stands to the Source of his being—his will to the Will whence it became a will, his love to the Love that kindled his power to love, his intellect to the Intellect that lighted his. If a man deal with these things only as things to be dealt with, as objects of thought, as ideas to be analysed and arranged in their due order and right relation, he treats them as facts and not as truths, and is no better, probably much the worse, for his converse with them, for he knows in a measure, and is false to all that is most worthy of his faithfulness.

But when the soul, or heart, or spirit, or what you please to call that which is the man himself and not his body, sooner or later becomes aware that he needs some one above him, whom to obey, in whom to rest, from whom to seek deliverance from what in himself is despicable, disappointing, unworthy even of his own interest; when he is aware of an opposition in him, which is not harmony; that, while he hates it, there is yet present with him, and seeming to be himself, what sometimes he calls *the old Adam,* sometimes *the flesh,* sometimes *his lower nature,* sometimes *his evil self;* and sometimes recognizes as simply that part of his being where God is not; then indeed is the man in the region of truth, and beginning to come true in himself.

Nor will it be long ere he discover that there is no part in him with which he would be at strife, so God were there, so that it were true, what it ought to be—in right relation to the whole; for, by whatever name called, the old Adam, or antecedent horse, or dog, or tiger, it would then fulfil its part holily, intruding upon nothing, subject utterly to the rule of the higher; horse or dog or tiger, it would be good horse, good dog, good tiger.

When a man is, with his whole nature, loving and willing the truth, he is then a live truth. But this he has not originated in himself. He has seen it and striven for it, but not originated it. The one originating, living, visible truth, embracing all truths in all relations, is Jesus Christ. He is true; He is the live Truth. His truth, chosen and willed by Him, is His absolute obedience to His Father. The obedient Jesus is Jesus the Truth.

He is true and the root of all truth and development of truth in men. Their very being, however far from the true human, is the undeveloped Christ in them, and his likeness to Christ is the truth of a man, even as the perfect meaning of a flower is the truth of a flower. Every man, according to the divine idea of him, must come to the truth of that idea; and under every form of Christ is the Christ. The truth of every man, I say, is the perfected Christ in him. As Christ is the blossom of humanity, so the blossom of every man is the Christ perfected in him.

He gives us the will wherewith to will and the power to use it, and the help needed to supplement the power, whatever in any case the need may be. But we ourselves must will the truth, and for that the Lord is waiting, for the victory of

God His Father in the heart of His child. In this alone can He see of the travail of His soul, in this alone be satisfied. The work is His, but we must take our willing share. The will, the power of willing, may be created, but the willing is begotten. Because God wills first, man wills also.

When my being is consciously and willedly in the hands of Him who called it to live and think and suffer and be glad —given back to Him by a perfect obedience—I thenceforward breathe the breath, share the life of God Himself. Then I am free, in that I am true—which means one with the Father. And freedom knows itself to be freedom.

When a man is true, if he were in hell he could not be miserable. He is right with himself because right with Him whence he came. To be right with God is to be right with the universe; one with the power, the love, the will of the mighty Father, the cherisher of joy, the lord of laughter, whose are all glories, all hopes, who loves everything, and hates nothing but selfishness, which He will not have in His kingdom.

Christ then is the Lord of life; His life is the light of men; the light mirrored in them changes them into the image of Him, the Truth; and thus the Truth, who is the Son, makes them free.

FOURTEEN

FREEDOM

...And the truth will make you free. . . . every one who commits sin is a slave to sin. The slave does not continue in the house for ever; the son continues for ever. So if the Son makes you free, you will be free indeed (John 8:32, 34-36).

Those to whom God is not all in all, are slaves. They may not commit great sins; they may be trying to do right; but so long as they *serve* God, as they call it, from duty, and do not know Him as their Father, the joy of their being, they are slaves—good slaves, but slaves.

If they did not try to do their duty, they would be bad slaves. They are by no means so slavish as those that serve from fear, but they are slaves; and because they are but slaves, they can fulfil no righteousness, can do no duty perfectly, but must ever be trying after it wearily and in pain, knowing well that if they stop trying, they are lost. They are slaves indeed, for they would be glad to be adopted by one who is their own Father!

Where then are the sons? I know none, I answer, who are yet utterly and entirely sons or daughters. There may be such—God knows; I have not known them; or, knowing them, have not been myself such as to be able to recognize them. But I do know some who are enough sons and daughters to be at war with the slave in them, who are not content to be slaves to their Father.

Nothing I have seen or known of sonship, comes near the glory of the thing. But there are thousands of sons and daughters, though their number be yet only a remnant, who are siding with the Father of their spirits against themselves, against all that divides them from Him from whom they have come. Such are not slaves; they are true though not perfect children.

They are children—with more or less of the dying slave in them; they know it is there, and what it is, and hate the slavery in them, and try to slay it. The real slave is he who does not seek to be a child; who does not desire to end his slavery; who looks upon the claim of the child as presumption; who never lifts up his heart to cry, "Father, what would you have me to do?"

The slaves of sin rarely grumble at that slavery; it is their slavery to God they grumble at; of that alone they complain —of the painful messengers He sends to deliver them from their slavery both to sin and to Himself. They must be sons or slaves. They cannot rid themselves of their owner. Whether they deny God, or mock Him by acknowledging and not heeding Him, or treat Him as an arbitrary, formal monarch; whether, taking no trouble to find out what pleases Him, they do dull things for His service He cares nothing about, or try to propitiate Him by assuming with strenuous effort some yoke the Son never wore, and never called on them to wear, they are slaves, and not the less slaves that they are slaves to God. They are so thoroughly slaves, that they do not care to get out of their slavery by becoming sons and daughters, by finding the good of life.

Could a Creator make a creature whose well-being should not depend on Himself? The whole question rests and turns on the relation of creative and created, of which relation few seem to have the consciousness yet developed. To live without the eternal creative life is an impossibility. Freedom from God can only mean an incapacity for seeing the facts of existence, an incapability of understanding the glory of the creature who makes common cause with his Creator in His creation of him, who wills that the lovely will calling him into life and giving him choice, should finish making him, should draw him into the circle of the creative heart, to joy that he lives by no poor power of his own will, but is one with the causing life of his life, in closest breathing and willing, vital and claimant oneness with the life of all life.

Such a creature knows the life of the infinite Father as the very flame of his life, and joys that nothing is done or will be done in the universe in which the Father will not make him all of a sharer that it is possible for perfect generosity to make him. If you say this is irreverent, I doubt if you have seen the God manifest in Jesus.

But one who reads may call out, in the agony and thirst of a child waking from a dream of endless seeking and no finding, "I am bound like Lazarus in his grave-clothes! what am I to do?" Here is the answer, drawn from this parable of our Lord; for the saying is much like a parable, teaching more than it utters, appealing to the conscience and heart, not to the understanding: "You are a slave; the slave has no hold on the house; only the sons and daughters have an abiding rest in the home of their father. God cannot have slaves about Him always. You must give up your slavery, and be set free from it. That is what I am here for.

"If I make you free, you shall be free indeed; for I can make you free only by making you what you were meant to be, sons like myself. That is how alone the Son can work. But it is you who must become sons; you must will it, and I am here to help you." It is as if He said, "You shall have the freedom of my Father's universe; for, free from yourselves, you will be free of His heart. Yourselves are your slavery. That is the darkness which you have loved rather than the light. You have given honor to yourselves, and not to the Father; you have sought honor from men, and not from the Father! Therefore, even in the house of your Father, you have been but sojourning slaves. We in His family are all one; we have no party-spirit; we have no self-seeking: fall in love with us, and you shall be free as we are free."

If then the poor starved child cry, "How, Lord?" the answer will depend on what he means by that *how*. If he means, "What plan will you adopt? What is your scheme for cutting my bonds and setting me free?" the answer may be a deepening of the darkness, a tightening of the bonds.

But if he means, "Lord, what would you have me to do?" the answer will not tarry. "Give yourself to me to do what I tell you, to understand what I say, to be my good, obedient little brother, and I will wake in you the heart that my Father put in you, the same kind of heart that I have, and it will grow to love the Father, altogether and absolutely, as mine does, till you are ready to be torn to pieces for Him. Then you will know that you are at the heart of the universe, at the heart of every secret—at the heart of the Father. Not till then will you be free, then free indeed!"

Christ died to save us, not from suffering, but from ourselves; not from injustice, far less from justice, but from being unjust. He died that we might live—but live as He lives, by dying as He died who died to Himself that He might live unto God.

If we do not die to ourselves, we cannot live to God, and he that does not live to God is dead. "You will know the truth," the Lord says, "and the truth will make you free. I am the truth, and you shall be free as I am free. To be free, you must be sons like me. To be free you must *be* that which you have to be, that which you are created. To be free you must give the answer of sons to the Father who calls you. To be free you must fear nothing but evil, care for nothing but the will of the Father, hold to Him in absolute confidence and infinite expectation. He alone is to be trusted."

He has shown us the Father not only by doing what the Father does, not only by loving his Father's children even as the Father loves them, but by His perfect satisfaction with Him, His joy in Him, His utter obedience to Him. He has shown us the Father by the absolute devotion of a perfect son.

He is the Son of God because the Father and He are one, have one thought, one mind, one heart. Upon this truth—I do not mean the dogma, but the truth itself of Jesus to His father—hangs the universe; and upon the recognition of this truth—that is, upon their becoming thus true—hangs the freedom of the children, the redemption of their whole world. "I and the Father are one," is the center-truth of the universe; and the circumfering truth is, "that they also may be one in us."

The only free man, then, is he who is a child of the Father. He is a servant of all, but can be made the slave of none: he is a son of the Lord of the universe. He is in himself, in virtue of his truth, free. He is in himself a king. For the Son rests his claim to royalty on this, that he was born and came into the world to bear witness to the truth.

FIFTEEN

THE CONSUMING FIRE

*O*ur God is a consuming fire
(Heb. 12:29).

Nothing is inexorable but love. Love which will yield to prayer is imperfect and poor. Nor is it then the love that yields, but its alloy. For if at the voice of entreaty love conquers displeasure, it is love asserting itself, not love yielding its claims. It is not love that grants a boon unwillingly; still less is it love that answers a prayer to the wrong and hurt of him who prays. Love is one, and love is changeless.

For love loves unto purity. Love has ever in view the absolute loveliness of that which it beholds. Where loveliness is incomplete, and love cannot love its fill of loving, it spends itself to make more lovely, that it may love more. It strives for perfection, even that itself may be perfected—not in itself, but in the object. As it was love that first created humanity, so even human love, in proportion to its divinity, will go on creating the beautiful for its own outpouring.

There is nothing eternal but that which loves and can be loved, and love is ever climbing towards the consummation when such shall be the universe, imperishable, divine.

Therefore all that is not beautiful in the beloved, all that comes between and is not of love's kind, must be destroyed.

And our God is a consuming fire.

If this be hard to understand, it is as the simple, absolute truth is hard to understand. It may be centuries of ages before a man comes to see a truth—ages of strife, of effort, of aspiration. But when once he does see it, it is so plain that he wonders he could have lived without seeing it. That he did not understand it sooner was simply and only that he did not see it. To see a truth, to know what it is, to understand it, and to love it, are all one.

The Fire of Love

Let us look at the utterance of the apostle which is crowned with this lovely terror: "Our God is a consuming fire."

"Therefore, let us be grateful for receiving a kingdom that cannot be shaken, and thus let us offer to God acceptable worship, with reverence and awe; for our God is a consuming fire." We have received a kingdom that cannot be moved—whose nature is immovable. Let us have grace to serve the Consuming Fire, our God, with divine fear; not with the fear that cringes and craves, but with the bowing down of all thoughts, all delights, all loves before Him who is the life of them all, and will have them all pure. The kingdom He has given us cannot be moved, because it has nothing weak in it. It is of the eternal world, the world of being, of truth. We, therefore, must worship Him with a fear pure as the kingdom is unshakable. He will shake heaven and earth, that only the unshakable may remain (v. 27).

He is a consuming fire, that only that which cannot be consumed may stand forth eternal. It is the nature of God, so terribly pure that it destroys all that is not pure as fire, which demands like purity in our worship. He will have purity. It is not that the fire will burn us if we do not worship thus; but that the fire will burn us until we worship thus; yea, will go on burning within us after all that is foreign to it has yielded to its force, no longer with pain and consuming, but as the highest consciousness of life, the presence of God.

When evil, which alone is consumable, shall have passed away in His fire from the dwellers in the immovable kingdom, the nature of man shall look the nature of God in the face, and His fear shall then be pure; for an eternal, that is a holy fear, must spring from a knowledge of the nature, not from a sense of the power. But that which cannot be consumed must be one within itself, a simple existence; therefore, in such a soul the fear towards God will be one with the homeliest love.

Yea, the fear of God will cause a man to flee, not from Him, but from himself; not from Him, but to Him, the Father of himself, in terror lest he should do Him wrong or his neighbor wrong. And the first words which follow for the setting forth of that grace whereby we may serve God acceptably are these: "Let brotherly love continue." To love our brother is to worship the Consuming Fire.

The symbol of *the consuming fire* would seem to have been suggested to the writer by the fire that burned on the mountain of the old law. That fire was part of the revelation of God there made to the Israelites. Nor was it the first instance of such a revelation. The symbol of God's presence, before which Moses had to put off his shoes, and to which it was not safe for him to draw near, was a fire that did not consume the bush in which it burned.

But the same symbol employed by a writer of the New Testament should mean more, not than it meant before, but than it was before employed to express; for it could not have been employed to express more than it was possible for them to perceive. What else than terror could a nation of slaves, into whose very souls the rust of their chains had eaten, in whose memory lingered the smoke of the flesh-pots of Egypt, who, rather than not eat of the food they liked best, would have gone back to the house of their bondage—what else could such a nation see in that fire than terror and destruction? How should they think of purification by fire? They had yet no such condition of mind as could generate such a thought.

And if they had had the thought, the notion of the suffering involved would soon have overwhelmed the notion of purification. Nor would such a nation have listened to any teaching that was not supported by terror. Fear was that for which they were fit. They had no worship for any being of whom they had not to be afraid.

Was then this show upon Mount Sinai a device to move obedience, such as bad nurses employ with children? a hint of vague and false horror? Was it not a true revelation of God?

If it was not a true revelation, it was none at all, and the story is either false, or the whole display was a political trick of Moses. Those who can read the mind of Moses will not easily believe the latter, and those who understand the scope of the pretended revelation, will see no reason for supposing the former. That which would be politic, were it a deception, is not therefore excluded from the possibility of another source. Some people believe so little in a cosmos or ordered world, that the very argument of fitness is a reason for unbelief.

At all events, if God showed them these things, God showed them what was true. It was a revelation of Himself. He will not put on a mask. He puts on a face. He will not speak out of flaming fire if that flaming fire is alien to Him, if there is nothing in Him for that flaming fire to reveal. Be His children ever so brutish, He will not terrify them with a lie.

A Partial Revelation

It was a revelation, but a partial one; a true symbol, not a final vision.

No revelation can be other than partial. If for true revelation a man must be told all the truth, then farewell to revelation; yea, farewell to the sonship. For what revelation, other than a partial, can the highest spiritual condition receive of the infinite God? But it is not therefore untrue because it is partial. Because of a lower condition of the receiver, a more partial revelation might be truer than that would be which constituted a fuller revelation to one in a higher condition; for the former might reveal much to him, the latter might reveal nothing.

Only, whatever it might reveal, if its nature were such as to preclude development and growth, thus changing the man to its incompleteness, it would be but a false revelation fighting against all the divine laws of human existence. The true revelation rouses the desire to know more by the truth of its incompleteness.

Here was a nation at its lowest: could it receive anything but a partial revelation, a revelation of fear? How should the Hebrews be other than terrified at that which was opposed to all they knew of themselves, beings judging it good to honor a golden calf? Such as they were, they did well to be afraid. They were in a better condition, acknowledging a terror *above* them, flaming on that unknown mountain height, than stooping to worship the idol below them. Fear is nobler than sensuality.

Fear is better than no God, better than a god made with hands. In that fear lay deep hidden the sense of the infinite. The worship of fear is true, although very low; and though not acceptable to God in itself, for only the worship of spirit and of truth is acceptable to Him, yet even in His sight it is precious. For He regards men not as they are merely, but as they shall be; not as they shall be merely, but as they are now growing, or capable of growing, towards that image after which He made them that they might grow to it.

Therefore a thousand stages, each in itself all but value-less, are of inestimable worth as the necessary and con-nected gradations of an infinite progress. A condition which of declension would indicate a devil, may of growth indicate a saint. So far then the revelation, not being final any more than complete, and calling forth the best of which they were now capable, so making future and higher reve-lation possible, may have been a true one.

But we shall find that this very revelation of fire is itself, in a higher sense, true to the mind of the rejoicing saint as to the mind of the trembling sinner. For the former sees far-ther into the meaning of the fire, and knows better what it will do to him. It is a symbol which needed not to be super-seded, only unfolded. While men take part *with* their sins, while they feel as if, separated from their sins, they would be no longer themselves, how can they understand that the lightning word is a Savior—that word which pierces to the dividing between the man and the evil, which will slay the sin and give life to the sinner? Can it be any comfort to them to be told that God loves them so that He will burn them clean? Can the cleansing of the fire appear to them any-thing beyond what it must always, more or less, be—a pro-cess of torture?

They do not want to be clean, and they cannot bear to be tortured. Can they then do other, or can we desire that they should do other, than fear God, even with the fear of the wicked, until they learn to love Him with the love of the holy? To them Mount Sinai is crowned with the signs of vengeance. And is not God ready to do unto them even as they fear, though with another feeling and a different end from any which they are capable of supposing? He is against sin: in so far as, and while, they and sin are one, He is against them—against their desires, their aims, their fears, and their hopes; and thus He is altogether and always *for them.*

That thunder and lightning and tempest, that blackness torn with the sound of a trumpet, that visible horror billowed with the voice of words, was all but a faint image to the senses of the slaves of what God thinks and feels against vileness and selfishness, of the unrest of unassuageable repulsion with which He regards such conditions. The intention was that so the stupid people, fearing somewhat to do as they would, might leave a little room for that grace to grow in them, which would at length make them see that evil, and not fire, is the fearful thing; yea, so transform them that they would gladly rush up into the trumpet-blast of Sinai to escape the flutes around the golden calf. Could they have understood this, they would have needed no Mount Sinai. It was a true, and of necessity a partial revelation—partial in order to be true.

What Is to Be Feared?

When we say that God is Love, do we teach men that their fear of Him is groundless? No. As much as they fear will come upon them, possibly far more. But there is something beyond their fear—a divine fate which they cannot withstand, because it works along with the human individuality which the divine individuality has created in them.

The wrath will consume what they *call* themselves; so that the selves God made shall appear, coming out with ten-fold consciousness of being, and bringing with them all that made the blessedness of the life the men tried to lead without God. They will know that now first are they fully themselves. The avaricious, weary, selfish, suspicious old man shall have passed away. The young, ever young self, will remain. That which they *thought* themselves shall have vanished: that which they *felt* themselves, though they misjudged their own feelings, shall remain—remain glorified in repentant hope. For that which cannot be shaken shall remain. That which is immortal in God shall remain in man. The death that is in them shall be consumed.

It is the law of Nature—that is, the law of God—that all that is destructible shall be destroyed. When that which is immortal buries itself in the destructible—when it receives all the messages from without, through the surrounding region of decadence, and none from within, from the eternal doors—it cannot, though immortal still, know its own immortality. The destructible must be burned out of it, or begin to be burned out of it, before it can *partake* of eternal life. When that is all burnt away and gone, then it has eternal life. Or rather, when the fire of eternal life has possessed a man, then the destructible is gone utterly, and he is pure.

Many a man's work must be burned, that by that very burning he may be saved—"so as by fire." Away in smoke go the lordships, the Rabbi-hoods of the world, and the man who acquiesces in the burning is saved by the fire; for it has destroyed the destructible, which is the vantage point of the deathly, which would destroy both body and soul in hell. If still he cling to that which can be burned, the burning goes on deeper and deeper into his bosom, till it reaches the roots of the falsehood that enslaves him—possibly by looking like the truth.

The man who loves God, and is not yet pure, courts the burning of God. Nor is it always torture. The fire shows itself sometimes only as light—still it will be fire of purifying. The consuming fire is just the original, the active form of Purity, that which makes pure, that which is indeed Love, the creative energy of God. Without purity there can be as no creation so no persistence. That which is not pure is corruptible, and corruption cannot inherit incorruption.

The man whose deeds are evil, fears the burning. But the burning will not come the less because he fears it or denies it. Escape is hopeless. For Love is inexorable. Our God is a consuming fire. He shall not come out till he has paid the last penny.

The Outer Darkness

If the man resists the burning of God, the consuming fire of Love, a terrible doom awaits him, and its day will come. He shall be cast into the outer darkness who hates the fire of God. What sick dismay shall then seize upon him! For let a man think and care ever so little about God, he does not therefore exist without God. God is here with him, upholding, warming, delighting, teaching him—making life a good thing to him. God gives him Himself, though he knows it not.

But when God withdraws from a man as far as that can be without the man's ceasing to be; when the man feels himself abandoned, hanging in a ceaseless vertigo of existence upon the verge of the gulf of his being, without support, without refuge, without aim, without end—for the soul has no weapons wherewith to destroy herself—with no in-breathing of joy, with nothing to make life good; then will he listen in agony for the faintest sound of life from the closed door. If the moan of suffering humanity ever reaches the ear of the outcast of darkness, he will be ready to rush into the very heart of the Consuming Fire to know life once more, to change this terror of sick negation, of unspeakable death, for that region of painful hope.

Imagination cannot mislead us into too much horror of being without God—that one living death. But with this divine difference: that the outer darkness is but the most dreadful form of the consuming fire—the fire without light—the darkness visible, the black flame. God hath withdrawn Himself, but not lost His hold. His face is turned away, but His hand is laid upon him still. His heart has ceased to beat into the man's heart, but He keeps him alive by His fire. And that fire will go searching and burning on in him, as in the highest saint who is not yet pure as He is pure.

But at length, O God, will you not cast Death and Hell into the lake of Fire—even into your own consuming self?

Death shall then die everlastingly,

> *And Hell itself will pass away,*
> *And leave her dolorous mansions to the peering day.*

Then indeed will you be all in all. For then our poor brothers and sisters, every one—O God, we trust in you, the Consuming Fire—shall have been burnt clean and brought home. For if their moans, myriads of ages away, would turn heaven for us into hell—shall a man be more merciful than God? Shall, of all His glories, His mercy alone not be infinite? Shall a brother love a brother more than The Father loves a son?—more than The Brother Christ loves His brother? Would He not die yet again to save one brother more?

As for us, now will we come to you, our Consuming Fire. And you will not burn us more than we can bear. But you will burn us. And although you seem to slay us, yet will we trust in you even for that which you have not spoken, if by any means at length we may attain unto the blessedness of those who have not seen and yet have believed.

SIXTEEN

THE LAST PENNY

*T*ruly I say to you, you will never get out till you have paid the last penny (Matt. 5:26).

There is a thing wonderful and admirable in the parables, not readily grasped, but specially indicated by the Lord Himself—their unintelligibility to the mere intellect. They are addressed to the conscience and not to the intellect, to the will and not to the imagination. They are strong and direct but not definite. They are not meant to explain anything, but to rouse a man to the feeling, "I am not what I ought to be, I do not the thing I ought to do!"

Many maundering interpretations may be given by the wise, with plentiful loss of labor, while the child who uses them for the necessity of walking in the one path will constantly receive light from them. The greatest obscuration of the words of the Lord, as of all true teachers, comes from those who give themselves to interpret rather than do them. Theologians have done more to hide the gospel of Christ than any of its adversaries.

It was not for our understandings, but our wills, that Christ came. He who does that which he sees, shall understand; he who is set upon understanding rather than doing, shall go on stumbling and mistaking and speaking foolishness. He has not that in him which can understand. The gospel itself, and in it the parables of the Truth, are to be understood only by those who walk by what they find. It is he that runs that shall read, and no other.

It is not intended by the speaker of the parables that any other should know intellectually what, known but intellectually, would be for his injury—what knowing intellectually he would imagine he had grasped, perhaps even appropriated. When the pilgrim of the truth comes on his journey to the region of the parable, he finds its interpretation. It is not a fruit or a jewel to be stored, but a well springing by the wayside.

What special meaning may be read in the different parts of magistrate, judge, and officer, beyond the general suggestion, perhaps, of the tentative approach of the final, I do not know; but I think I do know what is meant by "make friends . . . while you are going" and "the last penny." The parable is an appeal to the common sense of those that hear it, in regard to every affair of righteousness. Arrange what claim lies against you; compulsion waits behind it. Do at once what you must do one day. As there is no escape from payment, escape at least the prison that will enforce it. Do not drive Justice to extremities. Duty is imperative; it must be done. It is useless to think to escape the eternal law of things. Yield of yourself, nor compel God to compel you.

To the honest man, to the man who would fain be honest, the word is of right gracious import. To the untrue, it is a terrible threat; to him who is of the truth, it is sweet as most loving promise. He who is of God's mind in things, rejoices to hear the word of the changeless Truth. The voice of the Right fills the heavens and the earth, and makes his soul glad; it is his salvation. If God were not inexorably just, there would be no stay for the soul of the feeblest lover of right. "You are true, O Lord: one day I also shall be true!"

"You shall render the right, cost you what it may," is a dread sound in the ears of those whose life is a falsehood. What but the last penny would those who love righteousness more than life pay? It is a joy profound as peace to know that God is determined upon such payment, is determined to have His children clean, clear, pure as very snow; is determined that not only shall they with His help make up for whatever wrong they have done, but at length be incapable, by eternal choice of good, under any temptation, of doing the thing that is not divine, the thing God would not do.

No Escape

There has been much cherishing of the evil fancy, often without its taking formal shape, that there is some way of getting out of the region of strict justice, some mode of managing to escape doing *all* that is required of us; but there is no such escape. A way to avoid any demand of righteousness would be an infinitely worse way than the road to the everlasting fire, for its end would be eternal death.

No, there is no escape. There is no heaven with a little hell in it—no plan to retain this or that of the devil in our hearts or our pockets. Out Satan must go, every hair and feather! Neither shall you think to be delivered from the necessity of being good by being made good. God is the God of the animals in a far lovelier way, I suspect, than many of us dare to think, but He will not be the God of a man by making a good beast of him. You must be good; neither death nor any admittance into good company will make you good; though, doubtless, if you be willing and try, these and all other best helps will be given you.

There is no clothing in a robe of imputed righteousness, that poorest of legal cobwebs spun by spiritual spiders. To me it seems like an invention of well-meaning dullness to soothe insanity; and indeed it has proved a door of escape out of worse imaginations. It is apparently an old "doctrine," for St. John seems to point at it where he says, "Little children, let no one deceive you. He who does right is righteous, as He is righteous."

Christ is our righteousness, not that we should escape punishment, still less escape being righteous, but as the live potent Creator of righteousness in us, so that we, with our wills receiving His spirit, shall like Him resist unto blood, striving against sin; shall know in ourselves, as He knows, what a lovely thing is righteousness, what a mean, ugly, unnatural thing is unrighteousness. He is our righteousness, and that righteousness is no fiction, no pretense, no imputation.

One thing that tends to keep men from seeing righteousness and unrighteousness as they are, is that they have been told many things are righteous and unrighteous, which are neither the one nor the other. Righteousness is just fairness —from God to man, from man to God and to man; it is giving every one his due—his large mighty due. He is righteous, and no one else, who does this.

And any system which tends to persuade men that there is any salvation but that of becoming righteous even as Jesus is righteous; that a man can be made good, as a good dog is good, without his own willed share in the making; that a man is saved by having his sins hidden under a robe of imputed righteousness—that system, so far as this tendency, is of the devil and not of God. Thank God, not even error shall injure the true of heart. They grow in the truth, and as love casts out fear, so truth casts out falsehood.

I read, then, in this parable, that a man had better make up his mind to be righteous, to be fair, to do what he can to pay what he owes, in any and all the relations of life—all the matters, in a word, wherein one man may demand of another, or complain that he has not received fair play. Arrange your matters with those who have anything against you, while you are yet together and things have not gone too far to be arranged; *you will have to do it,* and that under less easy circumstances than now. Putting off is of no use. You must. The thing has to be done; there are means of compelling you.

It is a very small matter *to you* whether the man give you your rights or not; it is life or death to you whether or not you give him his. Whether he pay you what you count his debt or no, you will be compelled to pay him all you owe him. If you owe him a pound and he you a million, you must pay him the pound whether he pay you the million or not; there is no business-parallel here. If, owing you love, he gives you hate, you, owing him love, have yet to pay it. We have a good while given us to pay, but a crisis will come—come soon after all—comes always sooner than those expect it who are not ready for it—a crisis when the demand un-yielded will be followed by prison.

The same holds with every demand of God. By refusing to pay, the man makes an adversary who will compel him—and that for the man's own sake. If you or your life say, "I will not," then He will see to it. There is a prison, and the one thing we know about that prison is, that its doors do not open until entire satisfaction is rendered, the last penny paid.

The main debts whose payment God demands are those which lie at the root of all right, those we owe in mind, and soul, and being. Whatever in us can be or make an adversary, whatever could prevent us from doing the will of God, or from agreeing with our fellow—all must be yielded. Our every relation, both to God and our fellow, must be acknowledged heartily, met as a reality. Smaller debts, if any debt can be small, follow as a matter of course.

If the man acknowledge, and would pay if he could but cannot, the universe will be taxed to help him rather than he should continue unable. If the man accepts the will of

God, he is the child of the Father, the whole power and wealth of the Father is for him, and the uttermost penny will easily be paid. If the man denies the debt, or acknowledging does nothing towards paying it, then—at last—the prison.

God in the dark can make a man thirst for the light, who never in the light sought but the dark. The cells of the prison may differ in degree of darkness; but they are all alike in this, that not a door opens but to payment. There is no day but the will of God, and he who is of the night cannot be forever allowed to roam the day. Unfelt, unprized, the light must be taken from him, that he may know what the darkness is. When the darkness is perfect, when he is totally without the light he has spent the light in slaying, then will he know darkness.

The Final Prison

I think I have seen from afar something of the final prison of all, the innermost cell of the debtor of the universe; I will endeavor to convey what I think it may be.

It is the vast outside; the ghastly dark beyond the gates of the city of which God is the light—where the evil dogs go ranging, silent as the dark, for there is no sound any more than sight. The time of signs is over. Every sense has its signs, and they were all misused: there is no sense, no sign more—nothing now by means of which to believe.

The man wakes from the final struggle of death, in absolute loneliness—such a loneliness as in the most miserable moment of deserted childhood he never knew. Not a hint, not a shadow of anything outside his consciousness reaches him. All is dark, dark and dumb; no motion—not the breath of a wind! never a dream of change! not a scent from far-off field! nothing to suggest being or thing besides the man himself, no sign of God anywhere. God has so far withdrawn from the man, that he is conscious only of that from which He has withdrawn.

In the midst of the live world he cared for nothing but himself; now in the dead world he is in God's prison, his own separated self. But no liveliest human imagination could supply adequate representation of what it would be to be left without a shadow of the presence of God. If God gave it, man could not understand it. He knows neither God nor himself in the way of the understanding. For not he who cares least about God was in this world ever left as God could leave him. I doubt if any man could continue following his wickedness from whom God had withdrawn.

The most frightful idea of what could, to his own consciousness, befall a man, is that he should have to lead an existence with which God had nothing to do. The thing could not be; for being that is caused, the causation ceasing, must of necessity cease. It is always in, and never out of God, that we can live and do.

But I suppose the man so left that he seems to himself utterly alone, yet alas! with himself—smallest interchange of thought, feeblest contact of existence, dullest reflection from other being, impossible. In such evil case I believe the man would be glad to come in contact with the worst-loathed insect. It would be a shape of life, something beyond and besides his own huge, void, formless being! I imagine some such feeling in the prayer of the devils for leave to go into the swine.

His worst enemy, could he but be aware of him, he would be ready tò worship. For the misery would be not merely the absence of all being other than his own self, but the fearful, endless, unavoidable presence of that self. Without the correction, the reflection, the support of other presences, being is not merely unsafe, it is a horror—for anyone but God, who is His own being.

For him whose idea is God's, and the image of God, his own being is far too fragmentary and imperfect to be anything like good company. It is the lovely creatures God has made all around us, in them giving us Himself, that,

until we know Him, save us from the frenzy of aloneness—
for that aloneness is Self, Self, Self. The man who minds
only himself must at last go mad if God did not interfere.

Release

Can there be any way out of the misery? Will the soul that
could not believe in God, with all His lovely world around
testifying of Him, believe when shut in the prison of its own
lonely, weary all-and-nothing? It would for a time try to believe that it was indeed nothing, a mere glow of the setting
sun on a cloud of dust, a paltry dream that dreamed itself—
then, ah, if only the dream might dream that it was no
more! that would be the one thing to hope for.

Self-loathing, and that for no sin, from no repentance,
from no vision of better, would begin and grow and grow;
and to what it might not come no soul can tell—of essential,
original misery, uncompromising self-disgust! Only, then,
if a being be capable of self-disgust, is there not some room
for hope—as much as a pinch of earth in the cleft of a rock
might yield for the growth of a pine? Nay, there must be
hope while there is existence; for where there is existence
there must be God; and God is forever good nor can be
other than good.

But alas, the distance from the light! All his years in the
world he received the endless gifts of sun and air, earth and
sea and human face divine, as things that came to him because that was their way, and there was no one to prevent
them. Now the poorest thinning of the darkness he would
hail as men of old the glow of a descending angel; it would
be as a messenger from God. Not that he would think of
God! it takes long to think of God; but hope, not yet seeming hope, would begin to dawn in his bosom, and the thin-
ner darkness would be as a cave of light, a refuge from the
horrid self of which he used to be so proud.

A man may well imagine it impossible ever to think so
unpleasantly of himself! But he has only to let things go,

and he will make it the real, right, natural way to think of himself. True, all I have been saying is imaginary; but our imagination is made to mirror truth. All the things that appear in it are more or less after the model of things that are. I suspect it is the region whence issues prophecy; and when we are true it will mirror nothing but truth. I deal here with the same light and darkness the Lord dealt with, the same St. Paul and St. John and St. Peter and St. Jude dealt with. Ask yourself whether the faintest dawn of even physical light would not be welcome to such a soul as some refuge from the dark of the justly hated self.

And the light would grow and grow across the awful gulf between the soul and its haven—its repentance—for repentance is the first pressure of the bosom of God. And in the twilight, struggling and faint, the man would feel, faint as the twilight, another thought beside his, another thinking Something nigh his dreary self—perhaps the man he had most wronged, most hated, most despised—and would be glad that some one, whoever, was near him. The man he had most injured, and was most ashamed to meet, would be a refuge from himself—oh, how welcome!

So might I imagine a thousand steps up from the darkness, each a little less dark, a little nearer the light—but, ah, the weary way! He cannot come out until he have paid the last penny! Repentance once begun, however, may grow more and more rapid! If God once get a willing hold, if with but one finger He touch the man's self, swift as possibility will He draw him from the darkness into the light.

For that for which the forlorn, self-ruined wretch was made, was to be a child of God, a partaker of the divine nature, an heir of God and joint heir with Christ. Out of the abyss into which he cast himself, refusing to be the heir of God, he must rise and be raised. To the heart of God, the one and only goal of the human race—the refuge and home of all and each, he must set out and go, or the last glimmer of humanity will die from him.

Whoever will live must cease to be a slave and become a child of God. There is no half-way house of rest, where ungodliness may be dallied with, nor prove quite fatal. Be they few or many cast into such prison as I have endeavored to imagine, there can be no deliverance for human soul, whether in that prison or out of it, but in paying the last penny, in becoming lowly, penitent, self-refusing—so receiving the sonship, and learning to cry, *Father*!

SEVENTEEN

RIGHTEOUSNESS

...In order that I may gain Christ and be found in Him, not having a righteousness of my own, based on law, but that which is through faith in Christ, the righteousness from God that depends on faith (Phil. 3:8, 9).

What does the apostle mean by the righteousness that is of God by faith? He means the same righteousness Christ had by faith in God, the same righteousness God Himself has.

In his second epistle to the Corinthians he says, "He made Him to be sin who knew no sin, so that in Him we might become the righteousness of God"; [that is] "He gave him to be treated like a sinner, killed and cast out of His own vineyard by His husbandmen, that we might in Him be made righteous like God." As the antithesis stands it is rhetorically correct. But if the former half means, "He made Him to be treated as if He were a sinner," then the latter half should, in logical precision, mean, "that we might be treated as if we were righteous."

"That is just what Paul does mean," insist not a few. "He means that Jesus was treated by God as if He were a sinner, our sins being imputed to Him, in order that we might be treated as if we were righteous, His righteousness being imputed to us."

That is, that, by a sort of legal fiction, Jesus was treated as what He was not, in order that we might be treated as what we are not. This is the best device, according to the prevailing theology, that the God of truth, the God of mercy, whose glory is that He is just to men by forgiving their sins, could fall upon for saving His creatures!

It seems to me that, seeing much duplicity exists in the body of Christ, every honest member of it should protest against any word tending to imply the existence of falsehood in the indwelling spirit of that body. I now protest against this so-called *doctrine*, counting it the rightful prey of the foolishest wind in the limbo of vanities, whither I would gladly do my best to send it. It is the meagre misshapen offspring of the legalism of a poverty-stricken mechanical fancy, unlighted by a gleam of divine imagination. No one who knows his New Testament will dare to say that the figure is once used in it.

I have dealt already with the source of it. They say first, God must punish the sinner, for justice requires it; then they say He does not punish the sinner, but punishes a perfectly righteous man instead, attributes His righteousness to the sinner, and so continues just. Was there ever such a confusion, such an inversion of right and wrong! Justice *could not* treat a righteous man as an unrighteous; neither, if justice required the punishment of sin, *could* justice let the sinner go unpunished. To lay the pain upon the righteous in the name of justice is simply monstrous. No wonder unbelief is rampant. Believe in Moloch if you will, but call him Moloch, not Justice.

Be sure that the thing that God gives, the righteousness that is of God, is a real thing, and not a contemptible legalism. Pray God I have no righteousness imputed to me. Let me be regarded as the sinner I am; for nothing will serve my need but to be made a righteous man, one that will no more sin.

The Nature of Righteousness

We have the word *imputed* just once in the New Testament. Whether the evil doctrine may have sprung from any possible misunderstanding of the passage where it occurs, I hardly care to inquire. The word as Paul uses it, and the whole of the thought whence his use of it springs, appeals to my sense of right and justice as much as the common use of it arouses my abhorrence. The apostle says that a certain thing was imputed to Abraham for righteousness; or, as the revised version has it, "reckoned to him." What was it that was thus imputed to Abraham? The righteousness of another? God forbid! It was his own faith. The faith of Abraham is reckoned to him for righteousness.

To impute the righteousness of one to another, is simply to act a falsehood; to call the faith of a man his righteousness is simply to speak the truth. Was it not righteous in Abraham to obey God? The Jews placed righteousness in keeping all the particulars of the law of Moses; Paul says faith in God was counted righteousness before Moses was born. You may answer, Abraham was unjust in many things, and by no means a righteous man. True, he was not a righteous man in any complete sense. His righteousness would never have satisfied Paul; neither, you may be sure, did it satisfy Abraham. But his faith was nevertheless righteousness, and if it had not been counted to him for righteousness, there would have been falsehood somewhere, for such faith as Abraham's *is righteousness*.

It was that faith which is one with action: "He went out, not knowing where he was to go." The very act of believing in God after such fashion that, when the time of action comes, the man will obey God, is the highest act, the deepest, loftiest righteousness of which man is capable, is at the root of all other righteousness, and the spirit of it will work till the man is perfect.

If you define righteousness in the common-sense, that is, in the divine fashion—for religion is nothing if it be not the deepest common-sense—as a giving to everyone his due, then certainly the first due is to Him who makes us capable of owing, that is, makes us responsible creatures. You may say this is not one's first feeling of duty. True; but the first in reality is seldom the first perceived. The first duty is too high and too deep to come first into consciousness. If any one were born perfect, which I count an eternal impossibility, then the highest duty would come first into the consciousness. As we are born, it is the doing of, or at least the honest trying to do many another duty, that will at length lead a man to see that his duty to God is the first and deepest and highest of all, including and requiring the performance of all other duties whatever.

A man might live a thousand years in neglect of duty and never come to see that any obligation was upon him to put faith in God and do what He told him—never have a glimpse of the fact that he owed Him something. I would allow that if God were what he thinks Him he would indeed owe Him little; but he thinks Him such in consequence of not doing what he knows he ought to do. He has not come to the light. He has deadened, dulled, hardened his nature. He has not been a man without guile, has not been true and fair.

Faith Is Beginning of Righteousness

But while faith in God is the first duty, and may therefore well be called righteousness in the man in whom it is operative, even though it be imperfect, there is more reason than this why it should be counted to a man for righteousness. It is the one spiritual act which brings the man into contact with the original creative power, able to help him in every endeavor after righteousness, and ensure his progress to perfection. The man who exercises it may therefore also well be called a righteous man, however far from complete in righteousness.

We may call a woman beautiful who is not perfect in beauty; in the Bible men are constantly recognized as righteous men who are far from perfectly righteous. The Bible never deals with impossibilities, never demands of any man at any given moment a righteousness of which at that moment he is incapable; neither does it lay upon any man other law than that of perfect righteousness. It demands of him righteousness; when he yields that righteousness of which he is capable, content for the moment, it goes on to demand more: the common sense of the Bible is lovely.

To the man who has no faith in God, faith in God cannot look like righteousness; neither can he know that it is creative of all other righteousness toward equal and inferior lives. He cannot know that it is not merely the beginning of righteousness, but the germ of life, the active potency whence life-righteousness grows.

It is not like some single separate act of righteousness; it is the action of the whole man, turning to good from evil—turning his back on all that is opposed to righteousness, and starting on a road on which he cannot stop, in which he must go on growing more and more righteous, discovering more and more what righteousness is, and more and more what is unrighteous in himself. In the one act of believing in God—that is, of giving himself to do what He tells him—he abjures evil, both what he knows and what he does not yet know in himself.

A man may indeed have turned to obey God, and yet be capable of many an injustice to his neighbor which he has not yet discovered to be an injustice; but as he goes on obeying, he will go on discovering. Not only will he grow more and more determined to be just, but he will grow more and more sensitive to the idea of injustice—I do not mean in others, but in himself. A man who continued capable of a known injustice to his neighbor, cannot be believed to have turned to God.

At all events, a man cannot be near God, so as to be learning what is just toward God, and not be near his neighbor, so as to be learning what is unfair to him; for his will, which is the man, lays hold of righteousness, chooses to be righteous. If a man is to be blamed for not choosing righteousness, for not turning to the light, for not coming out of the darkness, then the man who does choose and turn and come out, is to be justified in his deed, and declared to be righteous. He is not yet thoroughly righteous, but is growing in and toward righteousness.

He needs creative God, and time for will and effort. Not yet quite righteous, he cannot yet act quite righteously, for only the man in whom the image of God is perfected can live perfectly. Born into the world without righteousness, he cannot see, he cannot know, he is not in touch with perfect righteousness, and it would be the deepest injustice to demand of him, with a penalty, at any given moment, more than he knows how to yield. But it is the highest love constantly to demand of him perfect righteousness as what he must attain to. With what life and possibility is in him, he must keep turning to righteousness and abjuring iniquity, ever aiming at the perfection of God.

Such an obedient faith is most justly and fairly, being all that God Himself can require of the man, called by God righteousness in the man. It would not be enough for the righteousness of God, or Jesus, or any perfected saint, because they are capable of perfect righteousness, and knowing what is perfect righteousness, choose to be perfectly righteous; but, in virtue of the life and growth in it, it is enough at a given moment for the disciple of the Perfect.

The righteousness of Abraham was not to compare with the righteousness of Paul. He did not fight with himself for righteousness, as did Paul—not because he was better than

Paul and therefore did not need to fight, but because his idea of what was required of him was not within sight of that of Paul. Yet he was righteous in the same way as Paul was righteous: he had begun to be righteous, and God called his righteousness righteousness, for faith is righteousness. His faith was an act recognizing God as his law, and that is not a partial act, but an all-embracing and all-determining action.

A single righteous deed toward one's fellow could hardly be imputed to a man as righteousness. A man who is not trying after righteousness may yet do many a righteous act: they will not be forgotten to him, neither will they be imputed to him as righteousness. Abraham's action of obedient faith was righteousness none the less that his righteousness was far behind Paul's. Abraham started at the beginning of the long, slow, disappointing preparation of the Jewish people. Paul started at its close, with the story of Jesus behind him. Both believe, obeying God, and therefore both were righteous. They were righteous because they gave themselves up to God to make them righteous; and not to call such men righteous, not to impute their faith to them for righteousness, would be unjust. But God is utterly just, and nowise resembles a legal-minded Roman emperor, or a bad pope formulating the doctrine of vicarious sacrifice.

Righteousness Describes Character

What, then, is the righteousness which is of God by faith? It is simply the thing that God wants every man to be, wrought out in him by constant obedient contact with God Himself. It is not an attribute either of God or man, but a fact of character in God and in man. It is God's righteousness wrought out in us, so that as He is righteous we too are righteous.

It does not consist in obeying this or that law; not even the keeping of every law, so that no hair's-breadth did we run counter to one of them, would be righteousness. To be righteous is to be such a heart, soul, mind, and will, as, with-

out regard to law, would recoil with horror from the lightest
possible breach of any law. It is to be so in love with what is
fair and right as to make it impossible for a man to do anything that is less than absolutely righteous. It is not the love
of righteousness in the abstract that makes anyone righteous, but such a love of fair play toward everyone with
whom we come into contact, that anything less than the fulfilling, with a clear joy, of our divine relation to him or her,
is impossible.

For the righteousness of God goes far beyond mere
deeds, and requires of us love and helping mercy as our
highest obligation and justice to our fellow men—those of
them too who have done nothing for us, those even who
have done us wrong. Our relations with others, God first
and then our neighbor in order and degree, must one day
become, as in true nature they are, the gladness of our being; and nothing then will ever appear good for us, that is
not in harmony with those blessed relations.

Every thought will not merely be just, but will be just because it is something more, because it is live and true.
What heart in the kingdom of heaven would ever dream of
constructing a metaphysical system of what we owed to God
and why we owed it? The light of our life, our sole, eternal,
and infinite joy, is simply God—God—God—nothing but
God, and all His creatures in Him. He is all and in all, and
the children of the kingdom know it. He includes all things;
not to be true to anything He has made is to be untrue to
Him. God is truth, is life; to be in God is to know Him and
need no law. Existence will be eternal Godness.

You would not like that way of it? There is, there can be,
no other; but before you can judge of it, you must know at
least a little of God as He is, not as you imagine Him. I say *as
you imagine Him*, because it cannot be that any creature
should know Him as He is and not desire Him. In proportion as we know Him we must desire Him, until at length we
live in and for Him with all our conscious heart. That is why

the Jews did not like the Lord: He cared so simply for His Father's will, and not for anything they called His will.

The righteousness which is of God by faith in the source, the prime of that righteousness, is then just the same kind of thing as God's righteousness, differing only as the created differs from the creating. The righteousness of him who does the will of his Father in heaven, is the right-eousness of Jesus Christ, is God's own righteousness. The righteousness which is of God by faith in God, is God's righteousness. The man who has this righteousness, thinks about things as God thinks about them, loves the things that God loves, cares for nothing that God does not care about.

Even while this righteousness is being born in him, the man will say to himself, "Why should I be troubled about this thing or that? Does God care about it? No. Then why should I care? I must not care. I will not care!" If he does not know whether God cares about it or not, he will say, "If God cares I should have my desire, He will give it me; if He does not care I should have it, neither will I care. In the mean-time I will do my work."

The man with God's righteousness does not love a thing merely because it is right, but loves the very rightness in it. He not only loves a thought, but he loves the man in his thinking that thought; he loves the thought alive in the man. He does not take his joy from himself. He feels joy in himself, but it comes to him from others, not from himself —from God first, and from somebody, anybody, everybody next.

He would rather, in the fulness of his content, pass out of being, rather himself cease to exist, than that another should. He could do without knowing himself, but he could not know himself and spare one of the brothers or sisters God had given him. The man who really knows God, is, and always will be, content with what God, who is the very self of his self, shall choose for him; he is entirely God's, and not at all his own. His consciousness of himself is the reflex from those about him, not the result of his own turning in of his regard upon himself.

It is not the contemplation of what God has made him, it is the being what God has made him, and the contemplation of what God Himself is, and what He has made his fellows, that gives him his joy. He wants nothing, and feels that he has all things, for he is in the bosom of his Father, and the thoughts of his Father come to him. He knows that if he needs anything, it is his before he asks it; for his Father has willed him, in the might and truth of His fatherhood, to be one with Himself.

This then, or something like this, for words are poor to tell the best things, is the righteousness which is of God by faith—so far from being a thing built on the rubbish heap of legal fiction called imputed righteousness, that only the child with the child-heart, so far ahead of and so different from the wise and prudent, can understand it. The wise and prudent interprets God by himself, and does not understand Him; the child interprets God by himself, and does understand Him. The wise and prudent must make a system and arrange things to his mind before he can say, *I believe*. The child sees, believes, obeys—and knows he must be perfect as his Father in heaven is perfect.

If any angel, seeming to come from heaven, told him that God had let him off, that He did not require so much of him as that, but would be content with less; that He could not indeed allow him to be wicked, but would pass by a great deal, modifying His demands because it was so hard for him to be quite good, and He loved him so dearly, the child of God would at once recognize, woven with the angel's starry brilliancy, the flicker of the flames of hell, and would say to the shining one, "Get thee behind me, Satan."

"But How Can God Bring This About in Me?"

Let Him do it, and perhaps you will know; if you never know, yet there it will be. Help Him to do it, or He cannot do it. He originates the possibility of your being His son, His daughter; He makes you able to will it, but you must will it. If He is not doing it in you—that is, if you have as yet prevented Him from beginning, why should I tell you, even if I knew the process, how He would do what you will not let Him do?

Why should you know? What claim have you to know? But indeed how should you be able to know? For it must deal with deeper and higher things than you *can* know anything of till the work is at least begun. Perhaps if you approved of the plans of the Glad Creator, you would allow Him to make of you something divine! To teach your intellect what has to be learned by your whole being, what cannot be understood without the whole being, what it would do you no good to understand save you understood it in your whole being—if this be the province of any man, it is not mine.

Let the dead bury their dead, and the dead teach their dead; for me, I will try to wake them. To those who are awake, I cry, "For the sake of your Father and the Firstborn among many brethren to whom we belong, for the sake of those He has given us to love the most dearly, let patience have her perfect work. Statue under the chisel of the Sculptor, stand steady to the blows of His mallet. Clay on the wheel, let the fingers of the Divine Potter model you at their will. Obey the Father's lightest word; hear the Brother who knows you, and died for you; beat down your sin, and trample it to death.

EIGHTEEN

LIFE

I came that they may have life, and have it abundantly (John 10:10).

In a word, He came to supply all our lack—from the root outward; for what is it we need but more life? What does the infant need but more life? What does the bosom of his mother give him but life in abundance? What does the old man need, whose limbs are weak and whose pulse is low, but more of the life which seems ebbing from him? Weary with feebleness, he calls upon death, but in reality it is life he wants. It is but the encroaching death in him that desires death. He longs for rest, but death cannot rest. Death would be as much an end to rest as to weariness. Even weakness cannot rest; it takes strength as well as weariness to rest.

How different is the weariness of the strong man after labor unduly prolonged, from the weariness of the sick man who in the morning cries out, "Would God it were evening!" and in the evening, "Would God it were morning!"

Low-sunk life imagines itself weary of life, but it is death, not life, it is weary of.

"More life!" is the unconscious prayer of all creation, groaning and travailing for the redemption of its lord, the son who is not yet a son. Is not the dumb cry to be read in the faces of some of the animals, in the look of some of the flowers, and in many an aspect of what we call Nature?

All things are possible with God, but all things are not easy. It is easy for Him *to be*, for there He has to do with His own perfect will. It is not easy for Him to create—that is, after the grand fashion which alone will satisfy His glorious heart and will, the fashion in which He is now creating us. In the very nature of being—that is, God—it must be hard —and divine history shows how hard—to create that which shall be not Himself, yet like Himself.

The problem is, so far to separate from Himself that which must yet on Him be ever and always and utterly dependent, that it shall have the existence of an individual, and be able to turn and regard Him—choose Him, and say, "I will arise and go to my Father," and so develop in itself the highest *Divine* of which it is capable—the will for the good against the evil—the will to be one with the life whence it has come, and in which it still is—to be the thing the Maker thought of when He willed, ere He began to work its being.

The Difficulty and Its Glory

I imagine the difficulty of doing this thing, of effecting this creation, this separation from Himself such that will in the creature shall be possible—I imagine, I say, the difficulty of such creation so great, that for it God must begin inconceivably far back in the infinitesimal regions of beginnings— not to say before anything in the least resembling man, but eternal miles beyond the last farthest-pushed discovery in *protoplasm*—to set in motion that division from Himself which in its grand result should be individuality, conscious-

ness, choice, and conscious choice—choice at last pure, being the choice of the right, the true, the divinely harmonious.

Hence the final end of the separation is not individuality;
that is but a means to it; the final end is oneness—an impossibility without it. For there can be no unity, no delight
of love, no harmony, no good in being, where there is but
one. Two at least are needed for oneness; and the greater
the number of individuals, the greater, the lovelier, the
richer, the diviner is the possible unity.

God is life, and the will-source of life. In the outflowing
of that life, I know Him; and when I am told that He is love,
I see that if He were not love He would not, could not
create. I know nothing deeper in Him than love, nor believe there is in Him anything deeper than love—nay, that
there can be anything deeper than love. The being of God is
love, therefore creation. I imagine that from all eternity He
has been creating. As He saw it was not good for man to be
alone, so has He never been alone Himself—from all eternity the Father has had the Son.

The never-begun existence of that Son I imagine an easy
outgoing of the Father's nature; while to make other
beings—beings like us, I imagine the labor of a God, an
eternal labor. Speaking after our poor human fashions of
thought—the only fashions possible to us—I imagine that
God has never been contented to be alone even with the Son
of His love, the prime and perfect idea of humanity, but
that He has from the first willed and labored to give existence to other creatures who should be blessed with His
blessedness—creatures whom He is now and always has
been developing into likeness with that Son—a likeness for
long to be distant and small, but a likeness to be forever
growing: perhaps never one of them yet, though unspeakably blessed, has had even an approximate idea of the blessedness in store for him.

Let no soul think that to say God undertook a hard labor

in willing that many sons and daughters should be sharers of the divine nature, is to abate His glory! The greater the difficulty, the greater is the glory of Him who does the thing He has undertaken—without shadow of compromise, with no half-success, but with a triumph of absolute satisfaction to innumerable radiant souls!

He knew what it would cost!—not energy of will alone, or merely that utterance and separation from Himself which is but the first of creation, though that may well itself be pain—but sore suffering such as we cannot imagine, and could only be God's, in the bringing out, call it birth or development, of the God-life in the individual soul—a suffering still renewed, a labor thwarted ever by that soul itself, compelling Him to take, still at the cost of suffering, the not absolutely best, only the best possible means left Him by the resistance of His creature.

Man finds it hard to get what he wants, because he does not want the best; God finds it hard to give, because He would give the best, and man will not take it. What Jesus did, was what the Father is always doing; the suffering He endured was that of the Father from the foundation of the world, reaching its climax in the person of His Son. God provides the sacrifice; the sacrifice is Himself. He is always, and has ever been, sacrificing Himself to and for His creatures. It lies in the very essence of His creation of them.

The worst heresy, next to that of dividing religion and righteousness, is to divide the Father from the Son—in thought or feeling or action or intent; to represent the Son as doing that which the Father does not Himself do. Jesus did nothing but what the Father did and does. If Jesus suffered for men, it was because His Father suffers for men; only He came close to men through His body and their senses, that He might bring their spirits close to His Father and their Father, so giving them life, and losing what could be lost of His own.

He is God our Savior: it is because God is our Savior that

Jesus is our Savior. The God and Father of Jesus Christ could never possibly be satisfied with less than giving Himself to His own! The unbeliever may easily imagine a better God than the common theology of the country offers him; but not the lovingest heart that ever beat can even reflect the length and breadth and depth and height of that love of God which shows itself in His Son—one, and of one mind, with Himself.

The whole history is a divine agony to give divine life to creatures. The outcome of that agony, the victory of that creative and again creative energy, will be radiant life, whereof joy unspeakable is the flower. Every child will look in the eyes of the Father and the eyes of the Father will receive the child with an infinite embrace.

The Joy of True Life

The life the Lord came to give us is a life exceeding that of the highest undivine man, by far more than the life of that man exceeds the life of the animal the least human. More and more of it is for each who will receive it, and to eternity. The Father has given to the Son to have life in Himself; that life is our light. We know life only as light; it is the life in us that makes us see. All the growth of the Christian is the more and more life he is receiving. At first his religion may hardly be distinguishable from the mere prudent desire to save his soul; but at last he loses that very soul in the glory of love, and so saves it; self becomes but the cloud on which the white light of God divides into harmonies unspeakable.

"In the midst of life we are in death," said one; it is more true that in the midst of death we are in life. Life is the only reality; what men call death is but a shadow—a word for that which cannot be—a negation, owing the very idea of itself to that which it would deny. But for life there could be no death. If God were not, there would not even be nothing. Not even nothingness preceded life. Nothingness owes its very idea to existence.

One form of the question between matter and spirit is, which was first, and caused the other—things or thoughts; whether things without thought caused thought, or thought without things caused things. To those who cannot doubt that thought was first, causally preceding the earliest material show, it is easily plain that death can be the cure for nothing, that the cure for everything must be life—that the ills which come with existence, are from its imperfection, not of itself—that what we need is more of it. We who *are*, have nothing to do with death; our relations are alone with life.

The thing that can mourn can mourn only from lack; it cannot mourn because of being, but because of not enough being. We are vessels of life, not yet full of the wine of life; where the wine does not reach, there the clay cracks, and aches, and is distressed. Who would therefore pour out the wine that is there, instead of filling to the brim with more wine! All the being must partake of essential being; life must be assisted, upheld, comforted, every part, with life. Life is the law, the food, the necessity of life. Life is everything.

Many doubtless mistake the joy of life for life itself; and, longing after the joy, languish with a thirst at once poor and inextinguishable; but even that thirst points to the one spring. These love self, not life, and self is but the shadow of life. When it is taken for life itself, and set as the man's center, it becomes a live death in the man, a devil he worships as his god; the worm of the death eternal he clasps to his bosom as his one joy!

The soul compact of harmonies has more life, a larger being, than the soul consumed of cares; the sage is a larger life than the clown; the poet is more alive than the man whose life flows out that money may come in; the man who loves his fellow is infinitely more alive than he whose endeavor is to exalt himself above him; the man who strives to be better, than he who longs for the praise of the many; but the man to whom God is all in all, who feels his life-roots hid with Christ in God, who knows himself the inheritor of all wealth and worlds and ages, yea, of power essential and in itself, that man has begun to be alive indeed.

When most inclined to sleep, let us rouse ourselves to live. Of all things let us avoid the false refuge of a weary collapse, a hopeless yielding to things as they are. It is the life in us that is discontented; we need more of what is discontented, not more of the cause of its discontent. Discontent, I repeat, is the life in us that had not enough of itself, is not enough to itself, so calls for more. He has the victory who, in the midst of pain and weakness, cries out, not for death, not for the repose of forgetfulness, but for strength to fight; for more power, more consciousness of being, more God in him: who, when sorest wounded, says with Sir Andrew Barton in the old ballad:—

Fight on my men, says Sir Andrew Barton,
I am hurt, but I am not slain;
I'll lay me down and bleed awhile,
And then I'll rise and fight again;

—and that with no silly notion of playing the hero—what have creatures like us to do with heroism who are not yet barely honest!—but because so to fight is the truth, and the only way.

The true man trusts in a strength which is not his, and which he does not feel, does not even always desire; believes in a power that seems far from him, which is yet at the root of his fatigue itself and his need of rest—rest as far from death as is labor. To trust in the strength of God in our weakness; to say, "I am weak, so let me be; God is strong"; to seek from Him who is our life, as the natural, simple cure of all that is amiss with us, power to do, and be, and live, even when we are weary—this is the victory that overcomes the world.

To believe in God our strength in the face of all seeming denial, to believe in Him out of the heart of weakness and unbelief, in spite of numbness and weariness and lethargy; to believe in the wide-awake real, through all the stupefying, enervating, distorting dream; to will to wake, when the very being seems athirst for a godless repose—these are the broken steps up to the high fields where repose is but a form of strength, strength but a form of joy, joy but a form of love. "I am weak," says the true soul, "but not so weak that I would not be strong; not so sleepy that I would not see the sun rise; not so lame but that I would walk! Thanks be to Him who perfects strength in weakness, and gives to His beloved while they sleep!"

If we will but let our God and Father work His will with us, there can be no limit to His enlargement of our existence, to the flood of life with which He will overflow our consciousness. We have no conception of what life might be, of how vast the consciousness of which we could be made capable. Many can recall some moment in which life seemed richer and fuller than ever before. To some, such moments arrive mostly in dreams. Shall soul, awake or asleep, infold a bliss greater than its Life, the living God, can seal, perpetuate, enlarge? Can the human twilight of a dream be capable of generating or holding a fuller life than the morning of divine activity?

God's Life in Us

I have been speaking as if life and the consciousness of it were one; but the consciousness of life is not life; it is only the outcome of life. The real life is that which is of and by itself—is life because it wills itself—which *is*, in the active, not the passive sense. This can only be God. But in us there ought to be a life correspondent to the life that is God's; in us also must be the life that wills itself—a life in so far resembling the self-existent life and partaking of its image, that it has a share in its own being.

A tree lives; I hardly doubt it has some vague consciousness, known by but not to itself, only to the God who made it. I trust that life in its lowest forms is on the way to thought and blessedness, is in the process of that separation, so to speak, from God, in which consists the creation of living souls; but the life of these lower forms is not life in the high sense—in the sense in which the word is used in the Bible. True life knows and rules itself; the eternal life is life come awake. The life of the most exalted of the animals is not such whatever it may become, and however I may refuse to believe their fate as being fixed as we see them.

But as little as any man or woman would be inclined to call the existence of the dog, looking strange lack out of his wistful eyes, an existence to be satisfied with, as little could I, looking on the human pleasure, the human refinement, the common human endeavor around me, consent to regard them as worthy the name of life. What in them is true dwells amidst an unchallenged corruption, demanding repentance and labor and prayer for its destruction. The condition of most men and women seems to me a life in death, an abode in unwhited sepulchres.

That they do not feel it so, is nothing. The sow wallowing in the mire may rightly assert it her way of being clean, but theirs is not the life of the God-born. The day must come when they will hide their faces with such shame as the good man yet feels at the memory of the time when he lived like them.

There is nothing for man worthy to be called life, but the life eternal—God's life, that is, after his degree shared by the man made to be eternal also. For he is in the image of God, intended to partake of the life of the Most High, to be alive as He is alive. Of this life the outcome and the light is righteousness, love, grace, truth; but the life itself is a thing that will not be defined, even as God will not be defined. It is a power, the formless cause of form. It has no limits whereby to be defined. It shows itself to the soul that is hungering and thirsting after righteousness, but that soul cannot show it to another, save in the shining of its own light.

The ignorant soul understands by this life eternal only an endless elongation of consciousness. What God means by it is a being like His own, a being beyond the attack of decay or death, a being so essential that it has no relation whatever to nothingness; a something which is, and can never go to that which is not, for with that it never had to do, but came out of the heart of Life, the heart of God, the fountain of being; an existence partaking of the divine nature, and having nothing in common, any more than the Eternal Himself, with what can pass or cease: God owed His being to no one, and His child has no lord but His Father.

This life, this eternal life, consists for man in absolute oneness with God and all divine modes of being, oneness with every phase of right and harmony. It consists in a love as deep as it is universal, as conscious as it is unspeakable; a love that can no more be reasoned about than life itself—a love whose presence is its all-sufficing proof and justification, whose absence is an annihilating defect. He who has it not cannot believe in it. How should death believe in life, though all the birds of God are singing jubilant over the empty tomb! The delight of such a being, the splendor of a consciousness rushing from the wide open doors of the fountain of existence, the ecstasy of the spiritual sense into which the surge of life essential, immortal, increate, flows in silent fullness from the heart of hearts—what may it, what must it not be, in the great day of God and the individual soul!

What Have We to Do?
What then is our practical relation to the life original? What have we to do towards the attaining to the resurrection from the dead? If we did not make, could not have made ourselves, how can we, now we are made, do anything at the unknown roots of our being? What relation of conscious

unity can be betwixt the self-existent God, and beings who live at the will of another, beings who could not refuse to be—cannot even cease to be, but must, at the will of that other, go on living, weary of what is not life, able to assert their relation to life only by refusing to be content with what is not life?

The self-existent God is that Other by whose will we live; so the links of the unity must already exist, and can but require to be brought together. For the link in our being wherewith to close the circle of immortal oneness with the Father, we must of course search the deepest of man's nature: there only, in all assurance, can it be found. And there we do find it. For the *will* is the deepest, the strongest, the divinest thing in man; so I presume, is it in God, for such we find it in Jesus Christ.

Here, and here only, in the relation of the two wills, God's and his own, can a man come into vital contact—on the eternal idea, in no one-sided unity of completest dependence, but in willed harmony of dual oneness—with the All-in-all. When a man can and does entirely say, "Not my will, but thine be done"—when he so wills the will of God as to do it, then is he one with God—one, as a true son with a true father.

When a man wills that his being be conformed to the being of his origin, *and sets himself to live the will of that causing life*, humbly eager after the privileges of his origin—thus receiving God—he becomes in the act, a partaker of the divine nature, a true son of the living God, and an heir of all He possesses. By the obedience of a son, he receives into himself the very life of the Father.

Obedience is the joining of the links of the eternal round. Obedience is but the other side of the creative will. Will is God's will, obedience is man's will; the two make one. The Root-Life, knowing well the thousand troubles it would bring upon Him, has created, and goes on creating other lives, that, though incapable of self being, they may, by willed obedience, share in the bliss of His essential self-ordained being. If we do the will of God, eternal life is ours —no mere continuity of existence, for that in itself is worthless as hell, but a being that is one with the essential Life, and so within His reach to fill with the abundant and endless outgoing of His love.

Our souls shall be vessels ever growing, and ever as they grow, filled with the more and more life proceeding from the Father and the Son, from God the ordaining, and God the obedient. What the delight of the being, what the abundance of the life He came that we might have, we can never know until we have it. But even now to the holy fancy it may sometimes seem too glorious to support—as if we must die of very life—of more being than we could bear—to awake to a yet higher life, and be filled with a wine which our souls were heretofore too weak to hold.

To be for one moment aware of such pure simple love towards but one of my fellows as I trust I shall one day have towards each, must of itself bring a sense of life such as the utmost effort of my imagination can but feebly shadow now—a mighty glory of consciousness! There would be, even in that one love, in the simple purity of a single affection such as we were created to generate, and intended to cherish, towards all, an expansion of life inexpressible, unutterable. For we are made for love, not for self.

Our neighbor is our refuge; *self* is our demon-foe. Every man is the image of God to every man, and in proportion as we love him, we shall know the sacred fact. The precious thing to human soul is, and one day shall be known to be, every human soul. And if it be so between man and man, how will it not be betwixt the man and his Maker, between the child and his eternal Father, between the created and the creating Life? Must not the glory of existence be endlessly redoubled in the infinite love of the creature (for all love is infinite) to the infinite God, the great One Life, than whom is no other—only shadows, lovely shadows of Him!

Reader to whom my words seem those of inflation and foolish excitement, it can be nothing to you to be told that I seem to myself to speak only the words of truth and soberness; but what if the cause why they seem other to your mind be—not merely that you are not whole, but that your being nowise thirsts after harmony, that you are not of the truth, and you have not yet begun to live?

How should the reveller, issuing worn and wasted from the haunts where the violent seize joy by force to find her perish in their arms—how should such reveller, I say, break forth and sing with the sons of the morning, when the ocean of light bursts from the fountain of the east? As little can you, with your mind full of petty cares, or still more petty ambitions, understand the groaning and travailing of the creation. It may indeed be that you are honestly desirous of saving your own wretched soul, but as yet you can know but little of your need of Him who is the First and the Last and the Living One.

NINETEEN

THE
HEART
WITH
THE
TREASURE

*D*o not lay up for yourselves
*treasures on earth, where moth and rust consume and where thieves
break in and steal, but lay up for yourselves treasures in heaven,
where neither moth nor rust consumes and where thieves do not
break in and steal. For where your treasure is, there will your heart
be also (Matt. 6:19-21).*

To understand the words of our Lord is the business of
life. For it is the main road to the understanding of The
Word Himself. And to receive Him is to receive the Father,
and so to have Life in ourselves. And Life, the higher, the
deeper, the simpler, the original, is the business of life.

The Word is that by which we live, namely, Jesus Himself; and His words represent, in part, in shadow, in suggestion, Himself. Any utterance worthy of being called *a truth,*
is human food: how much more *The Word,* presenting no
abstract laws of our being, but the vital relation of soul and
body, heart and will, strength and rejoicing, beauty and

light, to Him who first gave birth to them all! The Son came forth to *be*, before our eyes and in our hearts, that which He had made us for, that we might behold *the truth* in Him, and cry out for the living God, who, in the highest sense of all is The Truth, not as understood, but as understanding, living, and being, doing and creating the truth. "I am the truth," said our Lord; and by those who are in some measure like Him in being the truth, the Word can be understood. Let us try to understand Him.

What, I ask now, is the power of His word: "For where your treasure is, there will your heart be also"? The meaning of the reason thus added is not obvious upon its surface. It has to be sought for because of its depth at once and its simplicity. But it is so complete, so imaginatively comprehensive, so immediately operative on the conscience through its poetic suggestiveness, that when it is once understood, there is nothing more to be said, but everything to be done.

Does not *the heart* mean more than the heart? Does it not mean a deeper heart, the heart of your own self, not of your body? a heart which is the inmost chamber wherein springs the divine fountain of your being? a heart which God regards, though you may never have known its existence, not even when its writhings under the gnawing of the moth and the slow fire of the rust have communicated a dull pain to that outer heart which sends the blood to its appointed course through your body?

If God sees that heart corroded with the rust of cares, riddled into caverns and films by the worms of ambition and greed, then your heart is as God sees it, for God sees things as they are. And one day you will be compelled to see, nay, to *feel* your heart as God sees it; and to know that the cankered thing which you have within you, a prey to the vilest of diseases, is indeed the center of your being, your very heart.

Nor does the lesson apply to those only who worship

Mammon, who give their lives, their best energies to the accumulation of wealth: it applies to those equally who in any way worship the transitory; who seek the praise of men more than the praise of God; who would make a show in the world by wealth, by taste, by intellect, by power, by art, by genius of any kind, and so would gather golden opinions to be treasured in a storehouse of earth.

Nor to such only, but surely to those as well whose pleasures are of a more evidently transitory nature still, such as the pleasures of the senses in every direction—whether lawfully or unlawfully indulged, if the joy of being is centered in them—do these words bear terrible warning. For the hurt lies not in this—that these pleasures are false like the deceptions of magic, for such they are not. Pleasures they are. Nor is the hurt yet in this—that they pass away, and leave a fierce disappointment behind. That is only so much the better. But the hurt lies in this—that the immortal, the infinite, created in the image of the everlasting God, is housed with the fading and the corrupting, and clings to them as its good—clings to them till it is infected and interpenetrated with their proper diseases, which assume in it a form more terrible in proportion to the superiority of its kind, that which is mere decay in the one becoming moral vileness in the other. Therein lies the hurt.

TWENTY

THE
VOICE
OF
JOB

Oh that thou wouldest hide me in Sheol, that thou wouldest conceal me until thy wrath be past, that thou wouldest appoint me a set time, and remember me! If a man die, shall he live again? All the days of my service I would wait, till my release should come. Thou wouldest call, and I would answer thee; thou wouldest long for the work of they hands (Job 14:13-15).

The book of Job seems to me the most daring of poems: from a position of the most vantageless realism, it assaults the very citadel of the ideal! Its hero is a man seated among the ashes, covered with loathsome boils from head to foot, scraping himself with a potsherd. Sore in body, sore in mind, sore in heart, sore in spirit, he is the instance-type of humanity in the depths of its misery—all the waves and billows of a world of adverse circumstance rolling free over its head.

I would not be supposed to use the word *humanity* either

in the abstract, or of the mass concrete; I mean the humanity of the individual endlessly repeated: Job, I say, is *the human being*—a center to the sickening assaults of pain, the
ghastly invasions of fear. These, one time or another, I presume, threaten to overwhelm every man, reveal him to
himself as enslaved to the external, and stir him up to find
some way out into the infinite, where alone he can rejoice in
the liberty that belongs to his nature.

Seated in the heart of a leaden despair, Job cries aloud to
the Might unseen, scarce known, which yet he regards as
the God of his life.

He cannot, will not believe *Him* a tyrant; but, while he
pleads against His dealing with himself, [he] loves Him, and
looks to Him as the source of life, the power and gladness
of being. He dares not think God unjust, but not therefore
can he allow that he has done anything to merit the treatment he is receiving at His hands. Hence is he of necessity
in profoundest perplexity, for how can the two things be
reconciled?

The thought has not yet come to him that that which it
would be unfair to lay upon him as punishment, may yet be
laid upon him as favor—by a love supreme which would
give him blessing beyond all possible prayer—blessing he
would not dare to ask if he saw the means necessary to its
giving, but blessing for which, once known and understood,
he would be willing to endure yet again all that he had
undergone. Therefore is he so sorely divided in himself.
While he must not think of God as having mistaken him, the
discrepancy that looks like mistake forces itself upon him
through every channel of thought and feeling. He had nowise relaxed his endeavor after a godly life, yet is the hand
of the God he had acknowledged in all his ways uplifted
against him, as rarely against any transgressor!

He does not deny that there is evil in him; for—"Dost
thou open thine eyes upon such an one," he pleads, "and
bring him into judgment with *thee*?" but he does deny that

there is any guile in him. And who, because he knows and laments the guile in himself, will dare deny that there was once a Nathanael in the world?.

Job's Child-like Attitude

Had Job been Calvinist or Lutheran, the book of Job would have been very different. His perplexity would then have been—how God being just, could require of a man more than he could do, and punish him as if his sin were that of a perfect being who chose to do the evil of which he knew all the enormity. For me, I will call no one Master but Christ —and from Him I learn that His quarrel with us is that we will not do what we know, will not come to Him that we may have life. How endlessly more powerful with men would be expostulation grounded, not on what they have done, but on what they will not do!

Job's child-like judgment of God had never been vitiated and perverted, to the dishonoring of the great Father, by any taint of such low theories as, alas! we must call the popular. Explanations of God's ways by such as do not understand *Him*, they are acceptable to such as do not care to know Him, such as are content to stand afar off and stare at the cloud whence issue the thunders and the voices; but a burden threatening to sink them to Tophet, a burden grievous to be borne, to such as would arise and go to the Father. Job refused the explanation of his friends because he knew it false; to have accepted such as would by many in the present day be given him, would have been to be devoured at once of the monster. He simply holds on to God—keeps putting his question again and again, ever haunting the one source of true answer and reconciliation. No answer will do for him but the answer that God only can give; for who but God can justify God's ways to His creature?

From a soul whose very consciousness is contradiction, we must not look for logic; misery is rarely logical; it is itself a discord; yet is it nothing less than natural that, *feeling* as if

God wronged him, Job should yet be ever yearning after a sight of God, straining into His presence, longing to stand face to face with Him. He would confront the One. He is convinced, or at least cherishes as his one hope the idea, that, if he could but get God to listen to him, if he might but lay his case clear before Him, God would not fail to see how the thing was, and would explain the matter to him—would certainly give him peace. The man in the ashes would know that the foundations of the world yet stand sure; that God has not closed His eyes, or—horror of all horrors—ceased to be just! Therefore would he order his words before Him, and hear what God had to say. Surely the Just would set the mind of His justice-loving creature at rest!

His friends [were] good men, religious men, but of the pharisaic type—that is, men who would pay their court to God, instead of coming into His presence as children; men with traditional theories which have served their poor turn, satisfied their feeble intellectual demands, they think others therefore must accept or perish; men anxious to appease God rather than trust in Him; men who would rather receive salvation from God, than God their salvation. These his friends would persuade Job to the confession that he was a hypocrite, insisting that such things could not have come upon him but because of wickedness, and as they knew of none open, it must be for some secret vileness. They grow angry with him when he refuses to be persuaded against his knowledge of himself. They insist on his hypocrisy, he on his righteousness.

But let us look a little closer at Job's way of thinking and speaking about God, and his manner of addressing Him—so different from the pharisaic in all ages, in none more than in our own.

Waxing indignant at the idea that his nature required such treatment—"Am I a sea or a sea monster," he cries out, "that thou settest a guard over me?" "... Thou knowest that I am not guilty." To his friends he cries: "Will you speak falsely for God? and speak deceitfully for Him?" Do you not know that I am the man I say?

Such words are pleasing in the ear of the Father of spirits. He is not a God to accept the flattery which declares Him above obligation to His creatures: a God to demand of them a righteousness different from His own; a God to deal ungenerously with His poverty-stricken children; a God to make severest demands upon His little ones! Job is confident of receiving justice.

There is a strange but most natural conflict of feeling in him. His faith is in truth profound, yet is he always complaining. It is but the form his faith takes in his trouble. Even while he declares the hardness and unfitness of the usage he is receiving, he yet seems assured that, to get things set right, all he needs is admission to the presence of God—an interview with the Most High. To be heard must be to have justice.

He uses language which, used by any living man, would horrify the religious of the present day, in proportion to the lack of truth in them, just as it horrified his three friends, the honest pharisees of the time, whose religion was "doctrine" and rebuke. God speaks not a word of rebuke to Job for the freedom of his speech—He has always been seeking such as Job to worship Him.

It is those who know only and respect the outsides of religion, such as never speak or think of God but as *the Almighty* or *Providence*, who will say of the man who would go close up to God, and speak to Him out of the deepest in the nature He has made, "he is irreverent." They pay court to God, not love Him; they treat Him as one far away, not as one whose bosom is the only home.

Job's Rights

The grandeur of the poem is that Job pleads his cause with God against all the remonstrance of religious authority, recognizing no one but God, and justified therein. And the grandest of all is this, that he implies, if he does not actually say, that God *owes* something to His creature. This is the beginning of the greatest discovery of all—that God owes *Himself* to the creature He has made in His image, for so He has made him incapable of living without Him. This, His creatures' highest claim upon Him, is His divinest gift to them. For the fulfilling of this their claim He has sent His Son, that He may Himself, the Father of Him and of us, follow into our hearts.

Perhaps the worst thing in a theology constructed out of man's dull *possible*, and not out of the being and deeds and words of Jesus Christ, is the impression it conveys throughout that God acknowledges no such obligation. Are not we the clay, and He the potter? How can the clay claim from the potter? We are the clay, it is true, but *His* clay, but spiritual clay, live clay, with needs and desires—and *rights*; we are clay, but clay worth the Son of God's dying for, that it might learn to consent to be shaped unto honor.

We can have no merits—a *merit* is a thing impossible. But God has given us rights. Out of Him we have nothing; but, created by Him, come forth from Him, we have even rights towards Him—ah, never, never *against* Him! His whole desire and labor is to make us capable of claiming, and induce us to claim of Him the things whose rights He bestowed in creating us. No claim had we to be created: that involves an absurdity; but, being made, we have claims on Him who made us: our needs are our claims. A man who will not provide for the hunger of his child, is condemned by the whole world.

It is terrible to represent God as unrelated to us in the way of appeal to His righteousness. How should He be righteous without owing us anything? How would there be any right for the Judge of all the earth to do if He owed nothing? Verily He owes us nothing that He does not pay like a God; but it is of the devil to imagine imperfection and disgrace in obligation. So far is God from thinking so that in

every act of His being He lays Himself under obligation to
His creatures. Oh, the grandeur of His goodness, and righteousness, and fearless unselfishness! When doubt and
dread invade, and the voice of love in the soul is dumb, what
can please the Father of men better than to hear His child
cry to Him from whom he came, "Here I am, O God! You
have made me: give me that which you have made me needing."

God is the origin of both need and supply, the Father of
our necessities, the abundant Giver of the good things.
Right gloriously He meets the claims of His child! The story
of Jesus is the heart of His answer, not primarily to the
prayers, but to the divine necessities of the children He has
sent out into His universe.

Away with the thought that God could have been a perfect, an adorable Creator, doing anything less than He has
done for His children! that any other kind of being than
Jesus Christ could have been worthy of all-glorifying
worship! that His nature demanded less of Him than He
has done! that His nature is not absolute love, absolute self-
devotion—could have been without these highest splen-
dors!

I protest, therefore, against all such teaching as, originating in and fostered by the faithlessness of the human heart,
gives the impression that the exceeding goodness of God towards man is not the natural and necessary outcome of His
being. The root of every heresy popular in the church
draws its nourishment merely and only from the soil of unbelief. The idea that God would be God all the same, as glorious as He needed to be, had He not taken upon Himself
the divine toil of bringing home His wandered children,
had He done nothing to seek and save the lost, is false as
hell. Lying for God could go no farther.

As if the idea of God admitted of His being less than He
is, less than perfect, less than all-in-all, less than Jesus
Christ! less than Love absolute, less than entire unselfish-

ness! As if the God revealed to us in the New Testament were not His own perfect necessity of loving-kindness, but one who has made Himself better than, by His own nature, by His own love, by the laws which He willed the laws of His existence, He needed to be! They would have it that, being unbound, He deserves the greater homage! So it might be, if He were not our Father. But to think of the living God not as our Father, but as one who has condescended greatly, being nowise, in His own willed grandeur of righteous nature, bound to do as He has done, is killing to all but a slavish devotion. It is to think of Him as nothing like the God we see in Jesus Christ.

It will be answered that we have fallen, and God is thereby freed from any obligation, if any ever were. It is but another lie. No amount of wrong-doing in a child can ever free a parent from the divine necessity of doing all he can to deliver his child; the bond between them cannot be broken. It is the vulgar, slavish, worldly idea of freedom, that it consists in being bound to nothing. Not such is God's idea of liberty! To speak as a man—the more of vital obligation He lays on Himself, the more children He creates, with the more claims upon Him, the freer is He as creator and giver of life, which is the essence of His Godhead: to make scope for His essence is to be free.

If we dare, like Job, to plead with Him in any of the heart-eating troubles that arise from the impossibility of loving such misrepresentation of Him as is held out to us to love by our would-be teachers; if we think and speak out before Him that which seems to us to be right, will He not be heartily pleased with His children's love of righteousness—with the truth that will not part Him and His righteousness? Verily He will not plead against us with His great power, but will put strength in us, and where we are wrong will instruct us. For the heart that wants to do and think aright, the heart that seeks to worship Him as no tyrant, but as the perfectly, absolutely righteous God, is the delight of the Father.

A Prayer In Truth

To the heart that will not call that righteousness which it feels to be unjust, but lifts pleading eyes to His countenance —to that heart He will lay open the riches of His being— riches which it has not entered that heart to conceive. "O Lord, they tell me I have so offended against your law that, as I am, you can not look upon me, but threaten me with eternal banishment from your presence. But if you look not upon me, how can I ever be other than I am? Lord, remember I was born in sin: how then can I see sin as you see it? Remember, Lord, that I have never known myself clean: how can I cleanse myself? You must take me as I am and cleanse me.

"Is it not impossible that I should behold the final goodness of good, the final evilness of evil? How then can I deserve eternal torment? Had I known good and evil, seeing them as you see them, then chosen the evil, and turned away from the good, I know not what I should not deserve. But you know it has ever been something good in the evil that has enticed my selfish heart—nor mine only, but that of all my kind. You require of us to forgive: surely you forgive freely! Bound you may be to destroy evil, but are you bound to keep the sinner alive that you may punish him, even if it make him no better?

"Sin cannot be deep as life, for you are the life; and sorrow and pain go deeper than sin, for they reach to the divine in us: you can suffer, though you will not sin. To see men suffer might make us shun evil, but it never could make us hate it. We might see thereby that you hate sin, but we never could see that you love the sinner. Chastise us, we pray you, in loving kindness, and we shall not faint. We have done much that is evil, yea, evil is very deep in us, but we are not all evil, for we love righteousness; and are not you yourself, in your Son, the sacrifice for our sins, the atonement of our breach?

"You have made us subject to vanity, but have yourself

taken your godlike share of the consequences. Could we ever have come to know good as you know it, save by passing through the sea of sin and the fire of cleansing? They tell me I must say *for Christ's sake*, or you will not pardon. It takes the very heart out of my poor love to hear that you will not pardon me except because Christ has loved me; but I give you thanks that nowhere in the record of my gospel, does one of your servants say any such word.

"In spite of all our fears and grovelling, our weakness, and our wrongs, you will be to us what you are—such a perfect Father as no most loving child-heart of earth could invent the thought of! You will take our sins on yourself, giving us your life to live. You bear our griefs and carry our sorrows; and surely you will one day enable us to pay every debt we owe to each other! You will be to us a right generous, abundant Father! Then truly our heart shall be jubilant, because you are what you are—infinitely beyond all we could imagine. You will humble and raise us up. You have given yourself to us that, having you, we may be eternally alive with your life. We run within the circle of what men call your wrath, and find ourselves clasped in the zone of your love!"

But be it well understood that when I say *rights*, I do not mean *merits*—of any sort. We can deserve from Him nothing at all, in the sense of any right proceeding from ourselves. All our rights are such as the bounty of love inconceivable has glorified our being with—bestowed for the one only purpose of giving the satisfaction, the fulfilment of the same—rights so deep, so high, so delicate, that their satisfaction cannot be given until we desire it—yea long for it with our deepest desire.

But, lest it should be possible that any unchildlike soul might, in arrogance and ignorance, think to stand upon his rights against God, and demand of Him this or that after the will of the flesh, I will lay before such a possible one some of the things to which he has a right, yea, perhaps has

first of all a right to, from the God of his life, because of the
beginning He has given him—because of the divine germ
that is in him. He has a claim on God, then, a divine claim,
for any pain, want, disappointment, or misery, that would
help to show him to himself as the fool he is. He has a claim
to be punished to the last scorpion of the whip, to be spared
not one pang that may urge him towards repentance. He
has a claim to be sent out into the outer darkness, whether
what we call hell, or something speechlessly worse, if nothing less will do. He has a claim to be compelled to repent; to
be hedged in on every side; to have one after another of the
strong, sharptoothed sheepdogs of the great Shepherd sent
after him, to thwart him in any desire, foil him in any plan,
frustrate him of any hope, until he come to see at length
that nothing will ease his pain, nothing make life a thing
worth having, but the presence of the living God within
him; that nothing is good but the will of God; nothing noble
enough for the desire of the heart of man but oneness with
the eternal. For this God must make him yield his very being, that He may enter in and dwell with him.

That the man would enforce none of these claims, is
nothing; for it is not a man who owes them to him, but the
eternal God, who by His own will of right towards the creature He has made, is bound to discharge them. God has to
answer to Himself for His idea. He has to do with the need
of the nature He made, not with the self-born choice of the
self-ruined man. His candle yet burns dim in the man's
soul; that candle must shine as the sun. For what is the all-
pervading dissatisfaction of his wretched being but an unrecognized hunger after the righteousness of his Father?

The soul God made is thus hungering, though the selfish, usurping self, which is its consciousness, is hungering
only after low and selfish things, ever trying, but in vain, to
fill its mean, narrow content, with husks too poor for its
poverty-stricken desires. For even that most degraded
chamber of the soul which is the temple of the deified Self,

cannot be filled with less than God; even the usurping Self must be miserable until it cease to look at itself in the mirror of Satan, and open the door of its innermost closet to the God who means to dwell there, and make peace.

He that has looked on the face of God in Jesus Christ, whose heart overflows, if ever so little, with answering love, sees God standing with full hands to give the abundance for which He created His children, and those children hanging back, refusing to take, doubting the God-heart which knows itself absolute in truth and love.

God's Answer to Job

It is not at first easy to see wherein God gives Job any answer; I cannot find that He offers him the least explanation of why He has so afflicted him. He justifies him in his words. He says Job has spoken what is right concerning Him, and his friends have not; and He calls up before him, one after another, the works of His hands. The answer, like some of our Lord's answers if not all of them, seems addressed to Job himself, not to his intellect; to the revealing, God-like imagination in the man, and to no logical faculty whatever.

It consists in a setting forth of the power of God, as seen in His handiwork, and wondered at by the men of the time; and all that is said concerning them has to do with their show of themselves to the eyes of man. In what belongs to the deeper meanings of nature and her mediation between us and God, the appearances of nature are the truths of nature, far deeper than any scientific discoveries in and concerning them.

The show of things is that for which God cares *most*, for their show is the face of far deeper things than they; we see in them, in a distant way, as in a glass darkly, the face of the unseen. It is through their show, not through their analysis, that we enter into their deepest truths. What they say to the childlike soul is the truest thing to be gathered of them. To know a primrose is a higher thing than to know all the bot-

any of it—just as to know Christ is an infinitely higher thing
than to know all theology, all that is said about His person,
or babbled about His work.

The argument implied, not expressed, in the poem,
seems to be this—that Job, seeing God so far before him in
power, and His works so far beyond his understanding that
they filled him with wonder and admiration, beholding
these things, ought to have reasoned that He who could
work so grandly beyond his understanding, must certainly
use wisdom in things that touched him nearer, though they
came no nearer his understanding. Did he understand his
own being, history, and destiny? Should not God's ways in
these also be beyond his understanding? Might he not trust
Him to do him justice? In such high affairs as the rights of
a live soul, might not matters be involved too high for Job?
The Maker of Job was so much greater than Job, that His
ways with him might well be beyond his comprehension!
God's thoughts were higher than his thoughts, as the heavens were higher than the earth!

The true child, the righteous man, will trust absolutely,
against all appearances, the God who has created in him the
love of righteousness.

God does not, I say, tell Job why He had afflicted him: He
rouses his child-heart to trust. All the rest of Job's life on
earth, I imagine, his slowly vanishing perplexities would
yield him ever fresh meditations concerning God and His
ways, new opportunities of trusting Him, light upon many
things concerning which he had not as yet begun to doubt,
added means of growing in all directions into the knowledge of God.

But all that Job was required to receive at the moment
was the argument from God's loving wisdom in His power,
to His loving wisdom in everything else. For power is a real
and a good thing, giving an immediate impression that it
proceeds from goodness. Nor, however long it may last
after goodness is gone, was it ever born of anything but

goodness. In a very deep sense, power and goodness are one. In the deepest fact they are one.

Seeing God, Job forgets all he wanted to say, all he thought he would say if he could but see Him. The close of the poem is grandly abrupt. He had meant to order his cause before Him; he had longed to see Him that he might speak and defend himself, imagining God as well as his righteous friends wrongfully accusing him. But his speech is gone from him; he has not a word to say. To justify himself in the presence of Him who is Righteousness, seems to him what it is—foolishness and worthless labor. If God does not see him righteous, he is not righteous, and may hold his peace. If he is righteous, God knows it better than he does himself. Nay, if God does not care to justify him, Job has lost his interest in justifying himself. All the evils and imperfections of his nature rise up before him in the presence of the One [who is] pure, the One who is right, and has no selfishness in Him. "Behold," he cries, "I am of small account; what shall I answer thee? I lay my hand on my mouth."

Job had his desire: he saw the face of God—and abhorred himself in dust and ashes. He sought justification; he found self-abhorrence. Was this punishment? The farthest from it possible. It was the best thing—to begin with—that the face of God could do for him. Blessed gift is self-contempt, when the giver of it is the visible glory of the Living One.

Oh the divine generosity that will grant us to be abashed and self-condemned before the Holy!—to come so nigh Him as to see ourselves dark spots against His brightness! Verily we must be of His kind, else no show of Him could make us feel small and ugly and unclean! Oh the love of the Father, that He should give us to compare ourselves with Him, and be buried in humility and shame! To be rebuked before Him is to be His. Good man as Job was, he had never yet been right near to God; now God has come near to him, has become very real to him; he knows now in very deed that God is He with whom he has to do. He had laid all these troubles upon him that He might through them draw nigh to him, and enable him to know. Him.

Final Prosperity

For the prosperity that follows upon Job's submission is the embodiment of a great truth. Although a man must do right if it send him to Hades, yea, even were it to send him forever to hell itself, yet, while the Lord lives, we need not fear: *all* good things must grow out of and hang upon the one central good, the one law of life—the Will, the One Good. To submit absolutely to Him is the only reason. Circumstance as well as all being must then bud and blossom as the rose. And it will! What matter whether in this world or the next, if one day I know my life as a perfect bliss, having neither limitation nor hindrance nor pain nor sorrow more than it can dominate in peace and perfect assurance?

I care not whether the book of Job be a history or a poem. I think it is both—I do not care how much relatively of each. It was probably, in the childlike days of the world, a well-known story in the east, which some man, whom God had made wise to understand His will and His ways, took up, and told after the fashion of a poet. What its age may be, who can certainly tell!—it must have been before Moses.

The poem is for many reasons difficult, and in the original to me inaccessible; but, through all the evident inadequacy of our translation, who can fail to hear two souls, that of the poet and that of Job, crying aloud with an agonized hope that, let the evil shows around them be what they may, truth and righteousness are yet the heart of things. The faith, even the hope of Job seems at times on the point of giving way; he struggles like a drowning man when the billow goes over him, but with the rising of his head his courage revives. Christians we call ourselves!—what would not our faith be, were it as much greater than Job's as the word from the mouth of Jesus is mightier than that he heard out of the whirlwind! Here is a book of faith indeed, ere the law was given by Moses. Grace and Truth have visited us—but where is our faith?

Friends, our cross may be heavy, and the *via dolorosa* rough; but we have claims on God, yea the right to cry to Him for help. He has spent, and is spending Himself to give us our birthright, which is righteousness. Though we shall not be condemned for our sins, we cannot be saved but by leaving them. Though we shall not be condemned for the sins that are past, we shall be condemned if we love the darkness rather than the light, and refuse to come to Him that we may have life. God is offering us the one thing we cannot live without—His own self: we must make room for Him; we must cleanse our hearts that He may come in; we must do as the Master tells us, who knew all about the Father and the way to Him.

TWENTY-ONE

THE
FINAL
UNMASKING

*F*or nothing is covered that will
not be revealed, or hidden that will not be known (Matt. 10:26).

God is not a God that hides, but a God that reveals. His
whole work in relation to the creatures He has made—and
where else can lie His work?—is revelation—the giving
them truth, the showing of Himself to them, that they may
know Him, and come nearer and nearer to Him, and so
He have His children more and more of companions to
Him. That we are in the dark about anything is never because He hides it, but because we are not yet such that He is
able to reveal that thing to us.

That God could not do the thing at once which He takes
time to do, we may surely say without irreverence. His will
cannot finally be thwarted; where it is thwarted for a time,
the very thwarting subserves the working out of a higher
part of His will. He gave man the power to thwart His will,
that, by means of that same power, he might come at last to

do His will in a higher kind and way than would otherwise have been possible to him. God sacrifices His will to man that man may become such as Himself, and give all to the truth; He makes man able to do wrong, that he may choose and love righteousness.

The fact that all things are slowly coming into the light of the knowledge of men—so far as this may be possible to the created—is used in three different ways by the Lord, as reported by His evangelists. In one case, with which we will not now occupy ourselves—Mark 4:22; in Luke 8:16, He uses it to enforce the duty of those who have received light to let it shine: they must do their part to bring all things out. In Luke 12:2, He brought it to bear on hypocrisy, showing it uselessness; and, in the case recorded in Matthew 10:26, He uses the fact to enforce fearlessness as to the misinterpretation of our words and actions.

In whatever mode the Lord may intend that it shall be wrought out, He gives us to understand, as an unalterable principle in the government of the universe, that all such things as the unrighteous desire to conceal, and such things as it is a pain to the righteous to have concealed, shall come out into the light.

Hypocrisy

"Beware of hypocrisy," the Lord says. "Nothing is covered that will not be revealed, or hidden that will not be known." What is hypocrisy? The desire to look better than you are; the hiding of things you do, because you would not be supposed to do them, because you would be ashamed to have them known where you are known. The doing of them is foul; the hiding of them, in order to appear better than you are, is fouler still.

The man who does not live in his own consciousness as in the open heavens is a hypocrite—and for most of us the question is, are we growing less or more of such hypocrites? Are we ashamed of not having been open and clear?

Are we fighting the evil thing which is our temptation to hypocrisy?

The Lord has not a thought in Him to be ashamed of before God and His universe, and He will not be content until He has us in the same liberty. For our encouragement to fight on, He tells us that those that hunger and thirst after righteousness shall be filled, that they shall become as righteous as the Spirit of the Father and the Son in them can make them desire.

Misunderstanding

The Lord says also, "If they have called the master of the house Beelzebub, how much more will they malign those of his household! So have no fear of them; for nothing is covered that will not be revealed; or hidden that will not be known." To a man who loves righteousness and his fellow men, it must always be painful to be misunderstood. Misunderstanding is specially inevitable where he acts upon principles beyond the recognition of those around him, who, being but half-hearted Christians, count themselves the lawgivers of righteousness, and charge him with the very things it is the aim of his life to destroy. The Lord Himself was accused of being a drunkard and a keeper of bad company—and perhaps would in the present day be so regarded by not a few calling themselves by His name, and teaching temperance and virtue. He lived upon a higher spiritual plantform than they understand, acted from a height of the virtues they would inculcate, loftier than their eyes can scale. His Himalayas are not visible from their sand-heaps. The Lord bore with their evil tongues, and was neither dismayed nor troubled; but from this experience of His own, comforts those who, being His messengers, must fare as He. "Do not hesitate," says the Lord, "to speak the truth that is in you. Never mind what they call you. Proclaim from the housetop. Fear nobody."

He spoke the words to the men to whom He looked first

to spread the news of the kingdom of heaven; but they apply to all who obey Him. Few who have endeavored to do their duty, have not been annoyed, disappointed, enraged perhaps, by the antagonism, misunderstanding, and false representation to which they have been subjected, and which issues mainly from those and the friends of those who have benefited by their efforts to be neighbors to all.

If in the endeavor to lead a truer life, a man merely lives otherwise than his neighbors, strange motives will be invented to account for it. To the honest soul it is a comfort to believe that the truth will one day be known, that it will cease to be supposed that he was and did as dull heads and hearts reported of him. Still more satisfactory will be the unveiling where a man is misunderstood by those who ought to know him better—who, not even understanding the point at issue, take it for granted he is about to do the wrong thing, while he is crying for courage to heed neither himself nor his friends, but only the Lord.

How many hear and accept the words, "Be not conformed to this world," without once perceiving that what they call Society and bow to as supreme, is the World and nothing else, or that those who mind what people think, and what people will say, are conformed to—that is, take the shape of—the world. The true man feels he has nothing to do with society as judge or lawgiver. He is under the law of Jesus Christ, and it sets him free from the law of the world.

Let a man do right, nor trouble himself about worthless opinion. The less he heeds tongues, the less difficult will he find it to love men. Let him comfort himself with the thought that the truth must out. He will not have to pass through eternity with the brand of ignorant or malicious judgment upon him. He shall find his peers and be judged of them.

But, you who look for the justification of the light, are you verily prepared for yourself to encounter such expo-

sure as the general unveiling of things must bring? Are you
willing for the truth whatever it be? I nowise mean to ask,
Have you a conscience so void of offence, have you a heart
so pure and clean, that you fear no fullest exposure of what
is in you to the gaze of men and angels?—as to God, He
knows it all now! What I mean to ask is, Do you so love the
truth and the right, that you welcome, or at least submit
willingly to the idea of an exposure of what in you is yet
unknown to yourself—an exposure that may redound to
the glory of the truth by making you ashamed and humble?

Will you welcome any discovery, even if it work for the
excuse of others, that will make you more true, by revealing
what in you was false? Are you willing to be made glad that
you were wrong when you thought others were wrong? If
you can with such submission face the revelation of things
hid, then you are of the truth, and need not be afraid; for,
whatever comes, it will and can only make you more true
and humble and pure.

The Uncovering

Does the Lord mean that everything a man has ever done
or thought must be laid bare to the universe?

So far, I think, as is necessary to the understanding of
the man by those who have known, or are concerned to
know him. For the time to come, and for those who are yet
to know him, the man will henceforth, if he is a true man, be
transparent to all that are capable of reading him. A man
may not then, any more than now, be intelligible to those
beneath him, but all things will be working toward revelation, nothing toward concealment or misunderstanding.

Who in the kingdom will desire concealment, or be willing to misunderstand? Concealment is darkness; misunderstanding is a fog. A man will hold the door open for anyone
to walk into his house, for it is a temple of the living God—
with some things worth looking at, and nothing to hide.
The glory of the true world is, that there is nothing in it that

needs to be covered, while ever and ever there will be things uncovered. Every man's light will shine for the good and glory of his neighbor.

"Will all my weaknesses, all my evil habits, all my pettinesses, all the wrong thoughts which I cannot help—will all be set out before the universe?"

Yes, if they so prevail as to constitute your character—that is, if they are you. But if you have come out of the darkness, if you are fighting it, if you are honestly trying to walk in the light, you may hope in God your Father that what He has cured, what He is curing, what He has forgiven, will be heard of no more, not now being a constituent part of you. Or if indeed some of your evil things must yet be seen, the truth of them will be seen—that they are things you are at strife with, not things you are cherishing and brooding over.

God will be fair to you—so fair!—fair with the fairness of a father loving his own—who will have you clean, who will neither spare you any needful shame, nor leave you exposed to any that is not needful. The thing we have risen above, is dead and forgotten, or if remembered, there is God to comfort us. "If any one does sin, we have an advocate with the Father." We may trust God with our past as heartily as with our future. It will not hurt us so long as we do not try to hide things, so long as we are ready to bow our heads in hearty shame where it is fit we should be ashamed.

For to be ashamed is a holy and blessed thing. Shame is a thing to shame only those who want to appear, not those who want to be. Shame is to shame those who want to pass their examination, not those who would get into the heart of things. In the name of God let us henceforth have nothing to be ashamed of, and be ready to meet any shame on its way to meet us. For to be humbly ashamed is to be plunged in the cleansing bath of the truth.

Evildoers Will See Themselves

As to the revelation of the ways of God, I need not speak; He has been always, from the first, revealing them to His prophet, to His child, and will go on doing so for ever. But let me say a word about another kind of revelation—that of their own evil to the evil.

The only terrible, or at least the supremely terrible revelation is that of a man to himself. What a horror will it not be to a vile man—more than all to a man whose pleasure has been enhanced by the suffering of others—a man that knew himself such as men of ordinary morals would turn from with disgust, but who has hitherto had no insight into what he is—what a horror will it not be to him when his eyes are opened to see himself as the pure see him, as God sees him! Imagine such a man waking all at once, not only to see the eyes of the universe fixed upon him with loathing astonishment, but to see himself at the same moment as those eyes see him! What a waking!—into the full blaze of fact and consciousness, of truth and violation!

> *"To know my deed, 'twere best not know myself!"*

Or think what it must be for a man counting himself religious, orthodox, exemplary, to perceive suddenly that there was no religion in him, only love of self; no love of the right, only a great love of being in the right! What a discovery—that he was simply a hypocrite—one who loved to *appear,* and *was* not!

The rich seem to be those among whom will occur hereafter the sharpest reverses, if I understand aright the parable of the rich man and Lazarus. Who has not known the insolence of their meanness toward the poor, all the time counting themselves of the very elect! What riches and fancied religion, with the self-sufficiency they generate between them, can make man or women capable of, is appalling. Mammon, the most contemptible of deities, is the most

worshipped, both outside and in the house of God: to many
of the religious rich in that day, the great damning revelation will be their behavior to the poor to whom they thought
themselves very kind.

Of all who will one day stand in dismay and sickness of
heart, with the consciousness that their very existence is a
shame, those will fare the worst who have been consciously
false to their fellows; who, pretending friendship, have
used their neighbor to their own ends; and especially those
who, pretending friendship, have divided friends. To such
Dante has given the lowest hell. If there be one thing God
hates, it must be treachery.

Do not imagine Judas the only man of whom the Lord
would say, "Better were it for that man if he had never been
born!" Did the Lord speak out of personal indignation, or
did He utter a spiritual fact, a live principle? Did the word
spring from His knowledge of some fearful punishment
awaiting Judas, or from His sense of the horror it was to be
such a man? Beyond all things pitiful is it that a man should
carry about with him the consciousness of being such a person—should know himself and not another that false one!

"O God," we think, "how terrible if it were I!" Just so terrible is it that it should be Judas! And have I not done things
with the same germ in them, a germ which, brought to its
evil perfection, would have shown itself the canker-worm,
treachery? Except I love my neighbor as myself, I may one
day betray him! Let us therefore be compassionate and
humble, and hope for every man.

A man may sink by such slow degrees that, long after he
is a devil, he may go on being a good churchman or a good
dissenter, and thinking himself a good Christian. Continu-
ously repeated sin against the poorest consciousness of evil
must have a dread rousing. What if the only thing to wake
the treacherous, money-loving thief, Judas, to a knowledge
of himself, was to let the thing go on to the end, and his kiss
betray the Master? Judas did not hate the Master when he

kissed Him, but not being a true man, his very love betrayed him.

The good man, conscious of his own evil, and desiring no refuge but the purifying light, will chiefly rejoice that the exposure of evil makes for the victory of the truth, the kingdom of God and His Christ. He sees in the unmasking of the hypocrite, in the unveiling of the covered, in the exposure of the hidden, God's interference, for him and all the race, between them and the lie.

The only triumph the truth can ever have is its recognition by the heart of the liar. Its victory is in the man who, not content with saying, "I was blind and now I see," cries out, "Lord God, just and true, let me perish, but you endure! Let me live because you live, because you save me from the death in myself, the untruth I have nourished in me, and even called righteousness! Hallowed be your name, for you only are true; you only love; you only are holy, for you only are humble! You only are unselfish, you only have never sought your own, but the things of your children! Yea, O Father, be true, and every man a liar!"

There is no satisfaction of revenge possible to the injured. The severest punishment that can be inflicted upon the wrongdoer is simply to let him know what he is; for his nature is of God, and the deepest in him is the divine. Neither can any other punishment than the sinner's being made to see the enormity of his injury, give satisfaction to the injured. While the wrongdoer will admit no wrong, while he mocks at the idea of amends, or while, admitting the wrong, he rejoices in having done it, no suffering could satisfy revenge, far less justice. Both would continually know themselves foiled.

Therefore, while a satisfied justice is an unavoidable eternal event, a satisfied revenge is an eternal impossibility. For the moment that the sole adequate punishment, a vision of himself, begins to take true effect upon the sinner, that moment the sinner has begun to grow a righteous man, and the brother human whom he has offended has no choice, has nothing left him but to take the offender to his bosom—the more tenderly that his brother is a repentant brother, that he was dead and is alive again, that he was lost and is found.

Behold the meeting of the divine extremes—the extreme of punishment, the embrace of heaven! They run together; "the wheel is come full circle." For, I venture to think, there can be no such agony for created soul, as to see itself vile— vile by its own action and choice. Also I venture to think there can be no delight for created soul—short, that is, of being one with the Father—so deep as that of seeing the heaven of forgiveness open, and disclose the shining stair that leads to its own natural home, where the eternal Father has been all the time awaiting this return of His child.

So, friends, however indignant we may be, however intensely and however justly we may feel our wrongs, there is no revenge possible for us in the universe of the Father. I may say to myself with heartiest vengeance, "I should just like to let that man see what a wretch he is—what all honest men at this moment think of him!" But, the moment come, the man will loathe himself tenfold more than any other man could, and that moment my heart will bury his sin.

Let us try to antedate our forgiveness. Dares any man suppose that Jesus would have him hate the traitor through whom He came to the cross? Has He been pleased through all these ages with the manner in which those calling themselves by His name have treated, and are still treating His nation? We have not yet sounded the depths of forgiveness that are and will be required of such as would be His disciples!

Our friends will know us then: for their joy, will it be, or their sorrow? Will their hearts sink within them when they look on the real likeness of us? Or will they rejoice to find that we were not so much to be blamed as they thought, in this thing or that which gave them trouble?

Let us remember, however, that not evil only will be unveiled; that many a masking misconception will uncover a face radiant with the loveliness of the truth. And whatever disappointments may fall, there is consolation for every true heart in the one sufficing joy—that it stands on the border of the kingdom, about to enter into ever fuller, ever-growing possession of the inheritance of the saints in light.

TWENTY-TWO

THE
NEW
NAME

*To him who conquers I will give
some of the hidden manna, and I will give him a white stone, with a
new name written on the stone which no one knows except him who
receives it (Rev. 2:17).*

Truth is truth, whether from the lips of Jesus or Balaam.
But, in its deepest sense, *the truth* is a condition of heart,
soul, mind, and strength towards God and towards our fellow—not an utterance, not even a *right* form of words; and
therefore such truth coming forth in words is, in a sense,
the person that speaks. And many of the utterances of truth
in the *Revelation*, commonly called of St. John, are not
merely lofty in form, but carry with them the conviction
that the writer was no mere "trumpet of a prophecy," but
spoke that he did know, and testified that he had seen.

In this passage about the gift of the white stone, I think
we find the essence of religion.

What the notion in the mind of the writer with regard to

the white stone was, is, I think, of comparatively little moment. What his mystic meaning may be, must be taken differently by different minds. I think he sees in its whiteness purity, and in its substance indestructibility. But I care chiefly to regard the stone as the vehicle of the name—as the form whereby the name is represented as passing from God to the man, and what is involved in this communication is what I wish to show. If my reader will not acknowledge my representation as St. John's meaning, I yet hope so to set it forth that he shall see the representation to be true in itself, and then I shall willingly leave the interpretation to its fate.

What a Name Expresses

I say, in brief, the giving of the white stone with the new name is the communication of what God thinks about the man to the man. It is the divine judgment, the solemn holy doom of the righteous man, the "Come, thou blessed," spoken to the individual.

In order to see this, we must first understand what is the idea of a name—that is, what is the perfect notion of a name. For, seeing the mystical energy of a holy mind here speaks of God as giving something, we must understand that the essential thing, and not any of its accidents or imitations, is intended.

A name of the ordinary kind in this world, has nothing essential in it. It is but a label by which one man and a scrap of his external history may be known from another man and a scrap of his history. The only names which have significance are those which the popular judgment or prejudice or humor bestows, either for ridicule or honor, upon a few out of the many. Each of these is founded upon some external characteristic of the man, upon some predominant peculiarity of temper, some excellence or the reverse of character, or something which he does or has done well or ill enough, or at least, singularly enough, to render him, in the eyes of the people, worthy of such distinction from other men. As far as they go, these are real names, for, in some poor measure, they express individuality.

The true name is one which expresses the character, the nature, the being, the *meaning* of the person who bears it. It is the man's own symbol—his soul's picture, in a word—the sign which belongs to him and to no one else. Who can give a man this, his own name? God alone. For no one but God sees what the man is, or even, seeing what he is, could express in a name-word the sum and harmony of what He sees.

To whom is this name given? To him that overcomes. When is it given? When he has overcome. Does God then not know what a man is going to become? As surely as He sees the oak which He put there lying in the heart of the acorn. Why then does He wait till the man has become by overcoming ere He settles what his name shall be? He does not wait; He knows his name from the first. But as—although repentance comes because God pardons—yet the man becomes aware of the pardon only in the repentance; so it is only when the man has become his name that God gives him the stone with the name upon it, for then first can he understand what his name signifies.

It is the blossom, the perfection, the completion, that determines the name; and God foresees that from the first, because He made it so; but the tree of the soul, before its blossom comes, cannot understand what blossom it is to bear, and could not know what the word meant, which, in representing its own unarrived completeness, named itself. Such a name cannot be given until the man *is* the name.

God's name for a man must then be the expression in a mystical word—a word of that language which all who have overcome understand—of His own idea of the man, that being whom He had in His thought when He began to make the child, and whom He kept in His thought through the long process of creation that went to realize the idea. To tell the name is to seal the success—to say, "In you also I am well pleased."

But we are still in the region of symbol. The mystic symbol has for its center of significance the fact of the personal individual relation of every man to his God. That every man has affairs, and those his first affairs, with God stands to the reason of every man who associates any meaning or feeling with the words, Maker, Father, God. Were we but children of a day, with the understanding that someone had given us that one holiday, there would be something to be thought, to be felt, to be done, because we knew it. For then our nature would be according to our fate, and we could worship and die. But it would be only the praise of the dead, not the praise of the living, for death would be the deepest, the lasting, the overcoming. We should have come out of nothingness, not out of God. He could only be our Maker, not our Father, our Origin. But now we know that God cannot be the God of the dead—must be the God of the living; inasmuch as to know that our death would freeze the heart of worship, and we could not say "Our God," or feel him worthy of such worth-ship as we could render.

To him who offers unto this God of the living his own self of sacrifice, to him that overcomes, who knows that he is *one* of God's children, *this* one of the Father's making, He gives the white stone. To him who climbs on the stair of all his God-born efforts and God-given victories up to the height of his being—that of looking face to face upon his ideal self in the bosom of the Father—God's *him* realized in him through the Father's love in the Elder Brother's devotion—to him God gives the new name written.

The Sanctity of Individuality
But I leave this, because that which follows embraces and intensifies this individuality of relation in a fuller development of the truth. For the name is one "which no one knows except him who receives it." Not only then has each man

his individual relation to God, but each man has his peculiar relation to God. He is to God a peculiar being, made after his own fashion, and that of no one else; for when he is perfected he shall receive the new name which no one else can understand.

Hence he can worship God as no man else can worship Him—can understand God as no man else can understand Him. This or that man may understand God more, may understand God better than he, but no other man can understand God *as* he understands Him. God give me grace to be humble before you, my brother, that I drag not my simulacrum of you before the judgment seat of the unjust judge, but look up to yourself for what revelation of God you and no one else can give.

As the fir-tree lifts up itself with a far different need from the need of the palm-tree, so does each man stand before God, and lift up a different humanity to the common Father. And for each God has a different response. With every man He has a secret—the secret of the new name. In every man there is a loneliness, an inner chamber of peculiar life into which God only can enter. I say not it is *the innermost chamber*—but a chamber into which no brother, nay, no sister can come.

From this it follows that there is a chamber also—(O God, humble and accept my speech)—a chamber in God Himself, into which none can enter but the one, the individual, the peculiar man—out of which chamber that man has to bring revelation and strength for his brethren. This is that for which he was made—to reveal the secret things of the Father.

"But is there not the worst of all dangers involved in such teaching—the danger of spiritual pride?" If there be, are we to refuse the spirit for fear of the pride? Or is there any other deliverance from pride except the spirit? Pride springs from supposed success in the high aim: with attainment itself comes humility.

But here there is no room for ambition. Ambition is the desire to be above one's neighbor; and here there is no possibility of comparison with one's neighbor. No one knows what the white stone contains except the man who receives it. Here is room for endless aspiration towards the unseen ideal; none for ambition. Ambition would only be higher than others; aspiration would be high. Relative worth is not only unknown—to the children of the kingdom it is unknowable. Each esteems the other better than himself.

"God has cared to make me for Himself," says the victor with the white stone, "and has called me that which I like best; for my own name must be what I would have it, seeing it is myself. What matter whether I be called a grass of the field, or an eagle of the air? a stone to build into His temple, or a Boanerges to wield His thunder? I am His; His idea, His making; perfect in my kind, yea, perfect in His sight; full of Him, revealing Him, alone with Him. Let Him call me what He will. The name shall be precious as my life. I seek no more."

Gone then will be all anxiety as to what his neighbor may think about him. It is enough that God thinks about him. To be something to God—is not that praise enough? To be a thing that God cares for and would have complete for Himself, because it is worth caring for—is not that life enough?

Neither will he thus be isolated from his fellows. For that we say of one, we say of all. It is as *one* that the man has claims amongst his fellows. Each will feel the sacredness and awe of his neighbor's dark and silent speech with his God. Each will regard the other as a prophet, and look to him for what the Lord has spoken. Each, as a high priest returning from his Holy of Holies, will bring from his communion some glad tidings, some gospel of truth, which, when spoken, his neighbors shall receive and understand. Each will behold in the other a marvel of revelation, a present son or daughter of the Most High, come forth from Him to reveal Him afresh. In God each will draw nigh to each.

Yes, there will be danger—danger as everywhere; but He gives more grace. And if the man who has striven up the heights should yet fall from them into the deeps, is there not that fire of God, the consuming fire, which burns and destroys not?

To no one who has not already had some speech with God, or who has not at least felt some aspiration towards the fount of his being, can all this appear other than foolishness. So be it.

But, Lord, help them and us, and make our being grow into your likeness. If through ages of strife and ages of growth, yet let us at last see your face, and receive the white stone from your hand.

TWENTY-THREE

THE
GOD
OF
THE
LIVING

Now He is not God of the dead, but of the living: for all live to Him (Luke 20:33).

It is a recurring cause of perplexity in our Lord's teaching, that He is too simple for us; that while we are questioning with ourselves about the design of Solomon's carving upon some gold-plated door of the temple, He is speaking about the foundations of Mount Zion, yea, of the earth itself, upon which it stands. If the reader of the Gospel supposes that our Lord was here using a verbal argument with the Sadducees, namely, "I *am* the God of Abraham, Isaac, and Jacob; therefore they *are*," he will be astonished that no Sadducee was found with courage enough to reply: "All that God meant was to introduce Himself to Moses as the same God who had aided and protected his fathers while they were alive, saying, I am He that was the God of your fathers. They found me faithful. You, therefore, listen to me, and you too shall find me faithful *unto* the death."

But no such reply suggested itself even to the Sadducees of that day, for their eastern nature could see argument beyond logic. Shall God call Himself the God of the dead, of those who were alive once, but whom He either could not or would not keep alive? "Trust in me, for I took care of your fathers once upon a time, though they are gone now. Worship and obey me, for I will be good to you for threescore years and ten, or thereabouts; and after that, when you are not, and the world goes on all the same without you, I will call myself your God still." God changes not. Once God He is always God. If He has once said to a man, "I am your God," and that man has died the death of the Sadducee's creed, then we have a right to say that God is the God of the dead.

But "All Live to Him"

"And wherefore should He not be so far the God of the dead, if during the time allotted to them here, He was the faithful God of the living?" What God-like relation can the ever-living, life-giving, changeless God hold to creatures who partake not of His life, who have death at the very core of their being, are not worth their Maker's keeping alive? To let His creatures die would be to change, to abjure His God-hood, to cease to be that which He had made Himself. If they are not worth keeping alive, then His creating is a poor thing, and He is not so great, nor so divine as even the poor thoughts of those His dying creatures have been able to imagine Him.

But our Lord says, "All live to Him." With Him death is not. This that we call death is but a form in the eyes of men. It looks something final, an awful cessation, an utter change; it seems not probable that there is anything beyond. But if God could see us before we were, and make us after His ideal, that we shall have passed from the eyes of our friends can be no argument that He beholds us no longer. "All live to Him."

Let the change be ever so great, ever so imposing; let unseen life be ever so vague to our conception, it is not against reason to hope that God could see Abraham, after his Isaac had ceased to see him; saw Isaac after Jacob ceased to see him; saw Jacob after some of the Sadducees had begun to doubt whether there ever had been a Jacob at all. He remembers them; that is, He carries them in His mind: he of whom God thinks, lives. He takes to Himself the name of *Their God.* The Living One cannot name Himself after the dead, when the very Godhead lies in the giving of life. Therefore they must be alive. If He speaks of them, remembers His own loving thoughts of them, would He not have kept them alive if He could; and if He could not, how could He create them? Can it be an easier thing to call into life than to keep alive?

The Nature of Resurrection

"But if they live to God, they are aware of God. And if they are aware of God, they are conscious of their own being. Why then the necessity of a resurrection?"

For their relation to others of God's children in mutual revelation; and for fresh revelation of God to all. But let us inquire what is meant by the resurrection of the body. "With what kind of body do they come?"

Let us first ask what is the use of this body of ours. It is the means of revelation to us, the *camera* in which God's eternal shows are set forth. It is by the body that we come into contact with Nature, with our fellow-men, with all their revelations of God to us. It is through the body that we receive all the lessons of passion, of suffering, of love, of beauty, of science. It is through the body that we are both trained outwards from ourselves, and driven inwards into our deepest selves to find God.

We cannot yet have learned all that we are meant to learn through the body. How much of the teaching even of this world can the most diligent and most favored man have

exhausted before he is called to leave it! Is all that remains
to be lost? Who that has loved this earth can but believe that
the spiritual body of which St. Paul speaks will be a yet
higher channel of such revelation? The meek who have
found that their Lord spake true, and have indeed inherited the earth, who have seen that all matter is radiant of
spiritual meaning, who would not cast a sigh after the loss
of mere animal pleasure, would, I think, be the least willing
to be without a body, to be unclothed without being again
clothed upon.

All this revelation, however, would render only *a* body
necessary, not this body. The fullness of the word *Resurrection* would be ill met if this were all. We need not only a body
to convey revelation to us, but a body to reveal us to others.
The thoughts, feelings, imaginations which arise in us,
must have their garments of revelation whereby shall be
made manifest the unseen world within us to our brothers
and sisters around us; else is each left in human loneliness.

Now, if this be one of the uses my body served on earth
before, the new body must be like the old. Not that only, it
must be the same body, glorified as we are glorified, with
all that was distinctive of each from his fellows more visible
than ever before. The accidental, the non-essential, the un-
revealing, the incomplete will have vanished. That which
made the body what it was in the eyes of those who loved us
will be tenfold there. Will not this be the resurrection of the
body? of the same body though not of the same dead matter?

Every eye shall see the beloved, every heart will cry, "My
own again!—more mine because more himself than ever I
beheld him!" For do we not say on earth, "He is not himself
today," or "She looks her own self"; "She is more like herself than I have seen her for long"? And is not this when the
heart is glad and the face radiant? For we carry a better likeness of our friends in our hearts than their countenances,
save at precious seasons, manifest to us.

Who will dare to call anything less than this a resurrection? Oh, how the letter kills! There are people who can believe that the dirt of their bodies will rise the same as it went down to the friendly grave, who yet doubt if they will know their friends when they rise again. And they call *that* believing in the resurrection!

What! shall a man love his neighbor as himself, and must he be content not to know him in heaven? Better be content to lose our consciousness, and know ourselves no longer. What! shall God be the God of the families of the earth, and shall the love that He has thus created towards father and mother, brother and sister, wife and child, go moaning and longing to all eternity; or worse, far worse, die out of our bosoms? Shall God be God, and shall this be the end?

No, our God is an unveiling, a revealing God. He will raise you from the dead, that I may behold you; that that which vanished from the earth may again stand forth, looking out of the same eyes of eternal love and truth, holding out the same mighty hand of brotherhood, the same delicate and gentle, yet strong hand of sisterhood, to me, this me that knew you and loved you in the days gone by.

The new shall then be dear as the old, and for the same reason, that it reveals the old love. And in the changes which, thank God, must take place when the mortal puts on immortality, shall we not feel that the nobler our friends are, the more they are themselves; that the more the idea of each is carried out in the perfection of beauty, the more like they are to what we thought them in our most exalted moods, to that which we saw in them in the rarest moments of profoundest communion, to that which we beheld through the veil of all their imperfections when we loved them the truest?

Lord, evermore give us this Resurrection, like your own in the body of your Transfiguration. Let us see and hear, and know, and be seen, and heard, and known, as you see, hear, and know. Give us glorified bodies through which to reveal the glorified thoughts which shall then inhabit us, when not only shall you reveal God, but each of us shall reveal you.

And for this, Lord Jesus, come—the child, the obedient God—that we may be one with you and with every man and woman whom you have made, in the Father.

TWENTY-FOUR

THE INHERITANCE

Giving thanks to the Father, who has qualified us to share in the inheritance of the saints in light (Col. 1:12)

To have a share in any earthly inheritance, is to diminish the share of the other inheritors. In the inheritance of the saints, that which each has, goes to increase the possession of the rest. In this inheritance a man may desire and endeavor to obtain his share without selfish prejudice to others; nay, to fail of our share in it, would be to deprive others of a portion of theirs. Let us look a little nearer, and see in what the inheritance of the saints consists.

It might perhaps be to commit some small logical violence on the terms of the passage to say that "the inheritance of the saints in light" *must* mean purely and only "the possession of light which is the inheritance of the saints." At the same time the phrase is literally "the inheritance of the saints *in the light*," and this perhaps makes it the more

likely that, as I take it, Paul had in his mind the light as itself
the inheritance of the saints—that he held the very substance of the inheritance to be the light.

And if we remember that God is light; also that the highest prayer of the Lord for His friends was that they might
be one in Him and His Father; and recall what the apostle
said to the Ephesians, that "in Him we live and move and
have our being," we may be prepared to agree that, although he may not mean to include all possible phases of
the inheritance of the saints in the one word *light*, as I think
he does, yet the idea is perfectly consistent with his teaching. For the one only thing to make existence a good, the
one thing to make it worth having, is just that there should
be no film of separation between our life and the Life of
which ours is an outcome; that we should not only *know* that
God is our life, but be aware, in some grand consciousness
beyond anything imagination can present to us, of the presence of the making God, in the very process of continuing
us the live things He has made us.

This is only another way of saying that the very inheritance upon which, as the twice-born sons of our Father, we
have a claim—which claim His sole desire for us is that we
should, so to say, enforce—that this inheritance is simply
the light, God Himself, the Light. If you think of ten thousand things that are good and worth having, what is it that
makes them good or worth having but the God in them?
That the loveliness of the world has its origin in the making
will of God would not content me. I say, the very loveliness
of it is the loveliness of God, for its loveliness is His own
lovely thought, and must be a revelation of that which
dwells and moves in Himself.

Nor is this all: my interest in its loveliness would vanish, I
should feel that the soul was out of it, if you could persuade
me that God had ceased to care for the daisy, and now cared
for something else instead. The faces of some flowers lead
me back to the heart of God; and, as His child, I hope I feel,

in my lowly degree, what He felt when, brooding over them, He said, "They are good"; that is, "They are what I mean."

The thing I am reasoning toward is this: that, if everything were thus seen in its derivation from God, then the inheritance of the saints, whatever the form of their possession, would be seen to be light. All things are God's, not as being in His power—that of course—but as coming from Him. The darkness itself becomes light around Him when we think that verily He hath created the darkness, for there could have been no darkness but for the light. Without God there would not have existed the idea of nothing, any more than any reality of nothing, but that He exists and called *something* into being.

Nothingness owes its very name and nature to the being and reality of God. There is no word to represent that which is not God, no word for the *where* without God in it; for it is not, could not be. So I think we may say that the inheritance of the saints is the share each has in the Light.

The Meaning of Share

But how can any share exist where all is open?

The true share, in the heavenly kingdom throughout, is not what you have to keep, but what you have to give away. The thing that is mine is the thing I have with the power to give it. The thing I have *no* power to give a share in, is nowise mine. The thing I cannot share with everyone, cannot be essentially my own.

All the light is ours. God is all ours. Even that in God which we cannot understand is ours. If there were anything in God that was not ours, then God would not be one God. I do not say we must, or can ever know all in God; not throughout eternity shall we ever comprehend God, but He is our Father, and must think of us with every part of Him—so to speak; He must know us, and that in Himself which we cannot know, with the same thought, for He is one.

We and that which we do not or cannot know, come together in His thought. And this helps us to see how, claiming all things, we have yet shares. For the infinitude of God can only begin and only go on to be revealed, through His infinitely differing creatures—all capable of wondering at, admiring, and loving each other, and so bound all in one in Him, each to the others revealing Him.

For every human being is like a facet cut in the great diamond to which I may dare liken the Father of Him who likens His kingdom to a pearl. Every man, woman, child—for the incomplete also is His, and in its very incompleteness reveals Him as a progressive worker in His creation—is a revealer of God. I have my message of my great Lord, you have yours. Your dog, your horse tells you about Him who cares for all His creatures.

He knows His horses and dogs as we cannot know them, because we are not yet pure sons of God. When through our sonship, as Paul teaches, the redemption of these lower brothers and sisters shall have come, then we shall understand each other better. But now the Lord of Life has to look on at the wilful torture of multitudes of His creatures. It must be that offenses come, but woe unto that man by whom they come! The Lord may seem not to heed, but He sees and knows.

I say, then, that every one of us is something that the other is not, and therefore knows something—it may be without knowing that he knows it—which no one else knows. It is every one's business, as one of the kingdom of light, and inheritor in it all, to give his portion to the rest, for we are one family, with God at the head and the heart of it, and Jesus Christ, our Elder Brother, teaching us of the Father, whom He only knows.

We may say, then, that whatever is the source of joy or love, whatever is pure and strong, whatever wakes aspiration, whatever lifts us out of selfishness, whatever is beautiful or admirable—in a word, whatever is of the light—must make a part, however small it may then prove to be in its proportion, of the inheritance of the saints in the light. For, as in the epistle of James, "Every good endowment and every perfect gift is from above, coming down from the Father of lights with whom there is no variation or shadow due to change."

Our Hope of Heaven

Children fear heaven because of the dismal notions the unchildlike give them of it, who, without imagination, receive unquestioning what others, as void of imagination as themselves, represent concerning it. I do not see that one should care to present an agreeable picture of it; for, suppose I could persuade a man that heaven was the perfection of all he could desire around him, what would the man or the truth gain by it? If he knows the Lord, he will not trouble himself about heaven; if he does not know Him, he will not be drawn to *Him* by it.

I would not care to persuade the feeble Christian that heaven was a place worth going to; I would rather persuade him that no spot in space, no hour in eternity is worth anything to one who remains such as he is. But would that none presumed to teach the little ones what they know nothing of themselves! What have not children suffered from strong endeavor to desire the things they could not love! Well do I remember the pain of the prospect—no, the trouble at not being pleased with the prospect—of being made a pillar in the house of God, and going no more out! Those words were not spoken to the little ones. Yet are they, literally taken, a blessed promise compared with the notion of a continuous churchgoing.

Perhaps no one teaches such a thing; but somehow the children get the dreary fancy. There are ways of involuntary teaching more potent than words. What boy, however fain to be a disciple of Christ and a child of God, would prefer a sermon to his glorious kite, that divinest of toys, with

God Himself for his playmate, in the blue wind that tossed it hither and thither in the golden void! He might be ready to part with kite and wind and sun, and go down to the grave for his brothers—but surely not that they might be admitted to an everlasting prayer-meeting.

For my own part, I rejoice to think that there will be neither church nor chapel in the high countries; yea, that there will be nothing there called religion, and no law but the perfect law of liberty. For how should there be law or religion where every throb of the heart says *God!* where every song-throat is eager with thanksgiving! where such a tumult of glad waters is forever bursting from beneath the throne of God, the tears of the gladness of the universe! Religion? Where will be the room for it, when the essence of every thought must be God? Law? What room will there be for law, when everything upon which law could lay a *shalt not* will be too loathsome to think of? What room for honesty, where love fills full the law to overflowing—where a man would rather drop sheer into the abyss, than wrong his neighbor one hair's-breadth?

Heaven will be continuous touch with God. The very sense of being will in itself be bliss. For the sense of true life, there must be actual, conscious contact with the source of the life; therefore mere life—in itself, in its very essence good, good as the life of God which is our life—must be such bliss as, I think, will need the mitigation of the loftiest joys of communion with our blessed fellows; the mitigation of art in every shape, and of all combinations of arts; the mitigation of countless services to the incomplete, and hard toil for those who do not yet know their neighbor or their Father. The bliss of pure being will, I say, need these mitigations to render the intensity of it endurable by heart and brain.

To those who care only for things, and not for the souls of them, for the truth, the reality of them, the prospect of inheriting light can have nothing attractive. For their comfort—how false a comfort!—they may rest assured there is no danger of their being required to take up their inheritance at present. Perhaps they will be left to go on sucking *things* dry, constantly missing the loveliness of them, until they come at last to loathe the lovely husks, turned to ugliness in their false imaginations. The soul of Truth they have lost, because they never loved her. What may they not have to pass through, what purifying fires, before they can even behold her!

The notions of Christians, so called, concerning the state into which they suppose their friends to have entered, and which they speak of as a place of blessedness, are yet such as to justify the bitterness of their lamentation over them, and the heathenish doubt whether they shall know them again. Verily it were a wonder if they did! After a year or two of such a fate, they might well be unrecognizable! One is almost ashamed of writing about such follies. The nirvana is grandeur contrasted with their heaven.

The early Christians might now and then plague Paul with a foolish question, the answer to which plagues us to this day; but was there ever one of them doubted he was going to find his friends again? It is a mere form of Protean unbelief. They believe, they say, that God is love; but they cannot quite believe that He does not make the love in which we are most like Him, either a mockery or a torture.

Little would any promise of heaven be to me if I might not hope to say, "I am sorry; forgive me; let what I did in anger or in coldness be nothing, in the name of God and Jesus!" Many such words will pass, many a self-humiliation have place. The man or woman who is not ready to confess, who is not ready to pour out a heartful of regrets—can such a one be an inheritor of the light? It is the joy of a true heart, of an heir of light, of a child of that God who loves an open soul—the joy of any man who hates the wrong the more because he has done it, to say, "I was wrong; I am sorry."

Oh, the sweet winds of repentance and reconciliation

and atonement, that will blow from garden to garden of
God, in the tender twilights of His kingdom! Whatever the
place be like, one thing is certain, that there will be endless,
infinite atonement, ever-growing love. Certain too it is that
whatever the divinely human heart desires, it shall not
desire in vain. The light which is God, and which is our inheritance because we are the children of God, insures these
things. For the heart which desires is made thus to desire.

God is; let the earth be glad, and the heaven, and the
heaven of heavens! Whatever a father can do to make his
children blessed, that will God do for His children. Let us,
then, live in continual expectation, looking for the good
things that God will give to men, being their Father and
their everlasting Savior. If the things I have here come from
Him, and are so plainly but a beginning, shall I not take
them as an earnest of the better to follow?

How else can I regard them? For never, in the midst of
the good things of this lovely world, have I felt quite at
home in it. Never has it shown me things lovely or grand
enough to satisfy me. It is not all I should like for a place to
live in. It may be that my unsatisfaction comes from not having eyes open enough, or keen enough, to see and understand what He has given, but it matters little whether the
cause lie in the world or in myself, both being incomplete.
God is, and all is well.

All that is needed to set the world right enough for me—
and no empyrean heaven could be right for me without it—
is, that I care for God as He cares for me; that my will and
desires keep time and harmony with His music; that I have
no thought that springs from myself apart from Him; that
my individuality have the freedom that belongs to it as born
of His individuality, and be in no slavery to my body, or my
ancestry, or my prejudices, or any impulse whatever; that I
be free by obedience to the law of my being, the live and
live-making will by which life is life, and my life is myself.

What springs from myself and not from God, is evil; it is a perversion of something of God's. Whatever is not of faith is sin; it is a stream cut off—a stream that cuts itself off from its source, and thinks to run on without it. But light is my inheritance through Him whose life is the light of men, to wake in them the life of their Father in heaven. Loved be the Lord who in Himself generated that life which is the light of men!

III
THE
CREATION
OF
GOODNESS

"It is the one terrible heresy of the church, that it has always been presenting something else than obedience as faith in Christ."

TWENTY-FIVE

THE
CAUSE OF
SPIRITUAL
STUPIDITY

D_{o} *you not yet understand?*
(Mark 8:21).

After feeding the four thousand with seven loaves and a few small fishes, on the east side of the Sea of Galilee, Jesus, having crossed the lake, was met on the other side by certain Pharisees, whose attitude towards Him was such that He went again to the boat, and recrossed the lake. On the way the disciples considered that they had in the boat but a single loaf. Probably while the Lord was occupied with the Pharisees, one of them had gone and bought it, little thinking they were about to start again so soon.

Jesus, still occupied with the antagonism of the leaders of the people, and desirous of destroying their influence on His disciples, began to warn them against them. In so doing He made use of a figure they had heard Him use before—that of leaven as representing a hidden but potent and pervading energy. The kingdom of heaven, He had told them, was like leaven hid in meal, gradually leavening the whole of it. He now tells them to beware of the leaven of the Pharisees.

The disciples, whose minds were occupied with their lack of provisions, the moment they heard the word leaven, thought of bread, concluded it must be beause of its absence that He spoke of leaven, and imagined perhaps a warning against some danger of defilement from Pharisaical cookery: "It is because we have taken no bread!" A leaven like that of the Pharisees was even then at work in their hearts; for the sign the Pharisees sought in the mockery of unbelief, they had had a few hours before, and had already, in respect of all that made it of value, forgotten.

The Lesson of the Miracle
He addresses Himself to rouse in them a sense of their lack of confidence in God, which was the cause of their blunder as to His meaning. He reminds them of the two miracles with the loaves, and the quantity of fragments left beyond the need. From one of these miracles they had just come. It was not a day behind them, yet here they were doubting already!

He makes them go over the particulars of the miracles—hardly to refresh their memories—but to make their hearts dwell on them. For they had already forgotten or had failed to see their central revelation—the eternal fact of God's love and care and compassion. They knew the number of the men each time, the number of the loaves each time, the number of the baskets of fragments they had each time taken up, but they forgot the Love that had so broken the bread that its remnants twenty times outweighed its loaves.

Having thus questioned them like children, and listened as to the answers of children, He turns the light of their thoughts upon themselves, and, with an argument to the man which overleaps all the links of its own absolute logic, demands, "How is it that you do not understand?" Then

THE CAUSE OF SPIRITUAL STUPIDITY

they did understand, and knew that He did not speak to them of the leaven of bread, but of the teaching of the Pharisees and of the Sadducees. He who trusts can understand; he whose mind is set at ease can discover a reason.

The lesson He would have had them learn from the miracle, the natural lesson, the only lesson worthy of the miracle, was, that God cared for His children, and could, did, and would provide for their necessities. This lesson they had not learned. No doubt the power of the miracle was some proof of His mission, but the love of it proved it better, for it made it worth proving: it was a throb of the Father's heart.

The ground of the Master's upbraiding is not that they did not understand Him, but that they did not trust God. After all they had seen, they yet troubled themselves about bread. Because we easily imagine ourselves in want, we imagine God ready to forsake us. The miracles of Jesus were the ordinary works of His Father, wrought small and swift that we might take them in. The lesson of them was that help is always within God's reach when His children want it. Their design [was] to show what God is—not that Jesus was God, but that His Father was God—that is, was what He was. No other kind of God could be, or be worth believing in, no other notion of God be worth having.

The mission undertaken by the Son, was not to show Himself as having all power in heaven and earth, but to reveal His Father, to show Him to men such as He is, that men may know Him, and knowing, trust Him. It were a small boon indeed that God should forgive men, and not give Himself. It would be but to give them back themselves, and less than God just as He is will not comfort men for the essential sorrow of their existence. Only God the gift can turn that sorrow into essential joy: Jesus came to give them God, who is eternal life.

Those miracles of feeding gave the same lesson to their eyes, their hands, their mouths, that His words gave to their ears when He said, "Do not be anxious about what you shall eat, or what you shall drink. . . . your heavenly Father knows that you have need of these things. But seek first His kingdom and His righteousness, and all these things shall be yours as well." So little had they learned it yet, that they remembered the loaves but forgot the Father—as men in their theology forget the very Logos.

Thus forgetting, they were troubled about provision for the day, and the moment leaven was mentioned, thought of bread. "What else could He mean?" The connection was plain! The Lord reminds them of the miracle, which had they believed after its true value, they would not have been so occupied as to miss what He meant. It had set forth to them the truth of God's heart towards them; revealed the loving care without which He would not be God.

The care of the disciples was care for the day, not for the morrow; the word *morrow* must stand for any and every point of the future. The next hour, the next moment, is as much beyond our grasp and as much in God's care, as that a hundred years away. Care for the next minute is just as foolish as care for the morrow, or for a day in the next thousand years—in neither can we do anything, in both God is doing everything. Those claims only of the morrow which have to be prepared today are of the duty of today. The moment which coincides with work to be done, is the moment to be minded; the next is nowhere till God has made it.

Their lack of bread seems to have come from no neglect, but from the immediacy of the Lord's re-embarkation. At the same time, had there been a want of foresight, that was not the kind of thing the Lord cared to reprove. It was not this and that fault He had come to set right, but the primary evil of life without God, the root of all evils, from hatred to discourtesy. Certain minor virtues also, prudence among the rest, would thus at length be almost, if not altogether, superseded.

If a man forget a thing, God will see to that: man is not

lord of his memory or his intellect. But man is lord of his will, his action; and is then verily to blame when, remembering a duty, he does not do it, but puts it off, and *so* forgets it. If a man lay himself out to do the immediate duty of the moment, wonderfully little forethought, I suspect, will be found needful. That forethought only is right which has to determine duty, and pass into action. To the foundation of yesterday's work well done, the work of the morrow will be sure to fit. Work done is of more consequence for the future than the foresight of an archangel.

Barriers to Trust

With the disciples as with the rich youth, it was *Things* that prevented the Lord from being understood. Because of possession the young man had not a suspicion of the grandeur of the call with which Jesus honored him. *Things* filled his heart, so that the very God could not enter.

The disciples were a little further on than he; they had left all and followed the Lord; but neither had they yet got rid of *Things*. The paltry solitariness of a loaf was enough to hide the Lord from them, to make them unable to understand Him. Why, having forgotten, could they not trust?

In the former case it was the possession of wealth, in the latter the not having more than a loaf, that rendered [them] incapable of receiving the word of the Lord. The evil principle was precisely the same. If it be *Things* that slay you, what matter whether things you have, or things you have not? The youth, not trusting in God, the source of his riches, cannot receive the word of His Son, offering Him better riches, more direct from the heart of the Father. The disciples, forgetting who is lord of the harvests of the earth, cannot understand His word, because of the fear of a day's hunger. He did not trust in God as having given; they did not trust in God as ready to give.

We are like them when, in *any* trouble, we do not trust Him. It is hard on God, when His children will not let Him give; when they carry themselves so that He must withhold His hand, lest He harm them. To take no care that they acknowledge whence their help comes, would be to leave them worshippers of idols, trusters in that which is not.

The care that is filling your mind at this moment, or but waiting till you lay the book aside to leap upon you—that need which is no need, is a demon sucking at the spring of your life.

"No; mine is a reasonable care—an unavoidable care, indeed!"

"Is it something you have to do this very moment?"

"No."

"Then you are allowing it to usurp the place of something that is required of you this moment!"

"There is nothing required of me at this moment."

"Ah, but there is—the greatest thing that can be required of man."

"What is it?"

"Trust in the living God. His will is your life."

"He may not will I should have what I need!"

"Then you only think you need it. Is it a good thing?"

"Yes, it is a good thing."

"Then why doubt you shall have it?"

"Because God may choose to have me go without it."

"Why should He?"

"I cannot tell."

"Must it not be in order to give you something instead?"

"I want nothing instead."

"I thought I was talking to a Christian!"

"I can consent to be called nothing else."

"Do you not, then, know that, when God denies anything a child of His values, it is to give him something He values?"

"But if I do not want it?"

"You are none the less miserable just because you do not have it. Instead of his great possessions the young man was to have the company of Jesus, and treasure in heaven.

When God refused to deliver a certain man from a sore evil, concerning which he three times besought Him, unaccustomed to be denied, He gave him instead His own graciousness, consoled him in person for his pain."

"Ah, but that was St. Paul!"

"True; what of that?"

"He was one by himself!"

"God deals with all His children after His own father-nature. No scripture is of private interpretation even for a St. Paul. It sets forth God's way with man. If you are not willing that God should have His way with you, then, in the name of God, be miserable—till your misery drive you to the arms of the Father."

"I do trust Him in spiritual matters."

"Everything is an affair of the spirit. If God has a way, then that is the only way. Every little thing in which you would have your own way, has a mission for your redemption; and He will treat you as a naughty child until you take your Father's way for yours."

There will be this difference, however, between the rich that loves his riches and the poor that hates his poverty—that, when they die, the heart of the one will be still crowded with things and their pleasures, while the heart of the other will be relieved of their lack. The one has had his good things, the other his evil things. But the rich man who held his *things* lightly, nor let them nestle in his heart, who was a channel and no cistern—starts, in the new world, side by side with the man who accepted, not hated, his poverty. Each will say, "I am free!"

For the only air of the soul, in which it can breathe and live, is the present God and the spirits of the just: that is our heaven, our home, our all-right place. Cleansed of greed, jealousy, vanity, pride, possession, all the thousand forms of the evil self, we shall be God's children on the hills and in the fields of that heaven, not one desiring to be before another, any more than to cast that other out. For ambition and hatred will then be seen to be one and the same spirit. "What you have, I have; what you desire, I will; I give to myself ten times in giving once to you."

The Bane of Troubles

But let me be practical; for you are ready to be miserable over trifles, and do not believe God good enough to care for your care: I would reason with you to help you rid of your troubles, for they hide from you the thoughts of your God.

The things readiest to be done, those which lie not at the door but on the very table of a man's mind, are not merely in general the most neglected, but even by the thoughtful man, the most often let alone, the most often postponed. The Lord of life demanding high virtue of us, can it be that He does not care for the first principles of justice? May a man become strong in righteousness without learning to speak the truth to his neighbor?

Truth is one, and he who does the truth in the small thing is of the truth. He who will do it only in a great thing, who postpones the small thing near him to the great thing farther from him, is not of the truth. Let me suggest some possible parallels between ourselves and the disciples maundering over their one loaf—with the Bread of Life at their side in the boat. We, too, dull our understandings with trifles, fill the heavenly spaces with phantoms, waste the heavenly time with hurry. To those who possess their souls in patience come the heavenly visions.

When I trouble myself over a trifle, even a trifle confessed—the loss of some little article, say—spurring my memory, and hunting the house, not from immediate need, but from dislike of loss; when a book has been borrowed of me and not returned, and I have forgotten the borrower, and fret over the missing volume, while there are thousands on my shelves from which the moments thus lost might gather treasure holding relation with neither moth, nor rust, nor thief; am I not like the disciples? Am I not a fool whenever loss troubles me more than recovery would gald-den? God would have me wise, and smile at the trifle. Is it not time I lost a few things when I care for them so unreasonably? This losing of things is of the mercy of God; it comes to teach us to let them go.

Or have I forgotten a thought that came to me, which seemed of the truth, and a revealment to my heart? I wanted to keep it, to have it, to use it by and by, and it is gone! I keep trying and trying to call it back, feeling a poor man till that thought be recovered—to be far more lost, perhaps, in a note-book, into which I shall never look again to find it.

I forget that it is live things God cares about—live truths, not things set down in a book or in a memory, or embalmed in the joy of knowledge, but things lifting up the heart, things active in an active will. True, my lost thought might have so worked; but had I faith in God, the Maker of thought and memory, I should know that, if the thought was a truth, and so alone worth anything, it must come again; for it is in God—so, like the dead, not beyond my reach: kept for me, I shall have it again.

"These are foolish illustrations—not worth writing!"

If such things are not, then the mention of them is foolish. If they are, then he is foolish who would treat them as if they were not. I choose them for their smallness, and appeal especially to all who keep house concerning the size of trouble that suffices to hide word and face of God.

With every haunting trouble then, great or small, the loss of thousands or the lack of a dime, go to God, and appeal to Him, the God of your life, to deliver you, His child, from that which is unlike Him, therefore does not belong to you, but is antagonistic to your nature. If your trouble is such that you cannot appeal to Him, the more need you should appeal to Him! Where one cannot go to God, there is something specially wrong.

TWENTY-SIX

THE TEMPTATION IN THE WILDERNESS

Matthew 4:1-11.

How could the Son of God be tempted with evil—with that which must to Him appear in its true colors of discord, its true shapes of deformity? Or how could He then be the Son of His Father who cannot be tempted with evil?

In the answer to this lies the center, the essential germ of the whole interpretation: He was not tempted with evil but with good; with inferior forms of good, that is, pressing in upon Him, while the higher forms of good held themselves aloof, biding their time, that is, God's time. I do not believe that the Son of God could be tempted with evil, but I do believe that He could be tempted with good—to yield to which temptation would have been evil in Him—ruin to the universe.

But does not all evil come from good?

Yes; but it has come *from* it. It is no longer good. A good corrupted is no longer a good. Such could not tempt our

Lord. Revenge may originate in a sense of Justice, but it is revenge not justice; an evil thing, for it would be fearfully unjust. Evil is evil whatever it may have come from. The Lord could not have felt tempted to take vengeance upon His enemies, but He might have felt tempted to destroy the wicked from the face of the earth—to destroy them from the face of the earth, I say, not to destroy them for ever. To that I do not think He could have felt tempted.

But we shall find illustration enough of what I mean in the matter itself. Let us look at the individual temptations represented in the parable, and let us follow St. Matthew's record. We shall see how the devil tempted Him *to* evil, but not *with* evil.

Stones to Bread
First, He was hungry, and the devil said, "Make bread of this stone."

The Lord had been fasting for forty days—a fast impossible except during intense mental absorption. What a temptation was here! There is no sin in wishing to eat; no sin in procuring food honestly that one may eat. But it rises even into an awful duty, when a man knows that to eat will restore the lost vision of the eternal; will, operating on the brain, and thence on the mind, render the man capable of hope as well as of faith, of gladness as well as of confidence, of praise as well as of patience. Why then should He not eat? Why should He not put forth the power that was in Him that He might eat?

Because such power was His, not to take care of Himself, but to work the work of Him that sent Him. Such power was His not even to honor His Father save as His Father chose to be honored, who is far more honored in the ordinary way of common wonders, than in the extraordinary way of miracles. Because it was God's business to take care of Him, His to do what the Father told Him to do. To make that stone bread would be to take the care out of the

Father's hands, and turn the divinest thing in the universe into the merest commonplace of self-preservation.

And in nothing was He to be beyond His brethren, save in faith. No refuge for Him, any more than for them, save in the love and care of the Father. Other refuge, let it be miraculous power or what you will, would be but hell to Him. God is refuge. God is life.

"Was He not to eat when it came in His way? And did not the bread come in His way, when His power met that which could be changed into it?"

Regard that word *changed*. The whole matter lies in that. Changed from what? From what God had made it. Changed into what? Into what He did not make it. Why changed? Because the Son was hungry, and the Father would not feed Him with food convenient for Him! The Father did not give Him a stone when He asked for bread. It was Satan that brought the stone and told Him to provide for Himself. The Father said, That is a stone. The Son would not say, That is a loaf. No one creative *fiat* shall contradict another. The Father and the Son are of one mind. The Lord could hunger, could starve, but would not change into another thing what His Father had made one thing.

If we regard the answer He gave the devil, we shall see the root of the matter at once: "Man shall not live by bread alone, but by every word that proceeds from the mouth of God." Yea even by the word which made that stone that stone. Everything is all right. It is life indeed for Him to leave that a stone, which the Father had made a stone. It would be death to Him to alter one word that God had spoken.

In the higher aspect of this first temptation, arising from the fact that a man cannot feel the things he believes except under certain conditions of physical well-being dependent upon food, the answer is the same: A man does not live by his feelings any more than by bread, but by the Truth, that is, the Word, the Will, the uttered Being of God.

I am even ashamed to yield here to the necessity of writing what is but as milk for babes, when I would gladly utter, if I might, only that which would be as bread for men and women. What I must say is this: that, by *the Word of God*, I do not understand *The Bible*. The Bible is *a* Word of God, the chief of His written words, because it tells us of The Word, the Christ; but everything God has done and given man to know is a word of His, a will of His; and inasmuch as it is a will of His, it is a necessity to man, without which he cannot live: the reception of it is man's life. For inasmuch as God's utterances are a whole, every smallest is essential: He speaks no foolishness—there are with Him no vain repetitions. But by *the word* of the God and not Maker only, who is God just because He *speaks* to men, I must understand, in the deepest sense, every revelation of Himself in the heart and consciousness of man, so that the man knows that God is there, nay, rather, that He is here.

Even Christ Himself is not The Word of God in the deepest sense *to a man*, until He is this Revelation of God to the man—until the Spirit that is the meaning in the Word has come to him—until the speech is not a sound as of thunder, but the voice of words; for a word is more than an utterance —it is a sound to be understood. No word, I say, is fully a Word *of* God until it is a Word *to* man, until the man therein recognizes God. This is that for which the word is spoken. The words of God are as the sands and the stars—they cannot be numbered; but the end of all and each is this—to reveal God.

Nor, moreover, can the man know that any one of them is the word of God, save as it comes thus to him, is a revelation of God in him. It is *to* him that it may be *in* him; but till it is *in* him he cannot *know* that it was *to* him. God must be God *in* man before man can know that He is God, or that he has received aright—and for that for which it was spoken— any one of His words.

If, by any will of God—that is, any truth in Him—we live, we live by it tenfold when that will has become a word to us. When we receive it, His will becomes our will, and so we live by God. But the word of God once understood, a man must live by the faith of what God is, and not by his own feelings even in regard to God. It is the Truth itself, that which God is, known by what goes out of His mouth, that man lives by. And when he can no longer *feel* the truth, he shall not therefore die. He lives because God is true; and he is able to know that he lives because he knows, having once understood the word, that God is truth. He believes in the God of former vision, lives by that word therefore, when all is dark and there is no vision.

Trying God

We now come to the second attempt of the Enemy.

"Then if God is to be so trusted, try Him. Here is the word itself for it: He shall give His angels charge concerning you; not a stone shall hurt you. Take Him at His word. Throw yourself down, and strike the conviction into me that you are the Son of God."

Again, with a written word, in return, the Lord meets him. And He does not quote the Scripture for logical purposes—to confute Satan intellectually, but as giving even Satan the reason of His conduct. Satan quotes Scripture as a verbal authority; our Lord meets him with a Scripture by the truth in which He regulates His conduct.

If we examine it, we shall find that this answer contains the same principle as the former, namely this, that to the Son of God the will of God is Life. It was a temptation to show the powers of the world that He was the Son of God. But He was the *Son* of God: what was His *Father's* will? Such was not the divine way of convincing the world of sin, of righteousness, of judgment.

I think this will throw some light upon the words of our Lord, "If you have faith and never doubt . . ., if you say to this mountain, 'Be taken up and cast into the sea'; it will be done." Good people, among them John Bunyan, have been tempted to tempt the Lord their God upon the strength of this saying, just as Satan sought to tempt our Lord on the strength of the passage he quoted from the Psalms. Happily for such, the assurance to which they would give the name of faith generally fails them in time. Faith is that which, knowing the Lord's will, goes and does it; or, not knowing it, stands and waits, content in ignorance as in knowledge, because God wills; neither pressing into the hidden future, nor careless of the knowledge which opens the path of action. It is its noblest exercise to act with uncertainty of the result, when the duty itself is certain, or even when a course seems with strong probability to be duty.

But to put God to the question in any other way than by saying, What will you have me to do? is an attempt to compel God to declare Himself, or to hasten His work. This probably was the sin of Judas. It is presumption of a kind similar to the making of a stone into bread. It is, as it were, either a forcing of God to act where He has created no need for action, or the making of a case wherein He shall seem to have forfeited His word if He does not act. The man is therein dissociating himself from God so far that, instead of acting by the divine will from within, He acts in God's face, as it were, to see what He will do. Man's first business is, "What does God want me to do?" not "What will God do if I do so and so?"

God's Way of Deliverance
We shall now look at the third temptation. The first was to help Himself in His need; the second, perhaps to assert the Father; the third to deliver His brethren.

To deliver them, that is, after the fashion of men—from the outside still. Indeed, the whole Temptation may be regarded as the contest of the seen and the unseen, of the outer and inner, of the likely and the true, of the show and the reality. And as in the others, the evil in this last lay in that it was a temptation to save His brethren, instead of doing the will of His Father.

I will not inquire whether such an enterprise could be accomplished without the worship of Satan. I will ask whether to know better and do not so well, is not a serving of Satan. Not all the sovereignty of God, as the theologians call it, delegated to the Son, and administered by the wisdom of the Spirit that was given to Him without measure, could have wrought the kingdom of heaven in one corner of our earth. Nothing but the obedience of the Son, the obedience unto the death, the absolute *doing* of the will of God because it was the truth, could redeem the prisoner, the widow, the orphan.

The earth should be free because Love was stronger than Death. Therefore should fierceness and wrong and hypocrisy and God-service play out their weary play. He would take time; but the tree would be dead at last—dead, and cast into the lake of fire. It would take time; but His Father had time enough and to spare. It would take courage and strength and self-denial and endurance; but His Father could give Him all. It would cost pain of body and mind, yea, agony and torture; but those He was ready to take on Himself.

It would cost Him the vision of many sad and, to all but Him, hopeless sights; He must see tears without wiping them, hear sighs without changing them into laughter, see the dead lie, and let them lie; see Rachel weeping for her children and refusing to be comforted. He must look on His brothers and sisters crying as children over their broken toys, and must not mend them; He must go on to the grave, and they not know that thus He was setting all things right for them. His work must be one with and completing God's Creation and God's History.

The disappointment and sorrow and fear He could, He

would bear. The will of God should be done. Man should be free—not merely man as he thinks of himself, but man as God thinks of him. The divine idea shall be set free in the divine bosom; the man on earth shall see his angel face to face. He shall grow into the likeness of the divine thought, free not in his own fancy, but in absolute divine fact of being, as in God's idea. The great and beautiful and perfect will of God *must* be done.

TWENTY-SEVEN

SELF-DENIAL

*A*nd He said to all, If any man would come after me, let him deny himself and take up his cross daily and follow me. For whoever would save his life will lose it; and whoever loses his life for my sake, he will save it (Luke 9:23, 24).

Christ is the way out, and the way in; the way from slavery, conscious or unconscious, into liberty; the way from the unhomeliness of things to the home we desire but do not know.

To picture Him, we need not only endless figures, but sometimes quite opposing figures. He is not only the door of the sheepfold, but the shepherd of the sheep. He is not only the way, but the leader in the way, the rock that follows, and the captain of our salvation. We must become as little children, and Christ must be born in us. We must learn of Him, and the one lesson He has to give is Himself. He does first all He wants us to do; He is first all He wants us to be. We must not merely do as He did; we must see things as

He saw them, regard them as He regarded them. We must take the will of God as the very life of our being. We must neither try to get our own way, nor trouble ourselves as to what may be thought or said of us. The world must be to us as nothing.

I would not be misunderstood if I may avoid it: when I say *the world*, I do not mean the world God makes and means, yet less the human hearts that live therein; but the world man makes by choosing the perversion of his own nature—a world apart from and opposed to God's world. By the world I mean all ways of judging, regarding, and thinking, whether political, economical, ecclesiastical, social, or individual, which are not divine. They are not God's ways of thinking, regarding, or judging. They do not take God into account, do not set His will supreme, as the one only law of life. They do not care for the truth of things, but the customs of society, or the practice of the trade. They heed not what is right, but the usage of the time.

From everything that is against the teaching and thinking of Jesus, from the world in the heart of the best man in it, specially from the world in his own heart, the disciple must turn to follow Him. The first thing in all progress is to leave something behind; to follow Him is to leave one's self behind. "If any man would come after me, let him deny himself."

To Deny Is Not to Frustrate

Some seem to take this to mean that the disciple must go against his likings because they are his likings; must be unresponsive to the tendencies and directions and inclinations that are his, because they are such, and his. They seem to think something is gained by abstinence from what is pleasant, or by the doing of what is disagreeable—that to thwart the lower nature is in itself good. Now I will not dare say what a man may not get good from, if the thing be done in simplicity and honesty. I believe that when a man, for the sake of doing the thing that is right, does in mistake that which is not right, God will take care that he be shown the better way—will perhaps use the very thing which is his mistake to reveal to him the mistake it is. I will allow that the mere effort of will, arbitrary and uninformed of duty, partaking of the character of tyranny and even schism, may add to the man's power over his lower nature; but in that very nature it is God who must rule and not the man, however well he may mean.

From a man's rule of himself, in smallest opposition, however devout, to the law of his being, arises the huge danger of nourishing, by the pride of self-conquest, a far worse than even the unchained animal self—the demoniac self. True victory over self is the victory of God in the man, not of the man alone. It is not subjugation that is enough, but subjugation by God. In whatever man does without God, he must fail miserably—or succeed more miserably. No portion of a man can rule another portion, for God, not the man, created it, and the part is greater than the whole.

In effecting what God does not mean, a man but falls into fresh ill conditions. In crossing his natural, therefore in themselves right inclinations, a man may develop a self-satisfaction which in its very nature is a root of all sin. Doing the thing God does not require of him, he puts himself in the place of God, becoming not a law but a law-giver to himself, one who commands, not one who obeys. The diseased satisfaction which some minds feel in laying burdens on themselves, is a pampering, little as they may suspect it, of the most dangerous appetite of that self which they think they are mortifying.

All the creatures of God are good, received with thanksgiving. Then only can any one of them become evil, when it is used in relation in which a higher law forbids it, or when it is refused for the sake of self-discipline, in relations in which no higher law forbids, and God therefore allows it. For a man to be his own schoolmaster, is a right dangerous position; the pupil cannot be expected to make progress—except, indeed, in the wrong direction. To enjoy heartily and thankfully, and do cheerfully without, when God wills we should, is the way to live in regard to things of the lower nature; these must nowise be confounded with the things of *the world*. If any one say this is dangerous doctrine, I answer, "The law of God is enough for me, and for laws invented by man, I will none of them. They are false, and come all of rebellion. God and not man is our judge."

Verily it is not to thwart or tease the poor self Jesus tells us. That was not the purpose for which God gave it to us! He tells us we must leave it altogether—yield it, deny it, refuse it, lose it. Thus only shall we save it, thus only have a share in our own being. The self is given to us that we may sacrifice it; it is ours that we like Christ may have somewhat to offer—not that we should torment it, but that we should deny it; not that we should cross it, but that we should abandon it utterly. Then it can no more be vexed.

Positive Denial

"What can this mean?—we are not to thwart, but to abandon? How abandon, without thwarting?"

It means this: we must refuse, abandon, deny self altogether as a ruling, or determining or originating element in us. It is to be no longer the regent of our action. We are no more to think, "What should I like to do?" but "What would the Living One have me do?" It is not selfish to take that which God has made us to desire; neither are we very good to yield it. We should only be very bad not to do so, when He would take it from us; but to yield it heartily, without a struggle or regret, is not merely to deny the self a thing it would like, but to deny the self itself, to refuse and abandon it.

The self is God's making—only it must be the "slave of Christ," that the Son may make it also the free son of the same Father. It must receive all from Him—not as from no-

where. As well as the deeper soul, it must follow Him, not its
own desires. It must not be its own law; Christ must be its
law. The time will come when it shall be so possessed, so
enlarged, so idealized, by the indwelling God, who is its
deeper, its deepest self, that there will be no longer any en-
forced denial of it needful. It has been finally denied and
refused and sent into its own obedient place. It has learned
to receive with thankfulness, to demand nothing; to turn no
more upon its own center, or any more think to minister to
its own good.

God's eternal denial of Himself, revealed in Him who for
our sakes in the flesh took up His cross daily, will have been
developed in the man. His eternal rejoicing will be in God—
and in his fellows, before whom he will cast his glad self to
be a carpet for their walk, a footstool for their rest, a stair
for their climbing.

No grasping or seeking, no hungering of the individual,
shall give motion to the will; no desire to be conscious of
worthiness shall order the life; no ambition whatever shall
be a motive of action; no wish to surpass another be allowed
a moment's respite from death; no longing after the praise
of men influence a single throb of the heart. To deny the
self is to shrink from no dispraise or condemnation or contempt of the community, or circle, or country, which is
against the mind of the Living One. For no love or entreaty
of father or mother, wife or child, friend or lover, shall we
turn aside from following Him, but forsake them all as any
ruling or ordering power in our lives. We must do nothing
to please them that would not first be pleasing to Him.

Right deeds, and not the judgment thereupon; true
words, and not what reception they may have, shall be our
care. Not merely shall we not love money, or trust in it, or
seek it as the business of life, but, whether we have it or have
it not, we must never think of it as a windfall from the tree of
event or the cloud of circumstance, but as the gift of God.
We must draw our life, by the uplooking, acknowledging

will, every moment fresh from the Living One, the causing Life, not glory in the mere consciousness of health and being. It is God feeds us, warms us, quenches our thirst.

The will of God must be to us all in all. To our whole nature the life of the Father must be the joy of the child. We must know our very understanding His—that we live and feed on Him every hour in the closest way. To know these things in the depth of our knowing, is to deny ourselves, and take God instead. To try after them is to begin the denial, to follow Him who never sought His own. So must we deny all anxieties and fears.

When young we must not mind what the world calls failure; as we grow old, we must not be vexed that we cannot remember, must not regret that we cannot do, must not be miserable because we grow weak or ill. We must not mind anything. We have to do with God who can, not with ourselves where we cannot; we have to do with the Will, with the Eternal Life of the Father of our spirits, and not with the being which we could not make, and which is His care. He is our care; we are His; our care is to will His will; His care, to give us all things. This is to deny ourselves.

The Father's Yoke
And in this regard we must not fail to see, or seeing ever forget, that, when Jesus tells us we must follow Him, we must come to Him, we must believe in Him, He speaks first and always as *the Son* of the Father—and that in the active sense, as the obedient God, not merely as one who claims the sonship for the ground of being and so of further claim. He is the Son of the Father as the Son who obeys the Father, as the Son who came expressly and only to do the will of the Father, as the messenger whose delight it is to do the will of Him that sent Him.

At the moment He says *Follow me*, He is following the Father; His face is set homeward. He would have us follow Him because He is bent on the will of the Blessed. It is nothing even thus to think of Him, except thus we *believe* in Him. To believe in Him is to do as He does, to follow Him where he goes. We must believe in Him *practically*—altogether practically, as He believed in His Father; not as one concerning whom we have to hold something, but as one whom we have to follow out of the body of this death into life eternal.

It is not to follow Him to take Him in any way theoretically, to hold this or that theory about why He died, or wherein lay His atonement: such things can be revealed only to those who follow Him in His active being and the principle of His life—who do as He did, live as He lived. There is no other following. He is all for the Father; we must be all for the Father too, else are we not following Him. To follow Him is to be learning of Him, to think His thoughts, to use His judgments, to see things as He saw them, to feel things as He felt them, to be hearted, souled, minded, as He was—that so also we may be of the same mind with His Father. This it is to deny self and go after Him; nothing less, even if it be working miracles and casting out devils, is to be His disciple.

Busy from morning to night doing great things for Him on any other road, we should but earn the reception, "I never knew you." When He says, "Take my yoke upon you," He does not mean a yoke which He would lay upon our shoulders; it is His own yoke He tells us to take, and to learn of Him. It is the yoke He is Himself carrying, the yoke His perfect Father had given Him to carry.

The will of the Father is the yoke He would have us take, and bear also with Him. It is of this yoke that He says, "It is easy"; of this burden, "It is light." He is not saying, "The yoke I lay upon you is easy, the burden light." What He says is, "The yoke I carry is easy, the burden on my shoulders is light." With the garden of Gethsemane before Him, with the hour and the power of darkness waiting for Him, He declares His yoke easy, His burden light. There is no magnifying of Himself. He first denies Himself, and takes up His cross—then tells us to do the same. The Father magnifies the Son, not the Son Himself; the Son magnifies the Father.

We must be jealous for God against ourselves, and look well to the cunning and deceitful self—ever cunning and deceitful until it is informed of God—until it is thoroughly and utterly denied, and God is to it also All-in-All—till we have left it quite empty of our will and our regard, and God has come into it. Until then, its very denials, its very turnings from things dear to it for the sake of Christ, will tend to foster its self-regard, and generate in it a yet deeper self-worship. While it is not denied, only thwarted, we may through satisfaction with conquered difficulty and supposed victory, minister yet more to its self-gratulation. In a thousand ways will self delude itself, in a thousand ways befool its own slavish being. Christ sought not His own, sought not anything but the will of His Father: we have to grow diamond-clear, true as the white light of the morning. Hopeless task!—were it not that He offers to come Himself, and dwell in us.

But we must note that, although the idea of the denial of self is an entire and absolute one, yet the thing has to be done *daily*: we must keep on denying. It is a deeper and harder thing than any sole effort of most herculean will may finally effect. For indeed the will itself is not pure, is not free, until the self is absolutely denied. It takes long for the water of life that flows from the well within us, to permeate every outlying portion of our spiritual frame, subduing everything to itself, making it all of the one kind, until at last, reaching the outermost folds of our personality, it casts out disease, our bodies by indwelling righteousness are redeemed, and the creation delivered from the bondage of corruption into the liberty of the glory of the children of God. Every day till then we have to take up our cross; every hour to see that we are carrying it. A birthright may be lost for a mess of pottage, and what Satan calls a trifle must be a thing of eternal significance.

Is there not many a Christian who, having *begun* to deny himself, yet spends much strength in the vain and evil endeavor to accommodate matters between Christ and the dear self——seeking to save that which so he must certainly lose—in how different a way from that in which the Master would have him lose it! It is one thing to have the loved self devoured of hell in hate and horror and disappointment; another to yield it to conscious possession by the living God Himself, who will raise it then first and only to its true individuality, freedom, and life. With its cause within it, then, indeed, it shall be saved!—how then should it but live!

Here is the promise to those who will leave all and follow Him: "Whoever loses his life for my sake, he will save it"— in St. Matthew, "find it." What speech of men or angels will serve to shadow the dimly glorious hope! To lose ourselves in the salvation of God's heart! to be no longer any care to ourselves, but know God taking divinest care of us, His own! to be and feel just a resting-place for the divine love!

When we speak of a man and his soul, we imply a self and a self, reacting on each other: we cannot divide ourselves so; the figure suits but imperfectly. It was never the design of the Lord to explain things to our understanding—nor would that in the least have helped our necessity. What we require is a means, a word, whereby to think with ourselves of high things: that is what a true figure—for a figure may be true while far from perfect—will always be to us. But the imperfection of His figures cannot lie in excess. Be sure that, in dealing with any truth, its symbol, however high, must come short of the glorious meaning itself holds. It is the low stupidity of an unspiritual nature that would interpret the Lord's meaning as less than His symbols. The true soul sees, or will come to see, that His words, His figures always represent more than they are able to present. As the heavens are higher than the earth, so are the heavenly things higher than the earthly signs of them, let the signs be good as ever sign may be.

The Joy That Follows

There is no joy belonging to human nature, as God made it, that shall not be enhanced a hundredfold to the man who gives up himself—though, in so doing, he may seem to be yielding the very essence of life. To yield self is to give up grasping at things in their second causes, as men call them, but which are merely God's means, and to receive them direct from their source—to take them seeing whence they come, and not as if they came from nowhere, because no one appears presenting them.

The careless soul receives the Father's gifts as if it were a way things had of dropping into his hand. He thus grants himself a slave, dependent on chance and his own blundering endeavor—yet is he ever complaining, as if someone were accountable for the checks which meet him at every turn. For the good that comes to him, he gives no thanks—who is there to thank? At the disappointments that befall him he grumbles—there must be some one to blame! He does not think to what Power it could be of any consequence, nay, what power would not be worse than squandered, to sustain him after his own fashion, in his paltry, low-aimed existence!

How could a God pour out His being to uphold the merest waste of His creatures! No world could ever be built or sustained on such an idea. It is the children who shall inherit the earth; such as will not be children, cannot possess. The hour is coming when all that art, all that science, all that nature, all that animal nature, in ennobling subjugation to the higher even as man is subject to the Father, can afford, shall be the possession, to the endless delight, of the sons and daughters of God. To him to whom He is all in all, God is able to give these things; to another He cannot give them, for he is unable to receive them who is outside the truth of them.

Assuredly we are not to love God for the sake of what He can give us. It is impossible to love Him save because He is our God, and altogether good and beautiful. But neither may we forget what the Lord does not forget, that, in the end, when the truth is victorious, God will answer His creature in the joy of His heart. For what is joy but the harmony of the spirit! The good Father made His children to be joyful; only, ere they can enter into His joy, they must be like Himself, ready to sacrifice joy to truth.

No promise of such joy is an appeal to selfishness. Every reward held out by Christ is a pure thing; nor can it enter the soul save as a death to selfishness. The heaven of Christ is a loving of all, a forgetting of self, a dwelling of each in all, and all in each. Even in our nurseries, a joyful child is rarely selfish, generally righteous. It is not selfish to be joyful. What power could prevent him who sees the face of God from being joyful?—that bliss is his which lies behind all other bliss, without which no other bliss could ripen or last.

The one bliss of the universe is the presence of God—which is simply God being to the man, and felt by the man as being, that which in His own nature He is—the indwelling power of His life. God must be to His creature what He is in Himself, for it is by His essential being alone, that by which He *is*, that He can create. His presence is the unintermittent call and response of the creative to the created, of the father to the child.

Where can be the selfishness in being so made happy? It may be deep selfishness to refuse to be happy. Is there selfishness in the Lord's seeing of the travail of His soul and being satisfied? Selfishness consists in taking the bliss from another; to find one's bliss in the bliss of another is not selfishness. Joy is not selfishness; and the greater the joy thus reaped, the farther is that joy removed from selfishness.

The one bliss, next to the love of God is the love of our

neighbor. If any say, "You love because it makes you blessed," I deny it: "We are blessed, I say, because we love." No one could attain to the bliss of loving his neighbor who was selfish and sought that bliss from love of himself. Love is unselfishness. In the main we love because we cannot help it. There is no merit in it: how should there be in any love? But neither is it selfish.

There are many who confound righteousness with merit, and think there is nothing righteous where there is nothing meritorious. "If it makes you happy to love," they say, "where is your merit? It is only selfishness!" There is no merit, I reply; yet the love that is born in us is our salvation from selfishness. It is of the very essence of righteousness. Because a thing is joyful, it does not follow that I do it for the joy of it; yet when the joy is in others, the joy is pure.

That *certain* joys should be joys, is the very denial of selfishness. The man would be a demoniacally selfish man, whom love itself did not make joyful. It is selfish to enjoy in content beholding others' lack. Even in the highest spiritual bliss, to sit careless of others would be selfishness, and the higher the bliss, the worse the selfishness; but surely that bliss is right altogether of which a great part consists in labor that others may share it. Such, I will not doubt—the labor to bring others in to share with us—will be a great part of our heavenly content and gladness.

The making, the redeeming Father will find plenty of like work for His children to do. Dull are those—little at least can they have of Christian imagination—who think that where all are good, things must be dull. It is because there is so little good yet in them, that they know so little of the power or beauty of merest life divine. Let such make haste to be true. Interest will there be and variety enough, not without pain, in the ministration of help to those yet wearily toiling up the heights of truth—perhaps yet unwilling to part with miserable self, which cherishing they are not yet worth being, or capable of having.

The Forsakings That Are Most Difficult

Some of the things a man may have to forsake in following Christ, he has not to forsake because of what they are in themselves. Neither nature, art, science, nor fit society, is of those things a man will lose in forsaking himself. They are God's and have no part in the world of evil, the false judgments, low wishes, and unrealities generally, that make up the conscious life of the self which has to be denied. Such will never be restored to the man.

But in forsaking himself to do what God requires of him —his true work in the world, that is—a man may find he has to leave some of God's things, not to repudiate them, but for the time to forsake them, because they draw his mind from the absolute necessities of the true life in himself or in others. He may have to deny himself in leaving them—not as bad things, but as things for which there is not room until those of paramount claim have been so heeded, that these will no longer impede but further them.

Then he who knows God, will find that knowledge open the door of his understanding to all things else. He will become able to behold them from within, instead of having to search wearily into them from without. This gave to king David more understanding than had all his teachers. Then will the things he had had to leave be restored to him a hundred fold. So will it be in the forsaking of friends. To forsake them for Christ is not to forsake them as evil. It is not to allow their love to cast even a shadow between us and our Master; to be content to lose their approval, their intercourse, even their affection, where the Master says one thing and they another. It is to learn to love them in a far higher, deeper, tenderer, truer way than before—a way which keeps all that was genuine in the former way, and loses all that was false. We shall love *their* selves, and disregard our own.

I do not forget the word of the Lord about hating father and mother. I have a glimpse of the meaning of it, but dare not attempt explaining it now. It is all against the self—not against the father and mother.

There is another kind of forsaking that may fall to the lot of some, and which they may find very difficult: the forsaking of such notions of God and His Christ as they were taught in their youth—which they held, nor could help holding, at such time as they began to believe—of which they have begun to doubt the truth, but to cast which away seems like parting with every assurance of safety.

There are so-called doctrines long accepted of good people, which how any man can love God and hold, except indeed by fast closing of the spiritual eyes, I find it hard to understand. If a man care more for opinion than for life, it is not worth any other man's while to persuade him to renounce the opinions he happens to entertain. He would but put other opinions in the same place of honor—a place which can *belong* to no opinion whatever: it matters nothing what such a man may or may not believe, for he is not a true man. By holding with a school he supposes to be right, he but bolsters himself up with the worst of all unbelief—opinion calling itself faith, unbelief calling itself religion.

But for him who is in earnest about the will of God, it is of endless consequence that he should think rightly of God. He cannot come close to Him, cannot truly know His will, while his notion of Him is in any point that of a false god. The thing shows itself absurd. If such a man seem to himself to be giving up even his former assurance of salvation, in yielding such ideas of God as are unworthy of God, he must none the less, if he will be true, if he would enter into life, take up that cross also. He will come to see that he must follow *no* doctrine, be it true as word of man could state it, but the living Truth, the Master Himself.

Good souls many will one day be horrified at the things they now believe of God. If they have not thought about them, but given themselves to obedience, they may not have done them much harm as yet; but they can make little pro-

gress in the knowledge of God, while—if but passively—
holding evil things true of Him. If, on the other hand, they
do think about them, and find in them no obstruction, they
must indeed be far from anything to be called a true knowledge of God.

But there are those who find them a terrible obstruction, and yet imagine, or at least fear them true: such must
take courage to forsake the false in *any* shape, to deny their
old selves in the most seemingly sacred of prejudices, and
follow Jesus, not as He is presented in the tradition of the
elders, but as He is presented by Himself, His apostles, and
the spirit of truth. There are "traditions of men" after
Christ as well as before Him, and far worse, as "making of
none effect" higher and better things; and we have to look
how we have learned Christ.

TWENTY-EIGHT

LOVE YOUR NEIGHBOR

*Y*ou shall love your neighbor as
yourself (Matt. 22:39).

The original here quoted by our Lord is to be found in
the words of God to Moses, (Lev. 19:18): *"You shall not take
vengeance or bear any grudge against the sons of your own people,
but you shall love your neighbor as yourself: I am the Lord."* Our
Lord never thought of being original. The older the saying
the better, if it utters the truth He wants to utter. In Him it
becomes fact: The *Word* was made *flesh*. And so, in the
wondrous meeting of extremes, the words He spoke were
no more words, but spirit and life.

The same words are twice quoted by St. Paul, and once by
St. James, always in a similar mode: Love they represent as
the fulfilling of the law.

Is the converse true then? Is the fulfilling of the law love?
The apostle Paul says: "Love does no wrong to a neighbor;
therefore love is the fulfilling of the law." Does it follow that

working no ill is love? Love will fulfill the law: will the law fulfill love? No. If a man keeps the law, I know he is a lover of his neighbor. But he is not a lover because he keeps the law: he keeps the law because he is a lover. No heart will be content with the law for love. The law cannot fulfill love.

"But, at least, the law will be able to fulfill itself, though it reaches not to love."

I do not believe it. I am certain that it is impossible to keep the law towards one's neighbor except one loves him. The law itself is infinite, reaching to such delicacies of action, that the man who tries most will be the man most aware of defeat. We are not made for law, but for love. Love is law, because it is infinitely more than law. It is of an altogether higher region than law—is, in fact, the creator of law.

Had it not been for love, not one of the *shall-nots* of the law would have been uttered. True, once uttered, they show themselves in the form of justice, yea, even in the inferior and worldly forms of prudence and self-preservation; but it was love that spoke them first. Were there no love in us, what sense of justice could we have? Would not each be filled with the sense of his own wants, and be forever tearing to himself?

I do not say it is conscious love that breeds justice, but I do say that without love in our nature justice would never be born. For I do not call that justice which consists only in a sense of *our own* rights. True, there are poor and withered forms of love which are immeasurably below justice now; but even now they are of speechless worth, for they will grow into that which will supersede, because it will necessitate, justice.

The Use of Law

Of what use then is the law? To lead us to Christ, the Truth —to waken in our minds a sense of what our deepest nature, the presence, namely, of God *in* us, requires of us—to let us know, in part by failure, that the purest effort of will of which we are capable cannot lift us up even to the abstaining from wrong to our neighbor. What man, for instance, who loves not his neighbor and yet wishes to keep the law, will dare be confident that never by word, look, tone, gesture, silence, will he bear false witness against that neighbor? What man can judge his neighbor aright save him whose love makes him refuse to judge him? Therefore are we told to love, and not judge. It is the sole justice of which we are capable, and that perfected will comprise all justice.

Nay more, to refuse our neighbor love, is to do him the greatest wrong. But of this afterwards. In order to fulfill the commonest law, I repeat, we must rise into a loftier region altogether, a region that is above law, because it is spirit and life and makes the law: in order to keep the law towards our neighbor, we must love our neighbor. We are not made for law, but for grace—or for faith, to use another word so much misused. We are made on too large a scale altogether to have any pure relation to mere justice, if indeed we can say there is such a thing. It is but an abstract idea which, in reality, will not be abstracted. The law comes to make us long for the needful grace—that is, for the divine condition, in which love is all, for God is Love.

That our Lord meant by the love of our neighbor, not the fulfilling of the law towards him, but that condition of being which results in the fulfilling of the law and more, is sufficiently clear from His story of the good Samaritan. "Who is my neighbor?" said the lawyer. And the Lord taught him that everyone to whom he could be or for whom he could do anything was his neighbor; therefore, that each of the race, as he comes within the touch of one tentacle of our nature, is our neighbor.

Which of the inhibitions of the law is illustrated in the tale? Not one. The love that is more than law, and renders its breach impossible, lives in the endless story, coming out in active kindness, that is, the recognition of kind, of *kind*, and nighness, of *neighborhood*; yea, in tenderness and loving-kindness—the Samaritan-heart akin to the Jew-heart, the Samaritan hands neighbors to the Jewish wounds.

"You Shall Love Your Neighbor as Yourself"

So direct and complete is this parable of our Lord, that one becomes almost ashamed of further talk about it. Suppose a man of the company had put the same question to our Lord that we have been considering, had said, "But I may keep the law and yet not love my neighbor," would He not have returned: "Keep the law thus, not in the letter, but in the spirit, that is in the truth of action, and you will soon find, O Jew, that you love your Samaritan"?

And yet, when thoughts and questions arise in our minds, He desires that we should follow them. He will not check us with a word of heavenly wisdom scornfully uttered. He knows that not even *His* words will apply to every question of the willing soul; and we know that His spirit will reply. When we want to know more, that more will be there for us. Thus would we be ready for further teaching from that Spirit who is the Lord.

"But how," says a man, who is willing to recognize the universal neighborhood, but finds himself unable to fulfill the bare law towards the woman even whom he loves best, "How am I then to rise into that higher region, that empyrean of love?" And, beginning straightway to try to love his neighbor, he finds that the empyrean of which he spoke is no more to be reached in itself than the law was to be reached in itself. As he cannot keep the law without first rising into the love of his neighbor, so he cannot love his neighbor without first rising higher still.

The whole system of the universe works upon this law—the driving of things upward towards the center. The man who will love his neighbor can do so by no immediately operative exercise of the will. It is the man fulfilled of God from whom he came and by whom he is, who alone can as himself love his neighbor who came from God too and is by

God too. The mystery of individuality and consequent relation is deep as the beginnings of humanity, and the questions thence arising can be solved only by him who has, practically, at least, solved the holy necessities resulting from his origin.

In God alone can man meet man. In Him alone the converging lines of existence touch and cross not. When the mind of Christ, the life of the Head, courses through that atom which the man is of the slowly revivifying body, when he is alive too, then the love of the brothers is there as conscious life. From Christ through the neighbors comes the life that makes him a part of the body.

It *is* possible to love our neighbor as ourselves. Our Lord *never* spoke hyperbolically, although, indeed, that is the supposition on which many unconsciously interpret His words, in order to be able to persuade themselves that they believe them. We may see that it is possible before we attain to it; for our perceptions of truth are always in advance of our condition. True, no man can see it perfectly until he is it; but we must see it, that we may be it. A man who knows that he does not yet love his neighbor as himself may believe in such a condition, may even see that there is no other goal of human perfection, nothing else to which the universe is speeding, propelled by the Father's will. Let him labor on, and not faint at the thought that God's day is a thousand years. His millennium is likewise one day—yea, this day, for we have Him, The Love, in us, working even now the far end.

But while it is true that only when a man loves God with all his heart, will he love his neighbor as himself, yet there are mingled processes in the attainment of this final result. Let us try to aid such operation of truth by looking farther. Let us suppose that the man, who believes our Lord both meant what He said, and knew the truth of the matter, proceeds to endeavor obedience in this of loving his neighbor as himself. He begins to think about his neighbors generally, and he tries to feel love towards them. He finds at once that they begin to classify themselves. With some he feels no difficulty, for he loves them already, not indeed because they *are*, but because they have, by friendly qualities, by showing themselves lovable, that is loving, already, moved his feelings as the wind moves the waters, that is without any self-generated action on his part. And he feels that this is nothing much to the point; though, of course, he would be farther from the desired end if he had none such to love, and farther still if he loved none such.

He recalls the words of our Lord, "If you love those who love you, what reward have you?" and his mind fixes upon —let us say—one of a second class, and he tries to love him. The man is no enemy—we have not come to that class of neighbors yet—but he is dull, uninteresting—in a negative way, he thinks, unlovable. What is he to do with him? With all his effort, he finds the goal as far off as ever.

But let a man once love, and all those difficulties which appeared opposed to love will just be so many arguments for loving. Let a man once find another who has fallen among thieves; let him be a neighbor to him, pouring oil and wine into his wounds, and binding them up, and setting him on his own beast, and paying for him at the inn; let him do all this merely from a sense of duty; yet such will be the virtue of obeying an eternal truth even to his poor measure, that even if the truth does not after the deed give the faintest glimmer as truth in the man, he will yet be ages nearer the truth than before, for he will go on his way loving that Samaritan neighbor a little more than his Jewish dignity will justify.

Nor will he question the reasonableness of so doing, although he may not care to spend any logic upon its support. How much more, if he be a man who would love his neighbor if he could, will the higher condition unsought have been found in the action! For man is a whole; and so soon as he unites *himself* by obedient action, the truth that is in him makes itself known to him, shining from the new whole. For his action is his response to his Maker's design, his individual part in the creation of himself, his yielding to the All in all, to the tides of whose harmonious life all his being thenceforward lies open. When will once begins to aspire, it will soon find that action must precede feeling, that the man may know the foundation itself of feeling.

The whole system of divine education as regards the relation of man and man has for its end that a man should love his neighbor as himself. It is not a lesson that he can learn by itself, or a duty the obligation of which can be shown by argument, any more than the difference between right and wrong can be defined in other terms than their own.

Learning From One's Family

The whole constitution of human society exists for the express end of teaching the two truths by which man lives, Love to God and Love to Man. I will say nothing more of the mysteries of the parental relation, because they belong to the teaching of the former truth, than that we come into the world as we do, to look up to the love over us, and see in it a symbol, poor and weak, yet the best we can have or receive of the divine love. And thousands more would find it easy to love God if they had not such miserable types of Him in the self-seeking, impulse-driven, purposeless, faithless beings who are all they have for father and mother, and to whom their children are no dearer than her litter is to the unthinking dam.

What I want to speak of now, with regard to the second great commandment, is the relation of brotherhood and sisterhood. Why does my brother come of the same father and mother? Why do I behold the helplessness and confidence of his infancy? Is it not that Love may grow lord of all between him and me? Is it not that I may feel towards him what there are no words or forms of words to express—a love namely, in which the divine self rushes forth in utter self-forgetfulness to live in the contemplation of the brother? My brother according to the flesh is my first neighbor, that we may be very nigh to each other, whether we will or no, while our hearts are tender, and so may learn *brotherhood.* For our love to each other is but the throbbing of the heart of the great brotherhood, and could come only from the eternal Father, not from our parents.

Then my second neighbor appears, and who is he? Whom I come in contact with soever. He with whom I have any transactions, any human dealings whatever. Not the man only with whom I dine; not the friend only with whom I share my thoughts; not the man only whom my compassion would lift from some slough; but the man who makes my clothes; the man who prints my book; the man who drives me in his cab; the man who begs from me in the street, to whom, it may be, for brotherhood's sake, I must not give; yea, even the man who condescends to me.

With all and each there is a chance of doing the part of a neighbor, if in no other way yet by speaking truly, acting justly, and thinking kindly. Even these deeds will help to that love which is born of righteousness. All true action clears the springs of right feeling, and lets their waters rise and flow. A man must not choose his neighbor; he must take the neighbor that God sends him. In him, whoever he be, lies, hidden or revealed, a beautiful brother. The neighbor is just the man who is next to you at the moment, the man with whom any business has brought you in contact.

Thus will love spread and spread in wider and stronger pulses till the whole human race will be to the man sacredly lovely. Any rough-hewn semblance of humanity will at length be enough to move the man to reverence and affection. It is harder for some to learn this than for others. There are [those] whose first impulse is ever to repel and not to receive. But learn they may, and learn they must. Even these may grow in this grace until a countenance unknown will awake in them a yearning of affection rising to pain, because there is for it no expression, and they can only give the man to God and be still.

Is This Love Only for This Life?

When once to a man the human face is the human face divine, and the hand of his neighbor is the hand of a brother, then will he understand what St. Paul meant when he said, "I could wish that myself were accursed from Christ for my brethren." But he will no longer understand those who, so far from feeling the love of their neighbor an essential of their being, expect to be set free from its law in the world to come. There, at least, for the glory of God, they may limit its expansive tendencies to the narrow circle of their heaven. On its battlements of safety, they will regard hell from afar, and say to each other, "Hark! Listen to their moans. But do not weep, for they are our neighbors no more."

St. Paul would be wretched before the throne of God, if he thought there was one man beyond the pale of His mercy, and that as much for God's glory as for the man's sake. And what shall we say of the man Christ Jesus? Who, that loves his brother, would not, upheld by the love of Christ, and with a dim hope that in the far-off time there might be some help for him, arise from the company of the blessed, and walk down into the dismal regions of despair, to sit with the last, the only unredeemed, the Judas of his race, and be himself more blessed in the pains of hell, than in the glories of heaven?

But it is a wild question. God is, and shall be, All in all. Father of our brothers and sisters! You will not be less glorious than we, taught of Christ, are able to think you. When you go into the wilderness to seek, you will not come home until you have found. It is because we hope not for them in you, not knowing you, not knowing your love, that we are so hard and so heartless to the brothers and sisters whom you have given us.

Out of the Dungeon

One word more: This love of one's neighbor is the only door out of the dungeon of self. The man thinks his consciousness is himself; whereas his life consists in the inbreathing of God, and the consciousness of the universe of truth. To have himself, to know himself, to enjoy himself, he calls life; whereas, if he would forget himself, tenfold would be his life in God and his neighbors. The region of man's life is a spiritual region. God, his friends, his neighbors, his brothers all, is the wide world in which alone his spirit can find room. Himself is his dungeon.

If he feels it not now, he will yet feel it one day—feel it as a living soul would feel being prisoned in a dead body. His life is not in knowing that he lives, but in loving all forms of life. He is made for the All; for God, who is the All, is his life. And the essential joy of his life lies abroad in the liberty of the All. His delights, like those of the Ideal Wisdom, are with the sons of men. His health is in the body of which the Son of Man is the head. The whole region of life is open to him—nay, he must live in it or perish.

Nor thus shall a man lose the consciousness of well-being. Far deeper and more complete, God and his neighbor will flash it back upon him—pure as life. No more will he agonize to generate it in the light of his own decadence. For he shall know the glory of his own being in the light of God and of his brother.

But he may have begun to love his neighbor, with the hope of ere long loving him as himself, and notwithstanding start back affrighted at yet another word of our Lord, seeming to be another law yet harder than the first, although in truth it is not another, for without obedience to it the former cannot be attained. He has not yet learned to love his neighbor as himself whose heart sinks within him at the word, "I say to you, Love your enemies."

TWENTY-NINE

LOVE
YOUR
ENEMY

Matthew 5:43-48.

Is not this at length *too* much to expect? Will a man ever love his enemies? He may come to do good to them that hate him; but when will he pray for them that despitefully use him and persecute him? When? When he is the child of his Father in heaven. Then shall he love his neighbor as himself, even if that neighbor be his enemy. In the passage in Leviticus (19:18) already referred to as quoted by our Lord and His apostles, we find the neighbor and the enemy are one. "You shall not take vengeance or bear any grudge against the sons of your own people, but you shall love your neighbor as yourself: I am the Lord."

Look at the glorious way in which Jesus interprets the Scripture that went before Him. "*I am the Lord*;" You must be perfect, as your heavenly Father is perfect."

Is it then reasonable to love our enemies? God does; therefore it must be the highest reason. But is it reasonable to expect that man should become capable of doing so? Yes; on one ground: that the divine energy is at work in man, to render at length man's doing divine as his nature is. For this our Lord prayed when He said: "That they may all be one, even as thou, Father, art in me, and I in thee, that they also may be in us." Nothing could be less likely to human judgment: our Lord knows that one day it will come.

Why should we love our enemies? The deepest reason for this we cannot put in words, for it lies in the absolute reality of their being, where our enemies are of one nature with us, even of the divine nature. Into this we cannot see, save as into a dark abyss. It is in virtue of the divine essence which is in them, that pure essential humanity, that we call our enemies men and women. It is this humanity that we are to love—a something, I say, deeper altogether than and independent of the region of hate. It is the humanity that originates the claim of neighborhood; the neighborhood only determines the occasion of its exercise. "Is this humanity in every one of our enemies?" "Else there were nothing *to* love." "Is it there in very deed? Then we *must* love it, come between us and it what may."

Loving the Real Man
But how can we love a man or a woman who is cruel and unjust to us?—who sears with contempt, or cuts off with wrong every tendril we would put forth to embrace?—who is mean, unlovely, carping, uncertain, self-righteous, self-seeking, and self-admiring?—who can even sneer, the most inhuman of human faults, far worse in its essence than mere murder?

These things cannot be loved. The best man hates them most; the worst man cannot love them. But are these the man? Does a woman bear that form in virtue of these? Lies there not within the man and the woman a divine element of brotherhood, of sisterhood, a something lovely and lovable—slowly fading, it may be, dying away under the fierce heat of vile passions, or the yet more fearful cold of selfishness—but there? Shall that divine something—which, once awakened to be its own holy self in the man, will loathe these unlovely things tenfold more than we loathe them now—shall this divine thing have no recognition from us?

It is the very presence of this fading humanity that makes it possible for us to hate. If it were an animal only, and not a man or a woman that did us hurt, we should not hate: we should only kill. We hate the man just because we are prevented from loving him. We push over the verge of the creation—*we damn*—just because we cannot embrace. For to embrace is the necessity of our deepest being. That foiled, we hate.

Yet within the most obnoxious to our hate, lies that which, could it but show itself as it is, and as it will show itself one day, would compel from our hearts a devotion of love. It is not the unfriendly, the unlovely, that we are told to love, but the brother, the sister, who is unkind, who is unlovely. Shall we leave our brother to his desolate fate? Shall we not rather say, "With my love at least you shall be compassed about, for you have not your own lovingness to infold you; love shall come as near you as it may; and when yours comes forth to meet mine, we shall be one in the indwelling God"?

Let no one say I have been speaking in a figure merely. That I have been so speaking I know. But many things which we see most vividly and certainly are more truly expressed by using a right figure, than by attempting to give them a clear outline of logical expression. My figure means a truth.

If any one say, "Do not make such vague distinctions. There is the person. Can you deny that that person is unlovely? How then can you love him?" I answer, "That person, with the evil thing cast out of him, will be yet more the *person*, for he will be his real self. The thing that now makes you dislike him is separable from him, is therefore not he, makes himself so much less himself, for it is working death in him. Now he is in danger of ceasing to be a person at all. When he is clothed and in his right mind, he will be a person indeed.

"You *could* not then go on hating him. Begin to love now, and help him into the loveliness which is his. Do not hate him although you can. The personality, I say, though clouded, besmeared, defiled with the wrong, lies deeper than the wrong, and indeed, so far as the wrong has reached it, is by the wrong injured, yea, so far, it may be, destroyed."

But those who will not acknowledge the claim of love, may yet acknowledge the claim of justice. If it is impossible, as I believe, without love to be just, much more cannot justice coexist with hate. The pure eye for the true vision of another's claims can only go with the loving heart. The man who hates can hardly be delicate in doing justice, say to his neighbor's love, to his neighbor's predilections and peculiarities. It is hard enough to be just to our friends; and how shall our enemies fare with us? For justice demands that we shall think rightly of our neighbor as certainly as that we shall neither steal his goods nor bear false witness against him. Man is not made for justice from his fellow, but for love, which is greater than justice, and by including supersedes justice.

Mere justice is an impossibility, a fiction of analysis. It does not exist between man and man, save relatively to human *law*. Justice to be justice must be much more than justice. Love is the law of our condition, without which we can no more render justice than a man can keep a straight line walking in the dark. The eye is not single, and the body is not full of light. No man who is even indifferent to his brother can recognize the claims which his humanity has upon him. Nay, the very indifference itself is an injustice.

Who Is in the Wrong?

I have taken for granted that the fault lies with the enemy so considered, for upon the primary rocks would I build my foundation. But the question must be put to each man by himself, "Is my neighbor indeed my enemy, or am I my neighbor's enemy, and so take him to be mine?—awful thought! Or, if he be mine, am not I his? Am I not refusing to acknowledge the child of the kingdom within his bosom, so killing the child of the kingdom within my own?" Let us claim for ourselves no more indulgence than we give to him. Such honesty will end in severity at home and clemency abroad. For we are accountable for the ill in ourselves, and have to kill it; for the good in our neighbor, and have to cherish it. He only, in the name and power of God, can kill the bad in him; we can cherish the good in him by being good to it across all the evil fog that comes between our love and his good.

Nor ought it to be forgotten that this fog is often the result of misapprehension and mistake, giving rise to all kinds of indignations, resentments, and regrets. Scarce anything about us is just as it seems, but at the core there is truth enough to dispel all falsehood and reveal life as unspeakably divine. O brother, sister, across this weary fog, dimlighted by the faint torches of our truth-seeking, I call to the divine in you, which is mine, not to rebuke you, not to rouse you, not to say "Why do you hate me?" but to say "I love you; in God's name I love you." And I will wait until the true self looks out of your eyes, and knows the true self in me.

But in the working of the Divine Love upon the race, my enemy is doomed to cease to be my enemy, and to become my friend. One flash of truth towards me would destroy my enmity at once. One hearty confession of wrong, and our enmity passes away; from each comes forth the brother who was inside the enemy all the time. For this The Truth is at work. In the faith of this, let us love the enemy now, accepting God's work in reversion, as it were; let us believe as seeing His yet invisible triumph, clasping and holding fast our brother, in defiance of the changeful wiles of the wicked enchantment which would persuade our eyes and hearts that he is not our brother, but some horrible thing, hateful and hating.

But again I must ask, What if *we* are in the wrong and do the wrong, and hate because we have injured? What then? Why, then, let us cry to God as from the throat of hell that He would take pity upon us the chief of sinners, and send some help to lift us from the fearful pit and the miry clay. Nothing will help but the Spirit proceeding from the Father and the Son, the Spirit of the Father and the Brother casting out and revealing. It will be with tearing and foaming, with a terrible cry and a lying as one dead, that such a demon will go out. But what a vision will then arise in the depths of the purified soul!

"You therefore must be perfect, as your heavenly Father is perfect." "Love your enemies, and you shall be the children of the highest." It is the divine glory to forgive.

THIRTY

THE WORD
OF
JESUS
ON PRAYER

They ought always to pray...
(Luke 18:1).

The impossibility of doing what we would as we would, drives us to look for help. There is a reality of being in which all things are easy and plain—oneness, that is, with the Lord of Life; to pray for this is the first thing; and to the point of this prayer every difficulty hedges and directs us.

But if I try to set forth something of the reasonableness of all prayer, I beg my readers to remember that it is for the sake of action and not speculation. If prayer be anything at all, it is a thing to be done. What matter whether you agree with me or not, if you do not pray? I would not spend my labor for that. I desire it to serve for help to pray, not to understand how a man might pray and yet be a reasonable soul.

Here is a word of the Lord about prayer. It is a comfort that He recognizes difficulty in the matter—sees that we need encouragement to go on praying, that it looks as if we were not heard, that it is no wonder we should be ready to faint and leave off. He tells a parable in which the suppliant has to go often and often to the man who can help her, gaining her end only at the long last. Actual delay on the part of God, we know from what follows, He does not allow. He recognizes how the thing must look to those whom He would have go on praying. Here as elsewhere He teaches us that we must not go by the look of things, but by the reality behind the look.

A truth, a necessity of God's own willed nature, is enough to set up against a whole army of appearances. It looks as if He did not hear you. Never mind; He does. Go on as the woman did; you too will be heard. She is heard at last, and in virtue of her much going; God hears at once, and will avenge speedily. The unrighteous judge cared nothing for the woman; those who cry to God are His own chosen— plain in the fact that they cry to Him. He has made and appointed them to cry: they do cry: will He not hear them?

They exist that they may pray. He has chosen them that they may choose Him; He has called them that they may call Him—that there may be such communion, such interchange as belongs to their being and the being of their Father. The gulf of indifference lay between the poor woman and the unjust judge; God and those who seek His help, are closer than two hands clasped hard in love: He will avenge them speedily. It is a bold assertion in the face of what seems great delay—an appearance acknowledged in the very groundwork of the parable.

If there be a God, and I am His creature, there may be, there should be, there must be some communication open between Him and me. If anyone allow a God, but one scarce good enough to care about His creatures, I will yield him that it were foolish to pray to such a God; but the notion that, with all the good impulses in us, we are the offspring of a cold-hearted devil, is so horrible in its inconsistency, that I would ask that man what hideous and cold-hearted disregard to the truth makes him capable of the supposition! To such a one God's terrors, or, if not His terrors, then God's sorrow yet will speak; the divine something in him will love, and the love be left moaning.

If I find my position, my consciousness, that of one from home, nay, that of one in some sort of prison; if I find that I can neither rule the world in which I love nor my own thoughts or desires; that I cannot quiet my passions, order my likings, determine my ends, will my growth, forget when I would, or recall what I forget; that I cannot love where I would, or hate where I would; that I am no king over myself; that I cannot supply my own needs, do not even always know which of my seeming needs are to be supplied, and which treated as impostors; if, in a word, my own being is everyway too much for me; if I can neither understand it, be satisfied with it, nor better it—may it not well give me pause—the pause that ends in prayer?

He that is made in the image of God must know Him or be desolate: the child must have the Father! Witness the dissatisfaction, yea desolation of my soul—wretched, alone, unfinished, without Him! 'It cannot act from itself, save in God; acting from what seems itself without God, is no action at all. It is a mere yielding to impulse. All within is disorder and spasm. There is a cry behind me, and a voice before. Instincts of betterment tell I must rise above my present self—perhaps even above all my possible self. I see not how to obey, how to carry them out.

I am shut up in a world of consciousness, an unknown *I* in an unknown world. Surely this world of my unwilled, unchosen, compelled existence, cannot be shut out from Him, cannot be unknown to Him, cannot be impenetrable, impermeable, unpresent to Him from whom I am! Nay, is it not His thinking in which I think? Is it not by His consciousness that I am conscious?

Then shall I not think to Him? Shall I not tell Him my

troubles—how He, even He, has troubled me by making
me?—how unfit I am to be that which I am?—that my being
is not to me a good thing yet?—that I need a law that shall
account to me for it in righteousness—reveal to me how I
am to make it a good—how I am to *be* a good, and not an
evil?

If it be reasonable for me to cry thus, if I cannot but cry,
it is reasonable that God should hear. He cannot but hear.
A being that could not hear or would not answer prayer,
could not be God.

Prayer As Experience

But, I ask, all this admitted—is what you call a necessary
truth an existent fact? You say, "It must be so;" I say, "What
if there is no God!" Convince me that prayer is heard, and
I shall know.

I reply, What if God does not care to have you know it at
second hand? What if there would be no good in that?

The sole assurance worth a man's having, even if the
most incontestable evidence were open to him from a thousand other quarters, is that to be gained only from personal
experience—that assurance in himself which he can least
readily receive from another, and which is least capable of
being transmuted into evidence for another. The evidence
of Jesus Christ could not take the place of that.

A truth is of enormous import in relation to the life—that
is the heart, and conscience, and will; it is of little consequence merely as a fact having relation to the understanding. God may hear all prayers that ever were offered to
Him, and a man may believe that He does, nor be one whit
the better for it, so long as God has no prayers of his to hear,
he no answers to receive from God. Nothing in this quarter
will ever be gained by investigation.

Reader, if you are in any trouble, try whether God will
not help you; if you are in no need, why should you ask
questions about prayer? True, he knows little of himself

who does not know that he is wretched, and miserable, and poor, and blind, and naked; but until he begins at least to suspect a need, how can he pray? And for one who does not want to pray, I would not lift a straw to defeat such a one in the argument whether God hears or does not hear prayer: for me, let him think what he will! It matters nothing in heaven or in earth: whether in hell I do not know.

As to the so-called scientific challenge to prove the efficacy of prayer by the result of simultaneous petition, I am almost ashamed to allude to it. There should be light enough in science itself to show the proposal absurd. A God capable of being so moved in one direction or another, is a God not worth believing in—could not be the God believed in by Jesus Christ—and He said He knew. A God that should fail to hear, receive, attend to one single prayer, the feeblest or worst, I cannot believe in; but a God that would grant every request of every man or every company of men, would be an evil God—that is no God, but a demon.

That God should hang in the thought-atmosphere like a windmill, waiting till men enough should combine and send out prayer in sufficient force to turn His outspread arms, is an idea too absurd. God waits to be gracious, not to be tempted. A man capable of proposing such a test, could have in his mind no worthy representative idea of a God, and might well disbelieve in any. It is better to disbelieve than believe in a God unworthy.

The Problem of Unanswered Prayer

"But I want to believe in God. I want to know that there is a God that answers prayer, that I may believe in Him. There was a time when I believed in Him. I prayed to Him in great and sore trouble of heart and mind, and He did not hear me. I have not prayed since."

This only I will say: God has not to consider His children only at the moment of their prayer. Should He be willing to give a man the thing He knows he would afterwards wish

He had not given him? If a man be not fit to be refused, if he be not ready to be treated with love's severity, what he wishes may perhaps be given him in order that he may wish it had not been given him; but barely to give a man what he wants because he wants it, and without further purpose of his good, would be to let a poor ignorant child take his fate into his own hands—the cruelty of a devil. Yet is every prayer heard; and the real soul of the prayer may require, for its real answer, that it should not be granted in the form in which it is requested.

"To have a thing in another shape might be equivalent to not having it at all."

If you knew God, you would leave that to Him. He is not mocked, and He will not mock. But He knows you better than you know yourself, and would keep you from fooling yourself. He will not deal with you as the child of a day, but as the child of eternal ages. You shall be satisfied, if you will but let Him have His way with the creature He has made. The question is between your will and the will of God.

He is not one of those who give readiest what they prize least. He does not care to give anything but His best, or that which will prepare for it. Not many years may pass before you confess, "You are a God who hears prayer, and gives a better answer." You may come to see that the desire of your deepest heart would have been frustrated by having what seemed its embodiment then. That God should as a loving father listen, hear, consider, and deal with the request after the perfect tenderness of His heart, is to me enough; it is little that I should go without what I pray for.

If it be granted that any answer which did not come of love, and was not for the final satisfaction of him who prayed, would be unworthy of God; that it is the part of love and knowledge to watch over the wayward, ignorant child; then the trouble of seemingly unanswered prayers begins to abate, and a lovely hope and comfort takes its place in the child-like soul. To hear is not necessarily to grant—God forbid! But to hear is necessarily to attend to—sometimes as necessarily to refuse.

"Three times," says St. Paul, "I besought the Lord about this, that it should leave me; but He said to me, my grace is sufficient for you; for my power is made perfect in weakness." God had a better thing for Paul than granting his prayer and removing his complaint. The power of Christ should descend and remain upon him. He would make him stronger than his suffering, make him a sharer in the energy of God. Verily, if we have God, we can do without the answer to any prayer.

Why Pray?

"But if God is so good as you represent Him, and if He knows all that we need, and better far than we do ourselves, why should it be necessary to ask Him for anything?"

I answer, What if He knows prayer to be the thing we need first and most? What if the main object in God's idea of prayer be the supplying of our great, our endless need—the need of Himself? What if the good of all our smaller and lower needs lies in this, that they help to drive us to God?

Hunger may drive the runaway child home, and he may or may not be fed at once, but he needs his mother more than his dinner. Communion with God is the one need of the soul beyond all other need; prayer is the beginning of that communion, and some need is the motive of that prayer. Our wants are for the sake of our coming into communion with God, our eternal need.

If gratitude and love immediately followed the supply of our needs, if God our Savior was the one thought of our hearts, then it might be unnecessary that we should ask for anything we need. But seeing we take our supplies as a matter of course, feeling as if they came out of nothing, or from the earth, or our own thoughts—instead of out of a heart of love and a will which alone is force—it is needful that we should be made to feel some at least of our wants, that we may seek Him who alone supplies all of them, and find His every gift a window to His heart of truth.

So begins a communion, a talking with God, a coming-to-one with Him, which is the sole end of prayer, yea, of existence itself in its infinite phases. We must ask that we may receive; but that we should receive what we ask in respect of our lower needs, is not God's end in making us pray, for He could give us everything without that. To bring His child to His knee, God withholds that man may ask.

In regard, however, to the high necessities of our nature, it is in order that He may be able to give that God requires us to ask—requires by driving us to it—by shutting us up to prayer. For how can He give into the soul of a man what it needs, while that soul cannot receive it? The ripeness for receiving is the asking.

When the soul is hungry for the light, for the truth—when its hunger has waked its higher energies, thoroughly roused the will, and brought the soul into its highest condition, that of action—its only fitness for receiving the things of God—that action is prayer. Then God can give. Then He can be as He would towards the man; for the glory of God is to give Himself. We thank you, Lord Christ, for by your pain alone do we rise towards the knowledge of this glory of your Father and our Father.

For the real good of every gift it is essential, first, that the giver be in the gift—as God always is, for He is love—and next, that the receiver know and receive the giver in the gift. Every gift of God is but a harbinger of His greatest and only sufficing gift—that of Himself. No gift unrecognized as coming from God is at its own best; therefore many things that God would gladly give us, things even that we need because we are, must wait until we ask for them, that we may know whence they come. When in all gifts we find Him, then in Him we shall find all things.

Sometimes to one praying will come the feeling rather than question: "Were it not better to abstain? If this thing be

good, will He not give it me? Would He not be better
pleased if I left it altogether to Him?" It comes, I think, of
a lack of faith and childlikeness—taking form, perhaps, in a
fear lest, asking for what was not good, the prayer should be
granted. Such a thought has no place with St. Peter; he says,
"Cast all your anxieties upon him, for he cares about you."
It may even come of ambition after spiritual distinction.
In every request, heart and soul and mind ought to supply
the low accompaniment, "Thy will be done." But the making of any request brings us near to Him, into communion
with our Life. Does it not also help us to think of Him in all
our affairs, and learn in everything to give thanks? Anything large enough for a wish to light upon, is large enough
to hang a prayer upon: the thought of Him to whom that
prayer goes will purify and correct the desire. To say, "Father, I should like this or that," would be enough at once, if
the wish were bad, to make us know it and turn from it.

Such prayer about things must of necessity help to bring
the mind into true and simple relation with Him; to make us
remember His will even when we do not see what that will
is. Surely it is better and more trusting to tell Him all without fear or anxiety. Was it not thus the Lord carried Himself towards His Father when He said, "If it be possible, let
this cup pass from me"? But there was something He cared
for more than His own fear—His Father's will: "Nevertheless, not my will, but thine be done."

There is no apprehension that God might be displeased
with Him for saying what He would like, and not leaving it
all to His Father. Neither did He regard His Father's plans
as necessarily so fixed that they could not be altered to His
prayer. The true son-faith is that which comes with bold-
ness, fearless of the Father doing anything but what is right
fatherly, patient, and full of loving-kindness. We must not
think to please Him by any asceticism even of the spirit;
we must speak straight out to Him. The true child will not
fear, but lay bare his wishes to the perfect Father. The

Father may will otherwise, but His grace will be enough for the child.

There could be no riches but for need. God Himself is made rich by man's necessity. By that He is rich to give; through that we are rich by receiving.

As to any notion of prevailing by entreaty over an unwilling God, that is heathenish, and belongs to such as think Him a hard master, or one like the unjust judge. What so quenching to prayer as the notion of unwillingness in the ear that hears! And when prayer is dull, what makes it flow like the thought that God is waiting to give, wants to give us everything! "Let us then with confidence draw near to the throne of grace, that we may receive mercy and find grace to help in time of need." We shall be refused our prayer if that be better; but what is good our Father will give us with divine good will. The Lord spoke His parable "to the effect that they ought always to pray, and not lose heart."

THIRTY-ONE

MAN'S DIFFICULTY CONCERNING PRAYER

*A*nd *not lose heart" (Luke 18:*
11).

"How should any design of the All-wise be altered in response to prayer of ours! How are we to believe such a thing?"

By reflecting that He is the All-wise, who sees before Him, and will not block His path. Such objection springs from [the] poorest idea of God in relation to us. It supposes Him to have cares and plans and intentions concerning our part of creation, irrespective of us. What is the whole system of things for, but our education? Does God care for suns and planets and satellites, for divine mathematics and ordered harmonies, more than for His children? I venture to say He cares more for oxen than for those.

He lays no plans irrespective of His children; and, His design being that they shall be free, active, live things, He sees that space be kept for them. They need room to struggle out of their chrysalis, to undergo the change that comes with the waking will, and to enter upon the divine sports and labors of children in the house and domain of their Father. Surely He may keep His plans in a measure unfixed, waiting the free desire of the individual soul!

Is not the design of the first course of His children's education just to bring them to the point where they shall pray? and shall His system appointed to that end be then found hard and fast, tooth-fitted and inelastic, as if informed of no live causing soul, but an unselfknowing force—so that He cannot answer the prayer because of the system which has its existence for the sake of the prayer?

True, in many cases, the prayer, far more than the opportunity of answering it, is God's end; but how will the further end of the prayer be reached, which is oneness between the heart of the child and of the Father? How will the child go on to pray if he knows the Father cannot answer him? *Will not* may be for love, but how with a self-imposed *cannot?*

How could He be Father, who creating, would not make provision, would not keep room for the babbled prayers of His children? Is His perfection a mechanical one? Has He Himself no room for choice—therefore can give none? There must be a Godlike region of choice as there is a human, however little we may be able to conceive it.

What stupidity of perfection would that be which left no margin about God's work, no room for change of plan upon change of fact—yea, even the mighty change that, behold now at length, His child is praying! See the freedom of God in His sunsets—never a second like one of the foregone!— in His moons and skies—in the ever-changing solid earth! —all moving by no dead law, but in the harmony of the vital law of liberty, God's creative perfection—all ordered from within.

A divine perfection that were indeed, where was no liberty! where there could be but one way of a thing! I may move my arm as I please: shall God be unable so to move His? If but for Himself, God might well desire no change, but He is God for the sake of His growing creatures; all His making and doing is for them, and change is the necessity of their very existence.

Christ's Plans Modified

And as in all His miracles Jesus did only in miniature what His Father does ever in the great—in far wider, more elaborate, and beautiful ways, I will adduce from them an instance of answer to prayer that has in it a point bearing, it seems to me, most importantly on the thing I am now trying to set forth.

Poor, indeed, was the making of the wine in the earthen pots of stone, compared with its making in the lovely growth of the vine with its clusters of swelling grapes—the live roots gathering from the earth the water that had to be borne in pitchers and poured into the great vases. But it is precious as the interpreter of the same, even in its being the outcome of our Lord's sympathy with ordinary human rejoicing. There is however an element in its origin that makes it yet more precious to me—the regard of our Lord to a wish of His mother. Alas, how differently is the tale often received! how misunderstood!

His mother had suggested to Him that here was an opportunity for appearing in His own greatness, the potent purveyor of wine for the failing feast. It was not in His plan, as we gather from His words; for the Lord never pretended anything, whether to His enemy or His mother: He is The True. He lets her know that He and she have different outlooks, different notions of His work. "What have you to do with me?" He said; "my hour has not yet come." But there was that in His look and tone whence she knew that her desire, scarce half-fashioned into request, was granted.

What am I thence to conclude, worthy of the Son of God, and the Son of Mary, but that, at the prayer of His mother,

He made room in His plans for the thing she desired? It was not His wish then to work a miracle, but if His mother wished it, He would! He did for His mother what for His own part He would rather have let alone. Not always did He do as His mother would have Him; but this was a case in which He could do so, for it would interfere nowise with the will of His Father.

If it would have hurt His mother, if it had been in any way turning from the will of His Father in heaven, He would not have done it: that would have been to answer her prayer against her. His yielding makes the story doubly precious to my heart. The Son then could change His intent, and spoil nothing. So, I say, can the Father; for the Son does nothing but what He sees the Father do.

Prayer for Others

Finding it possible to understand, however, that God may answer prayers to those who pray for themselves, what are we to think concerning prayer for others? What fitness then can there be in praying for others? Will God give to another for our asking what He would not give without it? Would He not, if it could be done without the person's self, do it without a second person? If God were a tyrant, one whose heart might be softened by the sight of anxious love; or if He were one who might be informed, enlightened, reasoned with; or one in whom a setting forth of character, need, or claim might awake interest; then would there be plain reason in prayer for another.

But if we believe that God is the one unselfish, the one good being in the universe, and that His one design with His children is to make them perfect as He is perfect; if we believe that He not **only** would once give, but is always giving Himself to us for our life; if we believe that God does His best for *every* man; if also we believe that God knows every man's needs, and will, for love's sake, not spare one pang that may serve to purify the soul of one of His children; if we believe all this, how can we think He will in any sort alter His way with one because another prays for him? The prayer would arise from nothing in the person prayed for; why should it initiate a change in God's dealing with him?

The argument I know not how to answer. I can only, in the face of it, and feeling all the difficulty, say, and say again, "Yet I believe I may pray for my friend—for my enemy—for anybody! Yet and yet, there is, there must be some genuine, essential good and power in the prayer of one man for another to the Maker of both—and that just because their Maker is perfect, not less than very God."

I shall not bring authority to bear, for authority can at best but make us believe reason there; it cannot make us see it. The difficulty remains the same even when we hear the Lord Himself pray to His Father for those the Father loves because they have received His Son—loves therefore with a special love, as the foremost in faith, the elect of the world— loves not merely because they must die if He did not love them, but loves from the deeps of divine approval. Those who believe in Jesus will be satisfied in the face of the incomprehensible, that, in what He does, reason and right must lie; but not therefore do we understand. At the same time, though I cannot explain, I can show some ground upon which, even had he not been taught to do so, but left alone with his heart, a man might yet, I think, pray for another.

If God has made us to love like Himself, and like Himself long to help; if there are for whom we, like Him, would give our lives to lift them from the evil gulf of their ungodliness; and if all our hope for ourselves lies in God—what is there for us, what can we think of, what do, but go to God? —what but go to Him with this our own difficulty and need? If I can be helped through my friend, I think God will take the thing up, and do what I cannot do—help my friend that I may be helped—perhaps help me to help him.

You see, in praying for another we pray for ourselves—for the relief of the needs of our love; it is not prayer for another alone. Would God give us love, the root of power, in us, and leave that love whereby He Himself creates, altogether helpless in us? May He not at least expedite something for our prayers? Where He could not alter, He could perhaps expedite, in view of some help we might then be able to give. If He desire that we should work with Him, that work surely helps Him!

God is ever seeking to lift us up into the sharing of His divine nature; [to make us] God's kings, such men, namely, as with Jesus have borne witness to the truth, share His glory even on the throne of the Father. See the grandeur of the creative love of the Holy! Nothing less will serve it than to have His children, through His and their suffering, share the throne of His glory! If such be the perfection of the Infinite, should that perfection bring Him under bonds and difficulties, and not rather set Him freer to do the thing He would in the midst of opposing forces? If His glory be in giving Himself, and we must share therein, giving ourselves, why should we not begin here and now?

One way is clear: the prayer will react upon the mind that prays, its light will grow, will shine the brighter, and draw and enlighten the more. But there must be more in the thing. Prayer in its perfect idea being a rising up into the will of the Eternal, may not the help of the Father become one with the prayer of the child, and for the prayer of him He holds in His arms, go forth for him who wills not yet to be lifted to His embrace? To His bosom God Himself cannot bring His children at once, and not at all except through His own suffering and theirs. But will not any good parent find some way of granting the prayer of the child who comes to him, saying, "Father, this is my brother's birthday: I have nothing to give him, and I do love him so! could you give me something to give him, or give him something for me?"

"Still, could not God have given the gift without the prayer? And why should the good of any one depend on the prayer of another?"

I can only answer with the return question, "Why should my love be powerless to help another?" Surely the system of things would not be complete in relation to the best thing in it—love itself, if love had no help in prayer. If I love and cannot help, does not my heart move me to ask Him to help who loves and can? Will He answer, "Child, do not trouble me; I am already doing all I can"? If such answer came, who that loved would not be content to be nowhere in the matter? But how if the eternal, limitless Love, the unspeakable, self-forgetting God-devotion, which, demanding all, gives all, should say, "Pray on, my child; I am hearing you; it goes through me in help to him. We are of one mind about it; I help and you help. I shall have you all safe home with me by and by! There is no fear, only we must work, and not lose heart. Go, and let your light so shine before men that they may see your good things, and glorify me by knowing that I am light and no darkness"!—what then? Oh that lovely picture by Michelangelo, with the young ones and the little ones come to help God to make Adam!

Prayer Brings Communion

But it may be that the answer to prayer will come in a shape that seems a refusal. It may come even in an increase of that from which we seek deliverance. I know of one who prayed to love better: a sore division came between—out of which at length rose a dawn of tenderness.

There are some who would argue for prayer, not on the ground of any possible answer to be looked for, but because of the good to be gained in the spiritual attitude of the mind in praying. There are those even who, not believing in any ear to hear, any heart to answer, will yet pray. They say it does them good; they pray to nothing at all, but they get spiritual benefit.

I will not contradict their testimony. So needful is prayer to the soul that the mere attitude of it may encourage a good mood. Certainly to pray to that which is not, is in logic a folly. Yet the good that, they say, comes of it, may rebuke the worse folly of their unbelief, for it indicates that prayer is natural, and how could it be natural if inconsistent with the very mode of our being? Theirs is a better way than that of those who, believing there is a God, but not believing that He will give any answer to their prayers, yet pray to Him; that is more foolish and more immoral than praying to the No-god. Whatever the God be to whom they pray, their prayer is a mockery of Him, of themselves, of the truth.

On the other hand, let God give no assent to the individual prayer, let the prayer even be for something nowise good enough to be a gift of God, yet the soul that prays will get good of its prayer, if only in being thereby brought a little nearer to the Father, and making way for coming again. Prayer does react in good upon the praying soul, irrespective of answer.

There are moods of such satisfaction in God that a man may feel as if nothing were left to pray for, as if he had but to wait with patience for what the Lord would work. There are moods of such hungering desire, that petition is crushed into an inarticulate crying. There is a communion with God that asks for nothing, yet asks for everything. This last is the very essence of prayer, though not petition. It is possible for a man, not indeed to believe in God, but to believe that there is a God, and yet not desire to enter into communion with Him; but he that prays and does not faint will come to recognize that to talk with God is more than to have all prayers granted—that it is the end of all prayer, granted or refused. And he who seeks the Father more than anything He can give, is likely to have what he asks, for he is not likely to ask amiss.

Even such as ask amiss may sometimes have their prayers answered. The Father will never give the child a stone that asks for bread; but I am not sure that He will never give the child a stone that asks for a stone. If the Father say, "My child, that is a stone; it is no bread;" and the child answer, "I am sure it is bread; I want it;" may it not be well he should try his bread?

The Problem of Waiting

But now for another point in the parable, where I think I can give some help—I mean the Lord's apparent recognition of delay in the answering of prayer. In the very structure of the parable He seems to take delay for granted, and says notwithstanding, "He will vindicate them speedily!"

The reconciling conclusion is that God loses no time, though the answer may not be immediate.

He may delay because it would not be safe to give us at once what we ask: we are not ready for it. To give ere we could truly receive, would be to destroy the very heart and hope of prayer, to cease to be our Father. The delay itself may work to bring us nearer to our help, to increase the desire, perfect the prayer, and ripen the receptive condition.

Again, not from any straitening in God, but either from our own condition and capacity, or those of the friend for whom we pray, time may be necessary to the working out of the answer. God is limited by regard for our best; our best implies education; in this we must ourselves have a large share; this share, being human, involves time. And perhaps, indeed, the better the gift we pray for, the more time is necessary to its arrival.

To give us the spiritual gift we desire, God may have to begin far back in our spirit, in regions unknown to us, and do much work that we can be aware of only in the results. For our consciousness is to the extent of our being but as the flame of the volcano to the world-gulf whence it issues. In the gulf of our unknown being God works behind our consciousness. With His holy influence, with His own presence, the one thing for which most earnestly we cry, He may be approaching our consciousness from behind, coming forward through regions of our darkness into our light, long before we begin to be aware that He is answering our request—has answered it, and is visiting His child.

To vindicate speedily must mean to make no delay beyond what is absolutely necessary, to begin the moment it is possible to begin. Because the Son of Man did not appear for thousands of years after men began to cry out for a Savior, shall we imagine He did not come the first moment it was well He should come? Can we doubt that to come a moment sooner would have been to delay, not to expedite, His kingdom? For anything that needs a process, to begin to act at once is to be speedy. God does not put off like the unrighteous judge; He does not delay until irritated by the prayers of the needy. He will hear while they are yet speaking; yea, before they call He will answer.

God's Vengeance

Of course, no prayer for any revenge that would gratify the selfishness of our nature, a thing to be burned out of us by the fire of God, needs think to be heard. Be sure, when the Lord prayed His Father to forgive those who crucified Him, He uttered His own wish and His Father's will at once. God will never punish according to the abstract abomination of sin, as if men knew what they were doing. "Vengeance is mine," He says. With a right understanding of it, we might as well pray for God's vengeance as for His forgiveness. That vengeance is, to destroy the sin—to make the sinner abjure and hate it; nor is there any satisfaction in a vengeance that seeks or effects less. The man himself must turn against himself, and so be for himself. If nothing else will do, then hell-fire; if less will do, whatever brings repentance and self-repudiation, is God's repayment.

Friends, if any prayers are offered against us; if the vengeance of God be cried out for, because of some wrong you or I have done, God grant us His vengeance! Let us not think that we shall get off!

But perhaps the Lord was here thinking, not of persecution, or any form of human wrong, but of the troubles that most trouble His true disciple; and the suggestion is comforting to those whose foes are within them, for, if so, then He recognizes the evils of self, against which we fight, not as parts of ourselves, but as our foes, on which He will avenge the true self that is at strife with them.

And certainly no evil is, or ever could be, of the essential being and nature of the creature God made! The thing that is not good, however associated with our being, is against that being, not of it—is its enemy, on which we need to be avenged. When we fight, He will avenge. Till we fight, evil shall have dominion over us, a dominion to make us miserable. Other than miserable can no one be, under the yoke of a nature contrary to his own. Comfort yourself then, if you find your own heart and soul, or rather the things that move therein, too much for you: God will avenge His own elect. He is not delaying; He is at work for you. Only you must pray, and not faint. Ask, ask; it shall be given you. Seek most the best things; to ask for the best things is to have them. The seed of them is in you, or you could not ask for them.

But from whatever quarter come our troubles, whether from the world outside or the world inside, still let us pray. In His own right way, the only way that could satisfy us, for we are of His kind, will God answer our prayers with help. He will avenge us of our adversaries, and that speedily. Only let us take heed that we be adversaries to no man, but fountains of love and forgiving tenderness to all. And from no adversary, either on the way with us, or haunting the secret chamber of our hearts, let us hope to be delivered till we have paid the last penny.

THIRTY-TWO

THE
HANDS
OF THE
FATHER

*M*y God, my God, why hast
thou forsaken me? (Matt. 27:46).

I do not know that I should dare to approach this—of all
utterances into which human breath has ever been molded,
most awful in import—did I not feel that, containing both
germ and blossom of the final devotion, it contains therefore the deepest practical lesson the human heart has to
learn. The Lord, the Revealer, hides nothing that can be
revealed, and will not warn away the foot that treads in
naked humility even upon the ground of that terrible conflict between Him and Evil.

He will give us even to meditate the one thought that slew
Him at last, when He could bear no more, and fled to the
Father to know that He loved Him, and was well-pleased
with Him. For Satan had come at length yet again, to urge
Him with his last temptation; to tell Him that although He
had done His part, God had forgotten His. The Lord hides

not His sacred sufferings, for truth is light, and would be light in the minds of men. The Holy Child, the Son of the Father, has nothing to conceal, but all the Godhead to reveal. Let us then put off our shoes, and draw near, and bow the head, and kiss those feet that bear for ever the scars of our victory.

A Cry of Faith

It is with the holiest fear that we should approach the terrible fact of the sufferings of our Lord. Let no one think that those were less because He was more. The more delicate the nature, the more alive to all that is lovely and true, lawful and right, the more does it feel the antagonism of pain, the inroad of death upon life; the more dreadful is that breach of the harmony of things whose sound is torture. He felt more than man could feel, because He had a larger feeling.

He was even therefore worn out sooner than another man would have been. These sufferings were awful indeed when they began to invade the region about the will; when the struggle to keep consciously trusting in God began to sink in darkness; when the Will of The Man put forth its last determined effort in that cry after the vanishing vision of the Father: "My God, my God, why hast thou forsaken me?" Never had it been so with Him before. Never before had He been unable to see God beside Him. Yet never was God nearer Him than now. For never was Jesus more divine. He could not see, could not feel Him near; and yet it is "My God" that He cries.

Thus the Will of Jesus, in the very moment when His faith seems about to yield, is finally triumphant. It has no *feeling* now to support it, no beatific vision to absorb it. It stands naked in His soul and tortured, as He stood naked and scourged before Pilate. Pure and simple and surrounded by fire, it declares for God. The sacrifice ascends in the cry, *My God.* The cry comes not out of happiness, out of peace, out of hope. Not even out of suffering comes that cry. It was a cry *in* desolation, but it came out of Faith. It is the last voice of Truth, speaking when it can but cry.

The divine horror of that moment is unfathomable by human soul. It was blackness of darkness. And yet He would believe. Yet He would hold fast. God was His God yet. *My God*—and in the cry came forth the Victory, and all was over soon. Of the peace that followed that cry, the peace of a perfect soul, large as the universe, pure as light, ardent as life, victorious for God and His brethren, He Himself alone can ever know the breadth and length, and depth and height.

I do not think it was our Lord's deepest trial when in the garden He prayed that the cup might pass from Him, and prayed yet again that the will of the Father might be done. For that will was then present with Him. He was living and acting in that will. But now the foreseen horror has come. He is drinking the dread cup, and the Will has vanished from His eyes. Were that Will visible in His suffering, His will could bow with tearful gladness under the shelter of its grandeur. But now His will is left alone to drink the cup of The Will in torture. In the sickness of this agony, the Will of Jesus arises perfect at last; and of itself, unsupported now, declares for God in defiance of pain, of death, of apathy, of self, of negation, of the blackness within and around it; calls aloud upon the vanished God.

This is the Faith of the Son of God. God withdrew, as it were, that the perfect Will of the Son might arise and go forth to find the Will of the Father.

Is it possible that even then He thought of the lost sheep who could not believe that God was their Father; and for them, too, in all their loss and blindness and unlove, cried, saying the word they might say, knowing for them that *God* means *Father* and more, and knowing now, as He had never known till now, what a fearful thing it is to be without God and without hope? I dare not answer the question I put.

The Use of Spiritual Dryness

But wherein or what can this Alpine apex of faith have to do with the creatures who call themselves Christians, creeping about in the valleys, hardly knowing that there are mountains above them, save that they take offense at and stumble over the pebbles washed across their path by the glacier streams? I will tell you. We are and remain such creeping Christians, because we look at ourselves and not at Christ; because we gaze at the marks of our own soiled feet, and the trail of our own defiled garments, instead of up at the snows of purity, whither the soul of Christ climbed. Each, putting his foot in the footprint of the Master, and so defacing it, turns to examine how far his neighbor's footprint corresponds with that which he still calls the Master's, although it is but his own.

Or, having committed a petty fault, I mean a fault such as only a petty creature could commit, we mourn over the defilement to ourselves, and the shame of it before our friends or children, instead of hastening to make the due confession and amends to our fellow, and then, forgetting our paltry self with its well-earned disgrace, lift up our eyes to the glory which alone will quicken the true man in us, and kill the peddling creature we so wrongly call our *self*. The true self is that which can look Jesus in the face, and say *My Lord*.

It is easy in pain, so long as it does not pass certain undefinable bounds, to hope in God for deliverance, or pray for strength to endure. But what is to be done when all feeling is gone? when a man does not know whether he believes or not, whether he loves or not, when art, poetry, religion are nothing to him, so swallowed up is he in pain, or mental depression, or disappointment, or temptation, or he knows not what? It seems to him then that God does not care for him, and certainly he does not care for God. If he is still humble, he thinks that he is so bad that God cannot care for him. And he then believes for the time that God loves us only because and when and while we love Him; instead of believing that God loves us always because He is our God, and that we live only by His love. Or he does not believe in a God at all, which is better.

So long as we have nothing to say to God, nothing to do with Him, save in the sunshine of the mind when we feel Him near us, we are poor creatures, willed upon, not willing.

God does not, by the instant gift of His Spirit, make us always feel right, desire good, love purity, aspire after Him and His will. Therefore either He will not, or He cannot. If He will not, it must be because it would not be well to do so. If He cannot, then He would not if He could; else a better condition than God's is conceivable to the mind of God —a condition in which He could save the creatures whom He has made, better than He can save them.

The truth is this: He wants to make us in His own image, *choosing* the good, *refusing* the evil. How should He effect this if He were *always* moving us from within, as He does at divine intervals, towards the beauty of holiness? God gives us room *to be*; does not oppress us with His will; "stands away from us," that we may act from ourselves, that we may exercise the pure will for good.

Do not, therefore, imagine me to mean that we can do anything of ourselves without God. If we choose the right at last, it is all God's doing, and only the more His that it is ours, only in a far more marvellous way His than if He had kept us filled with all holy impulses precluding the need of choice. For up to this very point, for this very point, He has been educating us, leading us, pushing us, driving us, enticing us, that we may choose Him and His will, and so be tenfold more His children, of His own best making.

For God made our individuality as well as, and a greater marvel than, our dependence; made our *apartness* from Himself, that freedom should bind us divinely dearer to Himself, with a new and inscrutable marvel of love. For the

Godhead is still at the root, is the making root of our individuality, and the freer the man, the stronger the bond that binds him to Him who made his freedom. He made our wills, and is striving to make them free; for only in the perfection of our individuality and the freedom of our wills can we be altogether His children. This is full of mystery, but can we not see enough in it to make us very glad and very peaceful?

Not in any other act than one which, in spite of impulse or of weakness, declares for the Truth, for God, does the will spring into absolute freedom, into true life.

The Highest Condition of the Will

See, then, what lies within our reach every time that we are thus lapt in the folds of night. The highest condition of the human will is in sight, is attainable. I say not the highest condition of the Human Being; that surely lies in the Beatific Vision, in the sight of God. But the highest condition of the Human Will, as distinct, not as separated from God, is when, not seeing God, not seeming to itself to grasp Him at all, it yet holds Him fast. It cannot continue in this condition, for, not finding, not seeing God, the man would die; but the will thus asserting itself, the man has passed from death into life, and the vision is nigh at hand. Then first, thus free, in thus asserting its freedom, is the individual will one with the Will of God; the child is finally restored to the father; the childhood and the fatherhood meet in one; the brotherhood of the race arises from the dust; and the prayer of our Lord is answered, "I in them and thou in me, that they may become perfectly one." Let us then arise in God-born strength every time that we feel the darkness closing, or become aware that it has closed around us, and say, "I am of the Light and not of the Darkness."

Troubled soul, you are not bound to feel, but you are bound to arise. God loves you whether you feel or not. You cannot love when you will, but you are bound to fight the hatred in you to the last. Try not to feel good when you are not good, but cry to Him who is good. He changes not because you change. Nay, He has an especial tenderness of love towards you for that you are in the dark and have no light, and His heart is glad when you arise and say, "I will go to my Father." Then fold the arms of your faith, and wait in quietness until light goes up in your darkness. Fold the arms of your faith I say, but not of your action. Think of something that you ought to do, and go and do it, if it be but the sweeping of a room or the preparing of a meal, or a visit to a friend. Heed not your feelings: Do your work.

Then, if ever the time should come, as perhaps it must come to each of us, when all consciousness of well-being shall have vanished, when the earth shall be but a sterile promontory, and the heavens a dull and pestilent congregation of vapors, when no man or woman shall delight us, when God Himself shall be but a name, and Jesus an old story, then, even then, when a Death far worse than "that phantom of grisly bone" is griping at our hearts, and having slain love, hope, faith, forces existence upon us only in agony, then, even then, we shall be able to cry out with our Lord, "My God, my God, why hast thou forsaken me?" Nor shall we die then, I think, without being able to take up His last words as well, and say, "Father, into thy hands I commit my spirit."

The Hands of The Father

The cry, "Father, into thy hands I commit my spirit," meant, "It is finished." Every highest human act is just a giving back to God of that which He first gave to us. "God, you have given me: here again is your gift. I send my spirit home." Every act of worship is a holding up to God of what God has made us. "Here, Lord, look what I have got: feel with me in what you have made me, in this your own bounty, my being. I am your child, and know not how to thank you save by uplifting the overflowing of your life, and calling aloud, 'It is yours: it is mine. I am yours, and therefore I am mine.' " The vast operations of the spiritual as of the physical world, are simply a turning again to the source.

The last act of our Lord in thus commending His spirit at the close of His life, was only a summing up of what He had been doing all His life. He had been offering this sacrifice, the sacrifice of Himself, all the years, and in thus sacrificing He had lived the divine life. Every morning when He went out ere it was day, every evening when He lingered on the night-lapt mountain after His friends were gone, He was offering Himself to His Father in the communion of loving words, of high thoughts, of speechless feelings; and, between, He turned to do the same thing in deed, namely, in loving word, in helping thought, in healing action towards His fellows. For the way to worship God while the daylight lasts is to work; the service of God, the only "divine service," is the helping of our fellows.

I do not seek to point out this commending of our spirits to the Father as a duty: that is to turn the highest privilege we possess into a burden grievous to be borne. But I want to show that it is the most simple and blessed in the human world.

For the Human Being may say thus with himself: "Am I going to sleep—to lose consciousness—to be helpless for a time—thoughtless—dead? Or, more awful consideration, in the dreams that may come may I not be weak of will and scant of conscience?—Father, into your hands I commit my spirit. I give myself back to you. Take me, soothe me, refresh me, 'make me over again.' Am I going out into the business and turmoil of the day, where so many temptations may come to do less honorably, less faithfully, less kindly, less diligently than the Ideal Man would have me do? Father, into your hands. Am I going to do a good deed? Then, of all times, Father, into your hands; lest the enemy should have me now. Am I going to do a hard duty, from which I would gladly be turned aside,—to refuse a friend's re-

quest, to urge a neighbor's conscience?—Father, into your
hands I commit my spirit.

Am I in pain? Is illness coming upon me to shut out the
glad visions of a healthy brain, and bring me such as are
troubled and untrue? Take my spirit, Lord, and see that it
has no more to bear than it can bear. Am I going to die? Father, into your hands I commit my spirit. For it is your business, not mine. You will know every shade of my suffering;
You will care for me with your perfect fatherhood. As a
child I could bear great pain when my father was leaning
over me, or had his arm about me: how much nearer my
soul cannot your hands come!—yes, with a comfort, Father
of me, that I have never yet even imagined; for how shall
my imagination overtake your swift heart? I care not for the
pain, so long as my spirit is strong, and into your hands I
commit that spirit. If your love, which is better than life, receive it, then surely your tenderness will make it great."

God's Fatherhood

Think, brothers, think, sisters, we walk in the air of an eternal fatherhood Every uplifting of the heart is a looking up
to The Father. Graciousness and truth are around, above,
beneath us, yes *in* us. When we are least worthy, then, most
tempted, hardest, unkindest, let us yet commit our spirits
into His hands. Where else dare we send them? How the
earthly father would love a child who would creep into his
room with angry, troubled face, and sit down at his feet,
saying when asked what he wanted: "I feel so naughty,
papa, and I want to get good"! Would he say to his child:
"How dare you! Go away, and be good, and then come to
me"?

Would we not let all the tenderness of our nature flow
forth upon such a child? And shall we dare to think that if
we being evil know how to give good gifts to our children,
God will not give us His own spirit when we come to ask
Him?

Nor is there anything we can ask for ourselves that we may not ask for another. We may commit any brother, any sister, to the common fatherhood. And there will be moments when, filled with that spirit which is the Lord, nothing will ease our hearts of their love but the committing of all men, all our brothers, and all our sisters, to the one Father. Nor shall we ever know that repose in the Father's hands which the Lord knew when the agony of death was over and He entered the regions where there is only life, and therefore all that is not music is silence (for all noise comes of the conflict of Life and Death)—we shall never be able, I say, to rest in the bosom of the Father, till the fatherhood is fully revealed to us in the love of the brothers. For He cannot be our father save as He is their father; and if we do not see Him and feel Him as their father, we cannot know Him as ours. Never shall we know Him aright until we rejoice and exult for our race that He is *the* Father.

9 781573 832991